BUILDING THE ORANGE WAVE

BUILDING THE
ORAN

the **INSIDE STORY BEHIND** *the* **HISTORIC RISE** *of* **JACK LAYTON** *and the* **NDP**

G E

W A V E

BRAD LAVIGNE

foreword by **OLIVIA CHOW**

Douglas & McIntyre

Douglas and McIntyre (2013) Ltd.
PO Box 219 Madeira Park, B.C., VON 2HO
www.douglas-mcintyre.com

Cataloguing data available from Library and Archives Canada
ISBN 978-1-77162-017-8 (cloth)
ISBN 978-1-77162-018-5 (ebook)

Editing by Barbara Pulling
Copy editing by Shirarose Wilensky
Indexed by David Baughan
Jacket design by Naomi MacDougall
Text design by Anna Comfort O'Keeffe
Printed and bound in Canada
Distributed in the U.S. by Publishers Group West

We gratefully acknowledge the financial support of the
Canada Council for the Arts, the British Columbia Arts
Council, the Province of British Columbia through the
Book Publishing Tax Credit, and the Government of Canada
through the Canada Book Fund for our publishing activities.

FOR SARAH, ADDIE AND HARRY

CONTENTS

FOREWORD
— OLIVIA CHOW —

Jack Layton and I had been active in Toronto politics for years, championing causes with a large network of people, so I was surprised when I didn't recognize one of the guys sitting at our dining room table.

"Hello, I'm Olivia. You're here to help Jack get elected leader?"

"I'm here to help Jack get elected prime minister," he replied. "Nice to meet you. I'm Brad Lavigne."

It was the spring of 2002, and a small group of us had begun meeting at our house to map out Jack's run for the leadership of the New Democratic Party of Canada. Brad was a British Columbian who had moved to Toronto the previous year, and he was smart, witty and had connections all over Canada. Jack was on the road at the time, as he often was, but Brad pitched right in. He worked for weeks out of our house before even meeting Jack. On a rare day when Jack was actually at home, Brad was there too, trying to sign up yet another regional coordinator for the campaign on the phone. "Jack, go introduce yourself to this guy. We need him," I said.

The new guy became a constant in our lives over the next decade, as Jack and his team set out to revitalize the NDP. The goal of "the project," as we called it, was ambitious: turning a caucus of thirteen and a party with the support of only one in ten voters into a modern political force, ready to govern. The project required discipline and tenacity, as well as humour and optimism. With naysayers in our own party and beyond, Jack, an optimist to his very core, built a team of dedicated and talented people who worked tirelessly to build a better Canada. Brad was a cornerstone of that team.

Brad was the only member of Jack's team to be there through it all. From his start as a campaign volunteer on Jack's leadership run, Brad became the campaign manager for the historic 2011 election—the Orange Wave that propelled the NDP to Official Opposition. After that election, Brad was appointed Jack's principal secretary. Then, just a few months later, he had another role to play. He served as an honorary pall-bearer at Jack's state funeral.

Jack's family meant the world to him, and he always made time for us, no matter how crazy our lives were. But Jack had a second family—his political family—who also meant the world to him. They shared the lows and some spectacular highs, and they came to trust and love one another. Brad was part of that family. Brad is more than a witness to history; he helped shape it. His perspective is one of a kind. *Building the Orange Wave* gives Canadians from all walks of life a behind-the-scenes account of an extraordinary time in our country's history, a true sense of the scope of Jack's legacy. This is the definitive road map to fulfilling "the project"—working together to build a country where love, hope and optimism triumph over anger, fear and despair.

Olivia Chow
Toronto, July 2013

INTRODUCTION

It only took a few minutes.

It was election night, 2011, and I had stepped out of the makeshift war room on the top floor of the InterContinental Hotel in downtown Toronto to make congratulatory calls to our newly elected MPs in Atlantic Canada.

By the time I returned, our campaign team was verifying the names of Quebec ridings on flip-chart paper taped to the wall. "Are those the ridings we've won?" I asked.

"No. Those are the ridings we've lost. We can't list all the ridings we've won—there are too many for us to keep up," said a calm Nathan Rotman, the party's director of organization, who was on the phone getting the results from our Quebec ground troops. The room was quiet, the staffers too busy going about their work to stop and celebrate history unfolding.

"Holy shit," I whispered to myself. It was only then that it hit me that this thing was real.

It was the beginning of a historic night. In addition to the wave of seats in Quebec, the NDP had broken through right across the country, from Newfoundland to British Columbia. In the country's largest city, we'd captured eight seats. It was our best-ever showing in Toronto, and we'd won more seats than the Grits in a once-unshakable Liberal bastion.

In Quebec, we'd captured more than 40 per cent of the vote and won fifty-nine seats. We'd won the seats of former prime ministers Sir Wilfrid Laurier, Louis St. Laurent, Brian Mulroney, Jean Chrétien and Paul Martin. We'd beaten Bloc Québécois leader Gilles Duceppe in

Laurier–Sainte-Marie, the riding he had held for more than twenty years, by fifty-four hundred votes.

In the end, 4.6 million Canadians had voted for the New Democratic Party of Canada. We'd won 103 seats from every corner of the country to comprise the largest Official Opposition formed by any party since 1980. Even without the 1.3 million votes from Quebec, the 2011 election would have been the best election result in the party's fifty-year history.

It was an outcome that very few outside Jack Layton's inner circle had believed was possible, and one that even fewer had predicted. So how had it happened? Was it an accident? Were Jack and the NDP merely benefactors of lacklustre performances by the Liberals and the Bloc Québécois? Or was it something more?

To UNDERSTAND THE ORANGE WAVE that swept Canada on May 2, 2011, you have to go back to March 2002, when a small group convened at the Toronto home of Jack Layton and his wife, Olivia Chow. Together, we set out to get Jack elected leader of the NDP with a plan to professionalize the party's operations, transform its culture and expand its support to make the NDP a viable alternative to form the country's government.

Given the state of the party back when Jack was running for leader, it was an audacious goal, if not a downright absurd one. In the November 2000 election, the party had dropped from twenty-one seats to thirteen. We hadn't even cracked 10 per cent of the popular vote. When all the ballots were tallied, at the ripe old age of forty, the NDP was in a death spiral. Saving it would require changing the party from the inside. Beyond those boundaries, we would have to dislodge decades-old voting patterns and do nothing short of realigning federal politics. That included cracking Quebec, a province where the NDP, despite some Herculean efforts over the decades, had remained virtually invisible.

It would be intense, gruelling work, with many highs and many more lows. I signed on at the very beginning to be a part of what would become an inspiring and heartbreaking story that would forever reshape modern Canadian politics.

CHAPTER 1:
DECIDING TO GO FEDERAL

The only item on the agenda was very sensitive, so Jack had booked a table in the private room on the second floor of the Hey Lucy Café. The casual restaurant on King Street was not far from city hall, where Jack and Olivia both served as city councillors.

It was March 2002, and Toronto's progressive power couple had convened a meeting with some of their key political advisors. They were about to make a life-altering decision, and they wanted to talk through the feasibility—and the wisdom—of their tentative plan. The couple, married since 1988, had been wrestling with whether Olivia should run for mayor of Toronto or Jack should take a run at the leadership of the federal NDP. They had been discussing the two scenarios privately for months.

By then, it was clear that NDP leader Alexa McDonough's resignation was imminent, after the devastating federal election campaign in the fall of 2000. The mood in the party was gloomy. The 1997 results—McDonough expanded the NDP caucus from nine MPs to twenty-one with significant breakthroughs in Atlantic Canada—had given the party a false sense of hope that it was moving in the right direction. But the results of the November 27, 2000, election were a brutal reality check. The party was once again in decline, with little hope for growth.

No matter where they lived or to which wing of the party they belonged, NDP members shared one common sentiment: we can't keep going on as we have been. McDonough knew this, but she wanted her timing to be right. She also wanted to push through a major constitutional change inside the party before executing an exit strategy: to bring in a one-member, one-vote system to elect her successor.

McDonough handled the file deftly. She worked with party executives and local activists in the run-up to the party's convention in the fall of 2001 to secure support to revolutionize the way NDP leaders were elected. The new voting system meant every NDP member would now be able to cast a ballot for party leader, giving all members, not just the delegates at the convention, a direct say in who should lead the NDP.

The convention, though, had also turned out to be about something more fundamental: the future of the party itself. A group known as the New Politics Initiative (NPI), with the backing of NDP MPs Svend Robinson and Libby Davies, proposed to scrap the party altogether in favour of a more left-wing social movement entity. The idea was radical, and when 40 per cent of those at the convention backed the motion, many members were surprised.

Although some at convention felt this was a catalyst for a conversation about the direction the party needed to go, others believed this could be the beginning of the end of the NDP. But no one knew what was going to happen next.

Clearly, the party needed a new leader with popular appeal. McDonough had accomplished what she set out to do at the convention with the passage of the one-member, one-vote system, but with the closeness of the NPI vote, she decided to let a little more time pass before announcing her exit.

Jack Layton, a delegate at the convention, had left the meeting with the sense that the two factions could be brought together. Ultimately, he felt the goals of the NPI crowd and their opponents were not all that different. Neither camp was advocating for the status quo. Everyone wanted change. Jack, a confident optimist, thought he could revitalize and unite the party. The pending leadership race, as he saw it, was a make-or-break opportunity to get the party onto a fundamentally different path. The most important decision ever facing the party had arrived. Who, if anyone, would be up to the challenge of saving the party from oblivion? Jack thought he was.

This weighed heavily on the minds of Jack and Olivia at Hey Lucy that night in March 2002. Joined by close advisors Bob Gallagher, a long-time friend of the couple who first met Jack during the fight for gay rights in the 1980s, and Franz Hartmann, who had worked with Jack at city hall for the previous four years, the group decided to draw up a list of pros and cons for each option for Jack and Olivia.

The couple always made decisions together in a systematic way, and this would be their biggest decision yet. They first had to decide whether the federal NDP was the best vehicle to bring about the kind of change they had spent their lives working for. Would jumping to the federal scene be worth the risk? Their priorities at city hall fell under federal jurisdiction. Jack's two greatest passions were housing and the environment. Olivia cared deeply about child care. They knew solutions to these issues could only be realized with leadership at the federal level. From his time on the executive committee at the Federation of Canadian Municipalities, Jack understood this well. He had successfully pushed Finance Minister Paul Martin into partnership to secure federal funds for local infrastructure projects through the Green Municipal Fund.

The people around the table agreed that Jack winning the leadership contest would be one thing; getting elected to the House of Commons would be another. Even getting the federal NDP leader elected in Toronto was far from a certainty. At the time, the Liberals held all forty-two seats in the city and the surrounding suburbs.

Would it be practical for the NDP to have a leader who might not even be able to win a seat? Jack had already run as a candidate for the federal NDP—twice—and lost both times.

On the other side of the equation, Jack and Olivia had accomplished some great things on the municipal front, even during Mel Lastman's tenure as mayor. The flashy mayor, who was set to leave civic politics when his term ended in 2003, may have been conservative-minded, but Jack and Olivia had found ways to work with him and get things done, gaining governing experience for both of them. Jack's list of accomplishments included the wind turbine at Exhibition Place, the Out of the Cold housing project and the green bin composting program.

Jack running for mayor was a non-starter. He had run a decade earlier, prior to amalgamation of the Metro Toronto municipalities, and lost badly. Olivia as a candidate had fewer negatives, and, as the more practical of the two, had a reputation as a sound fiscal manager through her membership on Lastman's budget committee. She would play better with the more conservative voters outside the downtown core who made up an increasingly important segment of the Toronto municipal electorate.

The advisors around the table acknowledged the obvious: Jack running for federal leader had a road rife with obstacles, whereas Olivia running for mayor of Toronto had a clearer path forward. But the group also thought they could make significant movement on their core issues with stronger voices in Ottawa fighting for them.

Besides, Jack had been getting emails and phone calls from across Canada, encouraging him to throw his hat into the ring. "I even received one from a city councillor in Victoria," he said that night.

The group left Hey Lucy with the decision made and an action plan to follow. Jack would hit the road to assess how deep the support for his candidacy was on the ground. Olivia and her chief of staff, Bob Gallagher, would start building the campaign infrastructure for Jack's federal leadership run.

In the fall of 2000, I was living in Victoria, serving as chief of staff to Paul Ramsey, NDP minister of finance in the B.C. government. I'd been born and raised in B.C.'s Lower Mainland, and I'd jumped at the chance to return to my home province in the fall of 1998 to work for the NDP government. After becoming an NDP supporter and active in the student movement at Simon Fraser University in Burnaby, B.C., I had left in the fall of 1992 to continue my studies at Concordia University. I helped establish the Quebec branch of the Canadian Federation of Students during my time in Montreal, then went on to serve as head of the national student group in Ottawa from 1996 to 1998.

By the early fall of 2000, Heather Fraser, the federal NDP director of organization in Ottawa, was facing the prospect of staffing campaign headquarters in mere weeks amid rumours of a possible snap election. Heather reached out to me and other NDP government staffers and activists across the country to work on the election at campaign headquarters in Ottawa.

My boss, Paul Ramsey, agreed that it would be good experience for me to see what a federal campaign looked like up close. I took a short leave of absence and headed back to Ottawa. I arrived just days before the campaign was to begin, and the picture wasn't pretty. At the time, the NDP did not have a full-time electoral machine functioning between elections, so it was caught off guard in its preparations. It didn't help that the campaign's tour coordinator had quit in the weeks leading up to the campaign launch, leaving campaign director Dennis Young to scramble to both put together a leader's tour and get names on ballots. "We were not ready," Fraser recalls.

The federal party had little money and no internal capacity to produce national communications materials or to assist the local riding campaigns. All of that work was delegated to an advertising firm, Bleublancrouge, which only had time to focus on TV ads. By the time the central campaign managed to ship out CDs with leaflets on them, it was too late in the game for the local campaigns to use them.

That meant there was no message discipline. Essentially, local ridings were running by-elections, because headquarters had nothing to offer them. "It was a shit show," recalls Fraser, who kept a tally on how many local campaign managers hung up on her during the campaign. One campaign manager from Nova Scotia slammed the phone down eleven times.

By the last week of the campaign, the only remaining question was how many members of the NDP caucus would be left standing on election night. The results told the story: the party lost more than a third of its caucus and more than 340,000 votes, winning just thirteen seats.

With such a weak internal operation, the NDP had failed to become a relevant player in a campaign dominated by a familiar Liberal strategy: calling on progressives to vote Liberal—this time to block the election of Canadian Alliance leader Stockwell Day as prime minister. We were so weak in so many parts of the country that progressive voters could easily hold their noses and vote Liberal, despite Jean Chrétien's conservative record since coming to power in 1993.

After promising in 1993 to introduce a national child care program, expand medicare and initiate other social-policy initiatives, the Chrétien Liberals had done the exact opposite when they slashed billions in social transfers in the name of slaying the deficit. Once the books were in the black, the Liberals again promised ambitious social initiatives. But after winning the 1997 campaign, the Chrétien government pulled to the right, opting instead to use the surplus to dole out $100 billion in corporate tax cuts.

During the fall 2000 campaign, I worked in the NDP war room, where I produced opposition research and wrote memos on policies as well as backgrounders for stops on McDonough's tour. I wasn't involved in planning or strategy during the campaign, but serving as a staffer at campaign headquarters in Ottawa taught me some important lessons. Without advance preparation, a permanent electoral machine ready to hit the ground running and an adequate war chest to mount a big-league campaign, the federal NDP would remain insignificant.

I returned to Victoria feeling pessimistic. The staffers who remained in Ottawa felt the same way. The federal party could not continue to limp along in its current state. Without dramatic change, it would simply wither away.

In early January 2001, I had a drink to ring in the new year with Rob Fleming, an old friend of mine from the student movement and a local NDP activist. Fleming, today an NDP MLA in B.C., was then a city councillor in Victoria. We met at Bartholomew's pub in the Executive House Hotel, a favourite stomping ground for political staffers from the nearby legislature.

Naturally, our conversation turned to the state of the federal NDP and what needed to change if it were ever to become a viable political party. Leadership was key, and we agreed the next leader had to meet three criteria.

First, the person had to be fluently bilingual and able to hold their own in the nationally televised leader debates. Only then would Quebec, a province with strong social democratic leanings, look to the NDP as a viable alternative. "Our biggest concern during the French-language debate shouldn't be whether the leader understands the questions," I said to Rob.

Second, the person had to come from urban Canada. At the time, the NDP held no seats in Toronto, Ottawa or Montreal. In fact, our only urban seats were in East Vancouver and Halifax. Given that approximately 80 per cent of Canadian voters lived in urban areas, we needed someone who could appeal to the growing demographics that predominantly lived in big cities: young people, new Canadians and ethnic communities.

Third, the party needed someone who had governed. That meant a cabinet minister, a premier, a mayor—or even a city councillor, we agreed. Even without executive experience, a councillor oversees the administration of taxpayer dollars, drafts and passes legislation, and can lay claim to a record of achievement, Fleming pointed out.

So, who then? We ordered another round and ran through potential candidates from the west to the east. We listed everyone we could think of who met our three criteria. The list wasn't particularly robust when we hit Ontario. That's when our conversation turned to Jack.

"Ever heard of a Toronto city councillor named Jack Layton?" I asked Fleming. I had never met Jack, but I kept an eye on municipal politics in Canada's big cities as a barometer of local party strength. I knew Jack was a New Democrat, and I had often seen him in the news in his capacity as vice-president of the Federation of Canadian Municipalities (FCM). (Jack was elected president of the FCM in May 2001.)

"Yeah," Fleming replied. "Let's give him a shout; see if he's interested."

The next morning, Fleming sent an email to Jack's city hall office. He began with accolades about Jack's recent book on homelessness and his work at the FCM.

"Listen, to cut to the chase," Fleming continued. "Have you considered running for the national leadership position in our party? I know it would be a great loss for Riverdale and Toronto if you became national leader, but it is a great time of need for the NDP to present a new leader, and I think you are the guy for the job. Please consider it. I think you could galvanize a lot of support and help lead the crucial project of building a new social democratic politics in Canada."

Fleming didn't hear back, but his email had a profound effect on Jack. Just before the historic 2011 election, Jack referred to it when talking about his decision to run for leader in a never-released video shot by the NDP in January 2011 to use as material to be tested in focus groups. He'd kept Fleming's email all those years.

"I'd never thought about it," Jack said. "And I started talking to some of my friends from the Federation of Canadian Municipalities, and they said, 'Look, Jack, we've taught you a lot about this country. You've been on the federation boards for quite a few years, and we've told you everything about this country. We need a national government that starts to pay attention to our needs in our local communities, large and small, across the country. When you're finished your term as president, you should go, and yes, you should run for leader of the NDP and go and shake things up in Ottawa.'"

That evening in January 2001, though, Jack's words were far in the future. We were facing a more immediate challenge in B.C.: a provincial election in May, just four months away. The provincial NDP had been in government since 1991, but after our re-election in 1996, we had failed to capture the agenda. We were sitting well behind the B.C. Liberals in the polls, and we knew we were heading for a thumping.

That turned out to be putting it politely. It was a brutal campaign and a painful twenty-eight days on the campaign bus. As one of the premier's press secretaries, it was my job to spin for the disastrous campaign, alongside my friend Jim Rutkowski. We'd known it was going to be bad, but it was a massacre. The NDP went from being the government to holding only two seats. In this game, though, you learn more from bad campaigns than from the good ones, and in this campaign, I learned a lot. I also lost my job.

My wife and I pulled up stakes, as did many other NDP staffers, and moved to her hometown of Toronto, where I did environmental consulting work. After two very bad electoral campaigns in less than six months, it was nice to put party politics behind me for a little while.

Months rolled by. And then, in March 2002, Fleming phoned me with some surprising news. "You're never going to guess who just emailed me back," he said.

"Who?" I asked.

"A guy in Jack Layton's office," he said. "It's about the leadership. You should call him right away."

I hung up the phone and called Richard Barry, Jack's assistant at city hall. When I got Barry on the line, I laid it out.

"This is going to sound crazy," I told him. "I'm from B.C. and used to work for the NDP government there. I'm living in Toronto now and my friend from Victoria, city councillor Rob Fleming, said I should give you a call. I think Jack Layton should be the next leader of the NDP, and I want to help."

Barry didn't probe my credentials or ask about my organizing experience. Instead, he invited me to a meeting later that week at Jack and Olivia's house to explore the leadership bid. Before I knew it, I was sitting around their dining room table with other members of the steering committee for Jack's campaign. I was about to enter the inner workings of his political world and to embark on one of the greatest rides in Canada's political history.

JACK WAS NO "ORANGE DIAPER baby." He hadn't grown up in the party, and there were few roots for the NDP or its predecessor, the Co-operative Commonwealth Federation (CCF), in Quebec, where Jack grew up. His activism started in Hudson, an affluent community outside of Montreal. The Laytons had moved there in 1957, when Jack, the eldest of four children, was just seven. His parents had built a house in the middle of the woods, surrounded by farms.

Jack's great-grandfather, English immigrant Philip E. Layton, had set up a successful small business as a piano tuner and salesman after the job offer that brought him to Canada in 1887, for a church organist and choir director, was withdrawn when his potential employer discovered he was blind. Philip, who had been blinded in a woodworking accident as a teen, went on with his wife, Alice, to fundraise to buy land on which they built a school and a workshop for the visually impaired. In 1908, they founded the Montreal Association for the Blind. Philip Layton eventually helped found the Canadian Federation of the Blind.

"I'd start with my great-grampa," Jack said when asked about his political heroes in the 2011 NDP video. "He fought to help get the blind out of poverty. He was blinded himself as a teenager. He's always been my inspiration, even though I never knew him."

The Layton family's multi-generational run at electoral politics began when one of Philip and Alice's sons, Jack's grandfather Gilbert, was elected as a member of the Quebec National Assembly. Gilbert Layton quit Maurice Duplessis's Cabinet in 1939 to protest the Union Nationale's opposition to conscription for the Second World War. Gilbert's brother, George, was a city councillor in Montreal, where the family piano store, Layton Bros., thrived. It remains there today as Layton Audio.

"He ended up meeting with the leadership of the predecessor to the NDP, the CCF, people like J.S. Woodsworth campaigning for pensions for disabled people back in the forties," Jack said of his grandfather. "In fact, they won that fight. I guess that taught me you can make change. That was picked up from my dad: take the opportunity to make positive change happen working with other people. That's what he always encouraged us to do. He said, 'Never miss the opportunity to serve.'"

Jack's dad, engineer Robert Layton, was an active volunteer in the local United Church, where he and his wife, Doris, were leaders of a youth group. They set an example of community service that Jack embraced fully.

"All of the young people of Hudson would come down to the church—mostly to see their girlfriends, but they could say that they were going down to Mr. Layton's Bible class," Jack recounted with a smile in the video.

Jack's father, too, was drawn to politics during Quebec's transformative years. In 1962, Robert Layton served as a campaign manager for the local candidate under Jean Lesage's Liberal banner. And young Jack, then twelve, did his part, putting up Liberal posters around town alongside his dad. Robert Layton moved to electoral politics in 1984, when he ran successfully for Brian Mulroney's Progressive Conservatives and then served as a cabinet minister and the able and likeable caucus chairman. After ascending to high ranks within the provincial Liberals over the years, Jack's father had split with them in 1982 over Pierre Trudeau's repatriation of the constitution without the approval of the Quebec government.

"My dad was someone who believed in the possibility of change. He would get frustrated by people who wouldn't take the opportunity to go out and make positive change happen, including himself if he didn't. He'd push us to take those opportunities," Jack recalled in the 2011 video. "My dad had the most direct influence on me, because he was always involved in political change. In Quebec growing up, I saw him get involved in the Quiet Revolution. Not all of the English Canadians were as keen on the Quiet Revolution as my dad, but he felt taking advantage of the talent of French-Canadian people and having them learn the technical skills to take leadership positions was very important."

One of Jack's formative experiences during his Hudson days involved the prestigious yacht club to which his family belonged. The private club was a bastion for affluent anglophones. French-speaking members of the community were free to join the club, but they invariably didn't have the financial means, a testament to how language and class were intertwined.

Jack, a natural leader who had been elected student council president in high school, saw an opportunity to shake things up in 1967 while serving as "junior commodore" of the club's youth group. Finding a loophole in the club's rule book, he invited a bunch of low-income French teens to a summer party at the club. Turns out board members weren't pleased, but Jack sure was, he would later recount with glee. For him, it was about bringing young people who lived segregated lives together to socialize. On one level, it sounds simple. But for young Jack in a deeply divided Quebec, it was a cheeky and idealistic act of defiance.

As a young undergraduate at McGill University in the late 1960s, Jack took on new battles in the name of social and linguistic equality. Off campus, he supported the fight of the Front d'action politique against a plan to demolish homes and build pricey condominiums in the urban neighbourhood where he lived with his new wife, high school sweetheart Sally Halford.

On campus, he was an activist with the McGill français movement, calling for a more francophone and pro-worker institution. He also soaked up all he could from political philosopher Charles Taylor. Taylor would later earn world renown, but at the time, he was just an upstart professor Layton was drawn to because of his talk about compromise and the politics of polarization.

"Back in the day, they used to talk brokerage politics—smooth over all of the differences all of the time," Jack would later tell John Geddes of *Maclean's* magazine after the 2011 campaign. "Taylor's concept was that you want to bring out the different perspectives and have them stand in stark relief. Then what will emerge are the real solutions."

For Taylor, that also meant taking on, in his off hours, the party of chameleons that went where the wind was blowing: the Liberal Party of Canada. As a four-time candidate for the NDP in the 1960s in Montreal, he endured successive defeats to the Liberals, including to Pierre Trudeau in 1965 in the Liberal stronghold of Mount Royal.

Jack's own relationship with the NDP began in 1970. He was in his final year of undergraduate studies at McGill when the October Crisis erupted with the kidnapping of British trade commissioner James Cross on October 5. Jack was moved by a news report on October 16. NDP leader Tommy Douglas had delivered a speech in the House of Commons that day in response to the federal government's suspension of civil liberties under the War Measures Act: "We in the New Democratic Party recognize the need for prompt and energetic steps to stamp out terrorism, but we have insisted from the beginning that in the process of stamping out terrorism we must not abridge the freedoms that our people and our forefathers have won for us over the years." His words resonated deeply with the young Layton. The next day, Quebec labour minister Pierre Laporte was found dead in the trunk of a car at the Saint-Hubert airport, murdered by his FLQ kidnappers. The popularity of the

NDP and its leader took an immediate hit, but Jack felt the party's opposition to the War Measures Act was the right position: principled, if highly unfashionable at the time.

Jack responded by joining the NDP. He set off to pursue graduate studies in Toronto, and he would spend the next decade balancing his academic work as a graduate student at York University, and then a political science professor at Ryerson Polytechnic Institute (now Ryerson University), with his off-campus activism. He had always planned to return to Quebec after completing his graduate studies, but landing the job at Ryerson encouraged him to stay in Toronto.

Like his campus mentors in Toronto, including Mel Watkins and Terry Grier, Jack was never an armchair academic. He did the easy things—donate money to the NDP and display signs for the local NDP candidate at election time. But he also got his hands dirty with grassroots organizing. He immersed himself in fights in his community, from tenant rights to environmental initiatives. Years later, championing causes like same-sex marriage, he exhibited a depth of conviction more expedient political rivals would never possess. His was a personal history few national political leaders share.

A watershed moment for Jack came on February 5, 1981, when Toronto police raided four bathhouses and arrested nearly three hundred people. It was the largest mass arrest in Canada since the October Crisis, and the crackdown sparked outrage in the gay and lesbian community, which held an illegal march the following evening. Jack, a father of two young children at the time, was on Yonge Street with the marchers to show his support. He was always thinking about what the next step might be in a political fight, so he walked right up to the head marshal, a total stranger, and suggested they talk about what came next.

The marshal, Bob Gallagher, took up Jack's offer to hash out a political strategy. What followed was a decades-long political partnership that developed into a close friendship with both Jack and Olivia. Gallagher would later serve as chief of staff to Olivia at city hall and eventually became Jack's chief of staff in Ottawa.

By 1981, Jack had worked for a decade on the ground, assembling a network of allies and important mentors. One of those mentors was former Toronto mayor and progressive icon John Sewell. It was time for Jack to put those leadership skills to work and take the plunge into electoral politics, Sewell told him.

Jack made a big play by taking on incumbent Gordon Chong in a downtown ward dense with high-rises that was home to Toronto's business district. Chong was a conservative alderman who could count on the backing of Bay Street. Jack couldn't compete on the money front, but he had put together a small army of volunteers through his work on housing issues.

"We were given no chance to win, but the hundreds of tenants who had worked with us for fair and affordable housing over the past few years turned out to help. We ended up with 600 volunteers," Jack later recounted in his 2006 book, *Speaking Out Louder*. "On election night when some pundits declared me defeated, I said: Six hundred workers can defeat $60,000 anytime! That's just what occurred when all the votes from the high-rises rolled in. I learned that night democracy is finally about people, not money."

Jack would go on to be re-elected at the municipal level six times between 1984 and 2000. From his earliest years on council, he would rarely turn down an opportunity to use the media to highlight a cause. To his detractors he was a "showboat," but nobody drew attention to an issue like Jack. He was passionate about finding solutions to problems about which he cared deeply, such as housing, transit, equality, the environment and HIV/AIDS. In a move that hadn't been seen before at city hall, he transformed his small office into a base for community groups. He also evolved as a politician and learned how to get things done, setting in motion an ethos he would later bring to Ottawa. Years later, as NDP leader, he often spoke about being a politician of proposition, not just opposition. To some it sounded like a cliché, but Jack really meant it.

Jack's accomplishments at city hall showed how far ahead of the curve he was. He established the city's Environmental Protection Office in 1987, later chaired the Environmental Task Force created in 1998 and was tasked with drafting the first environmental plan for the amal-gamated City of Toronto. "I was once called the councillor for cycling and re-cycling," Jack, who was known for riding his bike to work and community events, later recalled with glee.

He chaired the Toronto Board of Health during the early years of the emerging AIDS crisis and did pioneering work to provide support and services for the gay community after watching many friends and political allies die. He secured $10 million from the city for an AIDS strategy that was praised worldwide and became a template for other cities around the world.

His big-picture accomplishments stood alongside smaller initiatives for his ward that required some tough slogging, like the seventeen-year-long effort to get sections of the Gardiner Expressway removed to make room for tree-lined boulevards.

After eight years on council, Jack decided to run for mayor in the 1991 election. He and his advisors at city hall, including Dan Leckie, felt that he could take on and beat the mayor at the time, the uninspiring Art Eggleton, who had collected some baggage. When Eggleton, first elected in 1980, announced he would not seek re-election, and a number of candidates on the right of the spectrum indicated they would throw their hats into the ring, Jack's campaign figured victory was possible. They devised a winning strategy dependent upon multiple candidates vying for the same right-of-centre votes, leaving the field clear for Jack on the left to capture 35 per cent of the vote with a targeted message. But as the campaign progressed, right-of-centre candidates Betty Disero and Susan Fish, pressured by the business community to prevent a Layton victory resulting from vote splitting on the right, had dropped out and coalesced around June Rowlands, and the mayoral race became a head-to-head contest.

This dynamic was not helpful.

Mel Watkins canvassed with Jack—and it wasn't going well, even in his own ward. But he was always full of good cheer with a big smile on his face, recalls Watkins. "The greatest thing I noticed about Jack was he didn't give up. We'd be in apartment buildings, he'd be running from one floor to the next, knocking on doors, where he generally got a good reception, but not so many votes. I admire Jack for many things, but one of the things I admire the most about him was that he was never a quitter, that he really was an optimist at heart."

Peter Tabuns, who shared office space with Jack during that election as a city council candidate, remembers Jack bouncing into the office one morning after campaigning at a subway stop. A "guy had come up to him to say: 'I wouldn't piss on your head if your brains were on fire.' Jack thought it was hilarious and went through the campaign office to make sure all heard the story. Then he headed back out to campaign in great spirits," recalls Tabuns, who is now an NDP member of the provincial legislature.

Jack took a drubbing at the polls. Rowlands bested him by a two-to-one margin. There was one important success that night, though. Olivia, who had worked with Toronto NDP MP Dan Heap before becoming a popular school board trustee, was elected a Metro councillor.

Jack and Olivia had met in 1985, a few years after Jack's marriage to his high school sweetheart had ended. Jack would later say it was "love at first sight"—at least for him. They married in 1988. Now, Olivia was making her debut as a councillor, and Jack was out, after an eight-year run. His trademark was his optimism, but the loss sent Jack into a real funk. Years later, he would tell Geddes of *Maclean's* that the defeat was a "skin-thickening experience." Olivia's take was more nuanced. "Jack didn't realize the impact it had on him," she recalls. "It was not easy because, before that, his career was going very smoothly. He was always employed. Now, he lost that and all of a sudden he wasn't sure what he wanted to do. Well, he knew what he wanted to do but he didn't have an outlet."

Jack ploughed ahead. He set up an office in the basement of the home he and Olivia shared with her mother, Ho Sze Chow, and founded the Green Catalysts consulting firm so that he could continue to work on issues that mattered to him. He started teaching part time and got involved in the Rotary Club. "Jack liked structure," says Olivia.

Jack also poured energy into an organization focussed on men combatting violence against women. He and Michael Kaufman co-founded White Ribbon, and together they built a grassroots campaign. To raise money for the public campaign, Kaufman put up his car as collateral to secure a loan. Jack and Olivia put up their home.

In 1993, Jack, keen to raise issues that needed to be on the federal agenda, agreed to serve as a sacrificial lamb for the federal NDP. As part of the national shellacking the party got that year, Jack lost to Liberal Bill Graham in the Toronto Centre riding. Jack's local campaign was more of a pro-forma effort than a realistic shot to win. But he got clobbered, coming in fourth with just 11 per cent of the vote. Even the Reform Party candidate beat him.

Jack rebounded in 1994, when he ran and won a three-year term for the Don River ward on Metro Council. But he was restless, and both he and Olivia wanted to raise the flagging NDP profile by becoming candidates. With a federal election coming in 1997, they decided to target the federal ridings that covered their local wards. Jack was selected as the NDP candidate for Toronto–Danforth, Olivia for Trinity–Spadina, where Jack and Olivia lived.

Victory was not their main goal, considering how poorly the federal NDP had done in the 1993 campaign. The party had garnered just 7 per cent of the national vote. But as organizers, Jack and Olivia also understood that if the NDP was to ever make a breakthrough in Canada's largest city, it would have to do a better job at identifying supporters and building stronger databases. The NDP also held both provincial seats and many city council seats within these two federal ridings, and strengthening that hold made strategic sense.

In the end, Jack garnered 33 per cent of the vote in Toronto–Danforth. The popular Liberal incumbent, Dennis Mills, was returned to Ottawa with 50 per cent. A handful of subway stops to the west, Olivia lost by just four points, even though it was her first time as a federal candidate. Liberal MP Tony Ianno was re-elected with 45 per cent of the vote. Olivia picked up an impressive 41 per cent.

Both Jack and Olivia were re-elected as city councillors in November 1997. By then, they had matured as politicians, and their ability to work with mayor Mel Lastman, who was loathed and lampooned by many on the left, was impressive.

ALTHOUGH JACK HAD RUN TWICE now for the federal NDP, he had also created headaches for the party, especially in Ontario. He had never been part of the establishment and was sometimes in direct conflict with party power-brokers in the province, at times because of issues he raised and other times because of his grassroots organizing methods.

Bob Rae and the provincial NDP government had made a commitment to extend rights to same-sex couples during their 1990 election campaign, but two years after Rae won a majority, the government had still not pressed ahead on this fundamental issue. When Ian Scott, the Liberal MP for the downtown Toronto riding of St. George–St. David, stepped down, NDP riding activists led by Bob Gallagher seized the opportunity of a forthcoming by-election to apply pressure on Rae and his Cabinet. The provincial riding had the highest percentage of lesbians and gays in the country, and there was growing frustration in the gay community. The NDP riding association presented an unprecedented ultimatum to the party brass: table legislation on spousal benefits for gays and lesbians or the local riding won't nominate a candidate, and if the party appoints a candidate, no local money would be spent on the campaign. The Ontario NDP appointed and bankrolled its own candidate. Jack, not a city councillor at the time, was still high profile, and he spoke out publicly in support of the ultimatum.

The gambit was a public relations disaster for the struggling Rae government. The party was furious at the riding association and other supporters of the uprising. In the end, Liberal candidate Tim Murphy, who went on to serve as chief of staff during Paul Martin's brief tenure as prime minister a decade later, won the by-election with more than 50 per cent of the vote. The NDP barely received a thousand votes and went from 36 per cent in the 1990 election to 8.5 per cent in the by-election of April 1, 1993. The following year, Rae finally introduced legislation on spousal benefits for same-sex couples and, surprisingly, made it a free vote in the legislature. The bill was defeated in yet another blunder by the Rae government, but Jack gained a reputation among the NDP establishment as someone who could not be counted on.

Jack's reputation as a shit disturber was enhanced during the 1999

Ontario election when he decided to support his old friend and mentor John Sewell, who was running as an independent in the Toronto Centre–Rosedale riding. The party brass were not amused. Jack and Olivia were both endorsing a candidate who would help split the vote, likely ensuring defeat. Liberal George Smitherman won the seat with nearly 40 per cent of the vote. Sewell came in third, behind the Progressive Conservatives, with 19 per cent. The New Democrat candidate, Helen Breslauer, came in last, receiving less than 9 per cent of the vote.

Now, Jack Layton, with Olivia Chow as his lead organizer, was set on trying to capture the leadership of the federal NDP. This outsider would have to convince party members not just that he could be trusted but that he was the guy who could pull everyone together to resuscitate a party in trouble. It was a tall order.

CHAPTER 2:
RUNNING THE OUTSIDER

When our small group started to meet regularly at Jack and Olivia's house, there was still no timeline for the leadership race. McDonough hadn't yet made her departure official. So our first order of business was to develop a coherent message and strategy that would carry Jack's candidacy through what would likely be a long campaign.

Historically, NDP leadership contests had been proxies for ideological debates within the party. The 1971 Waffle initiative, the Audrey McLaughlin versus Dave Barrett debate in 1989 and the Alexa McDonough versus Svend Robinson faceoff in 1995 were all battles over which direction, philosophically, the party should take.

This race would be different, we agreed. With the party struggling for relevancy, it didn't make sense to frame a leadership race around where candidates sat on the ideological spectrum. Jack's progressive credentials were well known in Toronto, and during the 2001 party convention, he'd shown NPI supporters, drawn from the anti-globalization and other social movements, that he embraced the issues that mattered to them with his passionate interventions at the convention floor mic.

Bill Blaikie, by contrast, had been so annoyed when Svend Robinson chastised the party for not being left wing enough in his pro-NPI speech that he'd spoken out against the initiative in a hard-hitting retort from the convention floor.

"That criticism really ticked me off," Blaikie told me years later, "because we had just come through a time where the caucus had opposed the anti-terrorism bill. Is that the mushy middle?" Blaikie made some fans that day, but he also made a lot of enemies. Even though he'd spear-headed the caucus fight against the Liberal government's deeply flawed anti-terrorism bill in the wake of the terrorist attacks in the U.S. on September 11, 2001, Blaikie's position on the NPI convinced many that he didn't appreciate the role of social movements in the party.

As we crafted Jack's campaign message, we decided he would speak to a much more pressing need, built around our desired ballot box question: Which candidate can bring attention to the issues that progressives care about? Nobody would be better at raising the profile of the party by drawing attention to the issues it championed than Jack. If that was the leadership race's ballot box question, we might just have a shot at this thing.

At Jack's insistence, the message would include making the case to build the party in Quebec. We couldn't call ourselves a truly national party if Quebec was not a part of it, he told the campaign's steering committee. His conviction on that front would play to the aspirations of New Democrat members for what the party could be. Jack also embodied a confidence that had been lacking in the party for many years. We need not just be the conscience of the nation, he was convinced. We could actually build the kind of Canada we wanted ourselves.

The campaign slogan we crafted, "New energy, new leadership," captured this optimistic sentiment. It was also a direct appeal to those who had become disillusioned with the party for being stale and lack-lustre. Our slogan was an unsubtle reference to the expected contenders in the race. Bill Blaikie, who declared on June 17, 2002, had been an MP since 1979, and Lorne Nystrom, who declared on July 31, was first elected in 1968 and had run unsuccessfully for the party leadership in 1975 and 1995.

As a counterpoint, we would present Jack as an outsider. He could claim roots within the party after years of membership, local involvement and having run in two federal elections as an NDP candidate. But he wouldn't have to wear any of the party's recent failings, unlike his opponents. It was a strong combination.

At its core, Jack's primary campaign message was that the party needed new blood. "New leadership" referred not only to the person who would occupy the post, but also to the way leadership would be practised. Not being associated with the party's recent failures was part of that. But Jack would offer a second piece of the puzzle: he planned to organize in key areas to build and strengthen the party's organizational capacity, its fundraising, its external communications and its brand.

It is very rare for a leadership candidate to have the whole package: the vision and the skills to attend to both internal and external considerations. You usually get one or the other, but Jack had an aptitude for both. He also knew from his city hall days and his days as a young activist that you needed both an infrastructure and the resources to win.

Through Jack's campaign, the choice of moving forward or embracing the status quo would be laid out plainly for party members to see. This approach redrew the terms of the debate, moving it away from "left versus right" to "modern politics versus the old way of looking at the world." That meant Jack didn't need to embark on any new, bold policy initiatives. In fact, although Jack would release numerous policy statements throughout his campaign, they did no more than highlight existing party policy or reiterate what he had been working for at city hall. Some said Jack's positions were refreshing, precisely what the party needed to modernize. Others argued that he was straying from the party's roots. Either way, what he was proposing was mostly existing party policy.

We were excited about how the campaign was shaping up, and we knew Jack's offer to the party was strong. We still had to develop a plan to inoculate against his weaknesses, though. Every candidate has weaknesses, and Jack was no exception. In fact, we assessed there would be plenty about him for the other candidates to attack.

Jack was too flashy, all show and no substance, they'd say. Sure, Jack could get elected as a city councillor, but he had run twice federally and lost badly. He'd also been beaten badly as a candidate for mayor. Jack was the epitome of Toronto, a place Canadians love to hate. How was this Torontonian, the ultimate urbanite, going to win in Saskatchewan or northern Ontario? Besides, the party had just tried someone without a seat in Parliament from outside of caucus in McDonough, and it hadn't worked. They would add that Layton's father was a Mulroney Conservative.

So our campaign plan couldn't be just about putting forward our message and promoting our ballot box question. We had to counter the criticisms we knew were coming, especially the overarching one about Jack being a shallow showboat. Luckily, between his time as president of the Federation of Canadian Municipalities and his substantive policy accomplishments in Toronto, we had plenty of ammunition to protect Jack against this critique. In fact, we could turn it into a strength. Jack would draw on his mantra at city hall and get the NDP into the business of proposition, not just opposition.

Our campaign also embraced an adage that Jack would stick with over the years: Don't just say you're going to do something; do it. We would have to out-organize, out-fundraise and operate a professional media relations and communications shop in our leadership campaign to show what the party would be capable of under Jack's leadership.

In terms of voting, the one-member, one-vote approach would be a first for the party, and we seized it. Tactically, the first question we had to get our heads around was whether to focus our organizational attention on the fifty-eight thousand existing NDP members or to sign up new members who would support Jack. We decided it wasn't an either-or option. The best way to show existing members that we could re-energize the party, we agreed, was to go out now and sign up new members, an effort to be spearheaded by Olivia and Bob Gallagher.

In fact, the initiative to get new members—and to keep existing members informed of our progress—would become the backbone of Jack's campaign message. The way to demonstrate new energy and new leadership was to attract new members. This emphasis on organizational muscle played to Jack's strengths. He and Olivia were organizers, first and foremost. That was their background, and they attracted other organizers, too. They liked results and outcomes. If you couldn't measure it, it wouldn't help you win.

Our campaign headquarters in the early days, Jack and Olivia's semi-detached Victorian house in Toronto's Chinatown, was a testament to their long-standing approach to politics. Their home had been transformed years earlier into an organizing centre. It was not uncommon for groups to be holding outreach meetings there about child care, AIDS action or affordable housing on any given night of the week. A sign-up sheet posted in Olivia's city hall office allowed people to book different rooms in their home, and the infrastructure at the house had evolved over the years. Extra phone lines had been in place since 1995, when Jack and Olivia had worked on Svend Robinson's campaign to lead the NDP. Multiple workstations had also been in place for years.

By the late spring of 2002, the Layton campaign took over the house. The living room, the dining room, the top floor balcony and the backyard, complete with a Chinese pond, were all serving as work areas. On most nights, there would be approximately forty campaign volunteers in the house, with five or six people on cordless phones pacing around the back garden, talking with organizers, party members and potential members. We would chase the time zones, starting off with calls to Newfoundland and Labrador, then the Maritimes, and ending at midnight Toronto time, when it became too late to call B.C. At one point, there were twenty-five keys to Jack and Olivia's house in circulation. The epicentre of the campaign was fuelled by the cooking of Olivia's mom, Ho Sze.

Locally, the campaign tapped into Jack and Olivia's extensive network of activists in Toronto. Nationally, our starting point was more modest, though not insignificant. Jack knew mayors and councillors from across Canada, and his long track record on environmental issues meant we could also tap into a network of green activists. Many of these activists were getting involved in the NDP for the first time. Many environmentalists were used to working quietly with the Liberals, evidence of the entrenched belief that the Grits were the least-worst governing option. But with the government's increasingly embarrassing record, environmentalists were growing more oppositional. Jack's campaign targeted these organizers with a modern message and a tactical approach to leadership that emphasized getting results.

My job during the early days was to enlist former student activists to work on Jack's campaign. From my nine years of involvement with the Canadian Federation of Students, I had friends and acquaintances all across Canada and appointed many of them to be in charge of organizing their province.

These provincial representatives were charged with finding others to help organize in their area. Each provincial and territorial lieutenant had a Toronto liaison with whom they spoke daily to maintain a strong connection with headquarters.

Planning for Jack's campaign launch took up a lot of time in those early months. Alexa McDonough had announced her departure on June 6, and the leadership convention was set for January. The stakes were high for Jack's campaign. A good launch, with the right message and mix of endorsers by Jack's side, would give his campaign a boost and symbolize the kind of party Jack would lead. A bad launch would embolden critics to detail why Jack wasn't ready for the national stage. That would play into the hands of veteran NDP MP Bill Blaikie, who had already jumped into the race. We needed to show the media—and the membership—that we were ready for prime time. By the morning of July 21, we were all set for Jack's official announcement, scheduled for the next day.

After thinking it through, Jack had decided the front lawn of Parliament Hill was the best place to announce his candidacy. The outsider from Toronto would be surrounded by a small army of supporters, also from outside Ottawa. Designated supporters would speak about Jack's record of getting things done on issues that mattered to progressives during his long career in municipal politics—and about what he could bring to the national stage.

Despite wariness from his advisory team about scheduling a laundry list of speakers, Jack insisted no group be left out of the launch. He wanted to showcase who he could bring into the struggling party. In addition to people from various social movements, he'd arranged for representatives from First Nations and the labour movement to be on hand, along with some old friends from a Quebec housing group. The housing activists had secured federal funding through an initiative of the

FCM under Jack's leadership, and he insisted they be there to illustrate how "flexible federalism," a big draw in Quebec, could work.

So the lineup for the open-air press conference was long—or, in the words of campaign communications director Jamey Heath, "a bit of a circus." With the launch just twenty-four hours away, and all decisions well in hand, Jamey took a stroll. It was mid-morning, and Heath was taking a break from polishing Jack's launch speech. He walked to Parliament Hill to clear his head.

Heath lived just a few blocks from the Hill, where he had settled a few months earlier. He was devoting all his time to Jack's campaign, though, so he'd never seen the bustle of the Hill on a summer day. Hundreds of tourists were snapping pictures and wandering the grounds. Then, a marching band began to play—very loudly. Heath looked at his watch and realized that Jack's press conference was scheduled to start at exactly the same time the next day. Panicked, he ran home and phoned officials to ask whether the changing of the guard took place every day on Parliament Hill. It did.

Heath rapidly drafted an updated media advisory with a new time for the launch and got it out to the press. Disaster averted. Jack's launch was not drowned out by bagpipes, and Jack was not subject to mockery in the media for how little he knew about how Ottawa worked. In fact, Jack got a clean hit in the press with great pictures of him standing on the steps of Parliament.

By Labour Day, we had a strong team of organizers in place. Except for Valerie Dugale, who was in charge of Jack's schedule and did other administrative work, and Heath, we were all volunteers, so we welcomed the arrival of Bruce Cox as full-time campaign manager. Cox and Jack went way back. They'd first met in the mid-1980s, when Cox worked for Toronto city councillor Joe Pantalone. Until recently, Cox had served as provincial secretary for the Ontario NDP, a position he'd held since 1999. When Jack first approached Cox about becoming his campaign manager, though, Cox wasn't sold on the idea. When they spoke at the close of the NDP's federal council meeting in Halifax in early June, Cox told Jack he'd decided to move on from party politics and devote himself to environmental advocacy work.

As it turned out, some of the internal discussions at the federal council meeting had reinforced Cox's decision to walk away. The group had convened to hammer out the rules for the NDP leadership race and make some key decisions, including where the convention would be held. Cox was flabbergasted at some of the ideas being entertained. "Why don't we hold this in Regina or Saskatoon?" he recalls a few people suggesting. "These were just bad decisions for the party. I was furious. The sentiment was, 'Let's stay small.' It was crazy."

Cox and others prevailed and the party opted instead for a Toronto leadership convention to guarantee that the national media would actually show up. Cox had had it, though, and he wanted out. Jack, who hadn't declared his candidacy yet, had other plans for him. "Let's go for a beer," he suggested to Cox as the meeting was winding down.

Cox encouraged Jack to run but explained he couldn't be counted on for help. Jack's counter-argument was simple and ultimately persuasive. "With all of the work you've done on the environment, you now have a bona fide environmentalist running. Take the summer off. Start after Labour Day," Jack suggested to Cox.

Cox agreed, to Jack's delight. Cox's party expertise was unquestionable, and the appointment was a very smart move: the outsider had landed an insider who was well liked by the NDP establishment. That would make Jack's campaign more attractive and build a bridge to the party.

Working from new office space just down the street from Jack and Olivia's home, Cox set out to strengthen the campaign infrastructure and to implement targeted strategies in the back half of the campaign in key regions. We knew we were signing up new members at a solid rate in Ontario, for example, but we needed to shore up support in Saskatchewan, where seventeen thousand of the fifty-eight thousand existing members—nearly one-third—lived.

Jack, who took weekly private French lessons throughout the campaign to brush up on his second language, continued to stress why Quebec mattered for the NDP, an argument that was easier to make once Quebec leadership candidate Pierre Ducasse entered the race. Ducasse, twenty-nine at the time, was not running to win but to raise some issues, including the

NDP's need to build in Quebec. "Just so you know, I'm doing this for the party," he told Jack when they met for the first time at an Ontario NDP convention just before Jack formally announced he was running. "I want to be clear I am not here to help another candidate, but I may hurt others more," said Ducasse, whose take on Bill Blaikie was unequivocal.

"It was pretty obvious pretty quickly that it was going to be between Jack and Bill," recalls Ducasse. "I absolutely believed that Bill was not right for the party. Project ourselves ten years to the future. We would not have won in Quebec. [Bill] just didn't have the sensitivity. He didn't have the personality. He would have been an actual disaster for Quebec."

Our Saskatchewan strategy was multi-pronged. In the fall, Bruce Cox assigned me the responsibility to liaise with our campaign organizers in Saskatchewan. I offered strategic advice on who to approach for endorsements and delivered feedback from our Saskatchewan organizers to the steering committee so that we could make needed regional adjustments.

A critical component of our Saskatchewan strategy was an endorsement letter from Saskatchewan deputy premier Clay Serby that would be mailed out to every new and existing NDP member, timed to arrive in their mailboxes at the same time their ballot arrived in the new year. We'd calculated that the majority of those voting would do so within the first twenty-four hours of receiving the ballot, so the timing of the mail-out was vital. We also poured resources into encouraging our supporters to mail in their ballots as soon as they got them, both to minimize chances of them not voting and to reduce our pull-the-vote work on election day.

For those on the outside looking in, it might have been hard to figure out what a Barenaked Ladies concert in Toronto in September had to do with our Saskatchewan strategy. Our detractors dismissed the concert as a stunt, like Stockwell Day arriving at his press conference on a Jet Ski wearing a wetsuit. The knock against Jack failed, but the concert was still a risky strategy for our campaign, given Jack's reputation as a bit of a showboat lacking in substance. On the surface, the event had all the trappings of a stunt: a popular band, a downtown venue and great visuals. But the real point of the concert was to reach thousands of people, especially young people, by meeting them where they hung out. The

Barenaked Ladies were the headliners, with sixteen acts in all. To get into the concert, you needed to sign up to join the party. If you were already a member, you could get in by signing up one friend. We turned the front parking lot of the Phoenix Concert Theatre into a giant membership sign-up assembly line, gathering names and contact information.

The media and the other leadership candidates pressed us about how we knew these young people would actually vote in the leadership race—or vote for Jack. The answer was simple: we didn't. But we did know definitively that these young people wouldn't vote in the leadership contest if they weren't NDP members. There was something more to the concert, too. Our target audience wasn't just the concert-goers in Toronto. It was also the long-time members of the party, many of whom were senior citizens, in places like Weyburn, Saskatchewan. Our hope was that they would hear about this candidate signing up young people in downtown Toronto and agree that's exactly what the party needed—more young people.

In the end, the concert would be one reason Jack did so well in rural Canada and among long-standing members. Nystrom and Blaikie were well known and well regarded, but neither of them could instill that sense of energy in people. Clay Serby's endorsement letter, sent from his hometown of Yorkton, Saskatchewan, reminded party members of this fact in a more subtle way:

> Yorkton is certainly not Toronto. We don't think about smog or subways and when it snows, we don't call in the army. But we do think about water quality and our rural roads. That's why I'm voting for Jack. Because he's worked with communities of all sizes and though their challenges are different, their solutions have much in common... Jack has brought thousands of new people in to our party, and that's one more reason I am on his team. He has proven he can broaden our base. We know we need to attract more people, particularly young people. Some may be thinking that getting 1,200 people into a concert where they hear our solutions is a "stunt," but I can't remember the last time the NDP got 1,200 young people out to hear our solutions... Ten years ago, our party had 44 Members of Parliament. Today, we have 14. That's got to change and Jack Layton is the candidate of change.

Another keystone of our campaign was that fundraising was a form of communication to deliver our message. This approach mattered, because although the party's leadership campaign rules stipulated you could spend up to $500,000 on your campaign, fundraising costs were excluded. Serby's pitch also asked for a donation, so it was excluded from our campaign costs. Jack's multilingual phone banks and mail program, run by Strategic Communications in Vancouver, were also excluded from campaign costs because they included a donation ask. Our campaign ultimately spent $500,000 to raise $1.2 million.

We raised eyebrows by holding fundraising receptions in martini bars. Some people thought Jack was trying to rebrand the party through the leadership race itself. He was. His unapologetic attempt to recast the NDP as younger, more modern and more confident was also on display in November, when we held a $125-per-plate dinner at the Liberty Grand ballroom at the CNE grounds in Toronto—an entry price unheard of in NDP circles at the time. The event raised $80,000.

Ed Broadbent was struck by how many young people were in attendance at the Liberty Grand ballroom dinner and by how many people he didn't recognize. Many of them had never been to an NDP event in their lives. The former party leader and respected elder statesman didn't know Jack personally, but their mutual friend Terry Grier had spoken to him about Jack as a serious prospect. Broadbent, deeply worried about the viability of the party going forward, had made a point of travelling to Toronto to speak with people who knew Jack's record in municipal politics and had watched him perform.

"It did not take me long at all to decide that Jack was what the party needed," Broadbent recalls. "Not only was he from an urban area, but he had an urbane outlook in terms of issues. He had taken concrete action. He had a reputation for reaching out as a municipal politician, and I thought it was important. The other thing that I think was very important is that, first and foremost, Jack's a doer."

A few days after the Liberty Grand fundraiser, on the night of the Toronto all-candidates meeting on October 29, Jack's BlackBerry rang. It was Broadbent. Jack left the room to take the call in private. He rejoined Cox, Heath and Gallagher with a big smile on his face.

"We got him," he told them.

"What do you mean?" Cox asked.

"Ed. He's in. He wants to endorse," Jack said.

We knew Broadbent's endorsement, to be announced November 27 on Parliament Hill, would be a game-changer. It would give all the party stalwarts who supported Broadbent permission to back Jack. That kind of boost just before the membership sign-up deadline of December 10 would help carry us through to the leadership convention.

Broadbent's announcement would also be a major blow for Bill Blaikie. Blaikie, a friend and long-time caucus colleague of Ed's, had never asked for Broadbent's support—he didn't think he had to. He had served under Broadbent's leadership for a decade, stick-handling some of the most difficult files the party had to deal with. They included the repatriation of the constitution, provincial rights, the national energy plan and the Canada Health Act.

"I have always had a high regard for Bill intellectually," Broadbent explained years later. "He is a very intelligent, bright guy. But in terms of political skills and outreach skills towards people who were not already with us, I thought he was limited—in terms of what was required to build the party to take it beyond its current base. Jack was a very intelligent man, but he was not an intellectual. David Lewis was an intellectual. Tommy Douglas was not. Bill Blaikie is an intellectual. Jack was not. Jack was a doer. He wanted to win. He wanted to build. He had a concreteness about him. This is what attracted me to Jack."

For Broadbent, the stakes in the leadership race could not have been higher: he believed the wrong choice could mean the end of the party. "I thought it was by no means self-evident in political life that the NDP would rebound," he recalled. "That we would just pick up where we left off with Alexa and start going up again. Other parties have disappeared in Canadian history. We could have gotten blown out of the water. History wasn't going to guarantee us a place in it. Bill was too much within the family for what I thought was needed."

The final phase of our Saskatchewan strategy, moving Jack and Olivia there during the Christmas holidays, was vital to showing long-time members how much the province mattered. The couple lived with supporters, going from house to house in town after town to work those communities. They never stayed in a hotel, and word quickly spread in some of the smaller towns that never had politicians visit that Jack Layton was staying there.

By the new year, we felt very good about where Jack's campaign stood heading into the leadership convention. We had impressed long-standing members. We had signed up eighty-one hundred new members, more than any other campaign. And we had raised $1.2 million and were debt-free.

THE CONVENTION KICKOFF, JANUARY 24, 2002, was my first day on the job as director of communications for the federal NDP. The position had been posted in December, as the party prepared to pull off a big-league show on a little-league budget.

Jack's campaign was in its final phase by then, and once the membership sign-up deadline had passed and the final mail-out had been delivered, all that was needed was to pull the vote. Before I applied, I'd talked to Cox, Heath and campaign volunteer Rick Smith, a good friend I'd met during my time with the Canadian Federation of Students. We figured if—or, more likely, when—Jack won, he could use some familiar faces and allies in Ottawa as he set out to modernize the party. It was so late in the game now that my stepping down from Jack's campaign would be inconsequential. Smith, who lived in Ottawa at the time, also understood how important it was for New Democrats to start taking up space in the national capital. Back then, the town was painted red. You couldn't walk a block in the downtown core without running into Liberal staffers. The NDP's unofficial bar in Ottawa back then, the Mayflower II, was a perfect metaphor for the rut we were in. It was dark and dingy, hidden away on the second floor of an ugly building. When I arrived in Ottawa after being offered the job, I remember looking around it and thinking, "For God's sake, if we do anything in this town, we need a better bar."

Heading into the leadership convention, Bruce Cox was feeling confident about Jack's ability to capture the necessary 50 per cent of the vote on the first ballot. As Jack's campaign team, we had never underestimated the organizational capacity of the other contenders. We'd even targeted the sign-ups of other campaigns in an effort to secure second-ballot support. Along with Blaikie, Nystrom and Ducasse, Joe Comartin and Bev Meslo were also contesting the leadership. But we knew Jack had been successful, particularly in Ontario, in attracting new members. Jack's pitch for change was playing well with long-standing members as well. The wild card was the labour vote. Unions affiliated with the party had been allocated 25 per cent of all votes cast, but it wasn't clear who would be voting on behalf of each affiliate. Besides, the labour vote hadn't coalesced around any one candidate.

The convention events would be largely pro forma and would have little impact on the outcome. The mail-in ballots had already been cast, and members could vote online during a set timeline up to January 25, when convention delegates could also vote in person. But there was huge excitement in the packed hall at the CNE's National Trade Centre, with the delegates sensing the party was on the brink of something big. Jack's campaign planned to use the fifteen minutes allotted for his nomination floor show to tell his story. The idea was to send the strong message that Jack had diverse support, from the old and the new. Ed Broadbent and a young university student, Willy Blomme, would nominate him from the floor. Jack would use the remaining time to deliver a speech timed to come in just under the fifteen minutes to avoid getting cut off.

Broadbent was scripted to deliver a concise line. "My name is Ed Broadbent, and I'm proud to nominate Jack Layton for leader." Full stop. That would be Blomme's cue to begin her short remarks in French about why Jack was so important for young people and the future of the party. The problem was that Broadbent didn't stop after his scripted line. Instead, he went on for a full five minutes. Blomme had lost her cue to start. Jack's speech cut down by Jamey Heath in real time, ended up being three minutes—about half of its original length. That was just the beginning of a convention that, on the surface, was going well for Jack. Jack's campaign did a very good job at executing under tough conditions. And although there was plenty of drama behind the scenes, delegates and reporters were too busy parsing the problems with the voting process itself to notice. For the first time ever at a leadership convention, in addition to the new one-member, one-vote system, the party was offering real-time Internet voting as an option alongside advance mail-in balloting and voting in person at the convention. The new technology was expensive, and the Internet option had plenty of detractors in the party, who feared that older, long-time members would feel alienated. But the party wanted the selection of the leader to be accessible, and they forged ahead. The party had hired a company called Election.com to oversee all aspects of the vote, and the process hit a snag soon after online voting opened up, encountering a targeted global worm designed to clog up our lines. (This was a different problem from the one the NDP would face during the 2012 vote, when the party was hit with a denial of service attack.)

In response to the glitch, voting time was extended, and the first-ballot results were delayed for hours. The crowd in the hall was restless, as were the radio and TV networks, forced to fill much more air time than originally planned. My first task as the party's new director of communications was to try to contain the negative press. The questions being tossed at me made for a gruelling afternoon, but the ordeal also proved to be good training for the decade to come. "Are you being hacked?" reporters asked me. "Have the results been compromised?"

Hours after the first results were supposed to be announced, we finally had the numbers. I waited in the staff area behind the main stage with my predecessor, Wayne Harding—who was on duty to ensure that the convention he had been working on for months went smoothly— and staff from the voting firm. When I saw the results on the backstage screen—53.5 per cent for Jack—I thought at first they couldn't be right. But Wayne printed off copies of the results, put them in an envelope and handed it to me. I was charged with providing the numbers, under embargo, to the reporters hovering at the back of the convention hall, where the media risers were stationed.

I was shaking as I walked through the crowd. People rushed over to me, pleading, "When are the results coming? C'mon."

I smiled calmly and said, "We'll have them soon." The delegates had no idea I had the results under my arm. I didn't look over at the Layton riser; I didn't want to tip my hand. I just kept my head down and wound my way through the packed hall.

Jack's campaign didn't need any tipoff from me, though. Norm MacAskill, Layton's Ontario organizer, had noticed that the party's two chief ushers, whose job was to keep order during the convention, had moved over to Jack's risers. That's when they knew that Jack, the outsider, had won.

It wasn't even close: Jack got 31,150 votes (53.5 per cent) compared with Blaikie's 14,365 votes (24.7 per cent). Nystrom failed to crack 10 per cent with 5,397 votes. Joe Comartin got 4,490 votes (7.7 per cent), Ducasse 2,155 votes (3.7 per cent) and Bev Meslo 645 votes (1.1 per cent).

"I didn't go in confident that I would win," Blaikie told me years later. "But I was thinking it was going to be closer than it was. I was surprised by the fact there was no second ballot."

The party didn't announce a breakdown province by province, but Jack's campaign knew from internal intelligence that he had won B.C., Ontario, Quebec, Newfoundland and Labrador, and likely Saskatchewan. We came in second in Manitoba. We knew it was important that Jack's win be a national victory, not just one region big-footing another. That way, a narrative about a Toronto takeover of the party wouldn't be able to gel.

Jack made his victory speech from the stage with his dad's parliamentary pin in his pocket. Immediately afterwards, he sent an important signal to Quebec. The networks all wanted to land the first post-victory interview with Jack, but he went to the CBC riser first, then to Radio-Canada. Networks fight like hell to get the winner first, and CTV and Global, private broadcasters with the largest share of the market, were upset. But the move signalled that, although the NDP had garnered only 2 per cent of the vote in Quebec in the most recent federal election, the province mattered to Jack. It was his first decision, moments after being elected leader. He had made Quebec his priority over reaching the largest English-speaking audience.

While Jack was doing the rounds with the various networks, Jamey Heath's phone rang. It was the prime minister's switchboard in Ottawa, asking if Mr. Layton had a few moments to accept a call from Jean Chrétien to congratulate him. Heath accepted graciously, saying he would hand over the phone to Jack as soon as the prime minister was ready. As the switchboard was transferring the call to Chrétien, Jamey's dad phoned to congratulate him on Jack's victory. Heath recognized the number and quickly took the call. "Hey, Dad, I'm just on the other line, hang on," he said. "I'm going to put you on hold for a sec." Instead of putting his dad on hold, Heath hung up on the Prime Minister's Office.

Accidentally hanging up on the prime minister was an embarrassment. Bungling your maiden speech on your first full day as NDP leader would be a public disaster, and it was one that was narrowly averted. Following Jack's victory on Saturday, Jack and Heath put the final touches on Jack's Sunday morning speech to convention. It was crafted to signal to the national press gallery and the country the approach Jack was going to take.

Heath and Bruce Cox insisted on a teleprompter. The party staff at the time had no experience running one, however, and just before Jack was set to go on, word got to Cox that there was a problem with the machine. The speech had been erased.

Cox turned to Heath, "Shit, we've got about fifteen minutes before he goes on. What do we do?"

"I'll re-type it directly into the machine," Heath said. "Here, you take a paper copy and have Jack practise it at his seat."

As a frantic Cox set out to find Jack, he dropped the speech, and the sheets of paper went flying everywhere. When Cox bent down to pick them up, he noticed the pages weren't numbered. He hadn't read the speech himself, so he scrambled to put the pages in order in the few minutes he had. The speech Heath was typing directly into the teleprompter, as fast as he could, was full of typos and missing words.

Jack, poised to take the stage, had no idea any of this was going on. Heath simply signalled to Cox that the teleprompter was all set to go.

Then the president of the party, André Foucault, called the new leader to the stage. The country was watching.

Jack gave a hard-hitting speech that focussed on the Iraq War, George W. Bush and the Liberal government's willingness to acquiesce to Washington on foreign policy. A week before the convention, 250,000 people had marched in Montreal to protest the U.S. invasion of Iraq, the largest of many rallies that galvanized progressives across Canada. Jack's speech also laid out his approach to politics. "It's whether we elect parliamentarians to bicker or build that will be the defining issue of our time. And we say, 'let's build,'" he told the receptive crowd.

Jack's speech achieved two significant things. First, it spoke with clarity and confidence about where Jack and the New Democrats stood on an important issue, in contrast to the always-waffling Liberal Party. Second, it announced a new way of doing things in Ottawa that would become Jack's hallmark leadership style.

The initial response from the press was good. But some of us wondered why Jack had been looking only at one side of the convention hall while he spoke. After the ovations, Jack came backstage, laughing hysterically.

"What is it? What's so funny?" asked Heath.

"The teleprompter," Jack said. "One of the paddles was on backwards, and I could only read from one side."

Paul Wells, writing in the *National Post,* spoke to a delegate who summed up the sentiment in many corners of the party. "There are an awful lot of people in the party who are sick of being off the radar screen. Jack is as much a vehicle for that as anything else." *Montreal Gazette* columnist L. Ian MacDonald noted that it was a "measure of how much the party thirsts for relevance again" that both Svend Robinson and Broadbent, "who can't stand each other, were both in Layton's camp."

STEP ONE OF THE PROJECT was complete. After a spectacularly successful campaign, Jack was leader of the federal NDP. But the party was still broke and dead last in the polls. Now we'd have to transfer the momentum from his decisive convention victory to the task of winning over caucus and the national media.

Excited and ready to implement the transition plan, the team, headed up by a newly appointed chief of staff and including Heath and me, headed back to Ottawa to begin the work. We didn't see it coming, but Jack was about to be handed a leadership-defining moment during his first hours on the job.

CHAPTER 3:
STUMBLING OUT OF THE GATES

Jack was in a buoyant mood. Two days earlier, he'd just won a decisive first-ballot victory in the leadership race. Now, he was standing at the front of the large boardroom in the NDP caucus services office on the tenth floor of the heritage building, just one block from Parliament Hill. "I've never had a staff this big before," he joked to the two dozen staffers, mostly young people, who worked as researchers or media officers for the NDP caucus.

Staff changes occur whenever a new party leader comes in, and Jack wanted to make sure everybody felt part of the new team. Jamey Heath would be director of communications in the new leader's office, and Rick Smith had been appointed Jack's chief of staff. Alexa McDonough's chief of staff, Hugh Blakeney, son of former Saskatchewan premier Allan Blakeney, would stay on for a month or so to help with the transition. Maureen Prebinski would continue as director of administration. Both Karl Bélanger, long-time press secretary to McDonough, and Jack would go on the party payroll, because Jack didn't have a seat in the House of Commons. This would put financial pressure on the party, but there wasn't any other option.

Looking out at all these caucus staffers, Jack drew on his experience in the swimming pool to rally the troops. As a teenager, he'd switched from competitive swimming to water polo, because he preferred team sports. "My friend was big and stocky, and after the first game, he turned to me and said, 'I don't think I can do this. I'm not keeping up. I'm holding everyone back,'" Jack told the group. Not content to leave it at that, Jack had consulted with the rest of their teammates, developed a plan and then gone back to tell his buddy, "Okay, there's been a change. You're big. You've got upper body strength. We're putting you in goal."

Jack's point was that everybody has a role to play, and he wanted to encourage NDP staffers to give it their all. Jack held up his BlackBerry and waved it around, "I want everybody on the team to feel like they can approach me with anything." It was a great moment, but things went downhill quickly from there.

The day after his victory, Jack had dispatched his old professor from Ryerson and long-time friend Terry Grier to ask Bill Blaikie if he would serve as the NDP's parliamentary leader. Jack wanted to send a strong signal to the caucus and the party that it was time to unite, bring the team together and get down to work. Since Jack was not yet an MP himself, Blaikie was the natural choice to lead the NDP in the House every day in Question Period. He was loved by the caucus and was a respected parliamentarian.

Blaikie accepted the offer, though he didn't like the underlying message of the leadership vote. He felt it diminished the role of the NDP MPs when, every time the party needed a new leader, they seemed to elect someone who wasn't an MP. "Experience as an MP was a liability," he says today.

Jack had rallied the troops with his upbeat staff meeting, but now, a week later, he was facing his caucus. As he took his seat in Room 371 on the third floor of the West Block, a space plenty big enough to hold the tiny NDP caucus of fourteen, he had only two supporters looking back at him. Three of the MPs in the room had run against him.

There was only one item on the agenda that day: Jack's appointment of Rick Smith as his chief of staff. Smith, who had led the local Ottawa leadership campaign for Jack, had been quietly working as head of the transition for a few months already, part of Jack's plan to make sure he had all his bases covered if he became leader. In the run-up to convention, Smith—tapped because he was a smart strategist who knew how Ottawa worked—had developed a comprehensive one-hundred-day plan.

Smith's appointment as chief of staff became official on the night of

Jack's win. Word spread quickly through the hospitality suites, and the rumblings began immediately. Since 1997, Smith had served as the executive director of the Canadian office of the International Fund for Animal Welfare (IFAW). A marine biologist by training, he was well known in the environmental community for IFAW's work on endangered species. Smith was also a household name in Newfoundland and Labrador, where his organization was leading the campaign against the commercial seal hunt, a symbol of great cultural pride for islanders. The Newfoundland provincial party, though small at the time, was vocal in its opposition to Jack's pick. Party stalwarts like Jack Harris and Nancy Riche made it clear that unless Smith was dropped, they'd go public with their opposition.

Reporters had picked up a strong whiff of dissent at the hospitality suites on Saturday night after Jack's leadership win. Jack's new press secretary, Karl Bélanger, who had met Jack for the first time that day, had fielded informal queries that night from Quebec journalists Michel Vastel from *Le Soleil* and Maurice Godin from Radio-Canada. "Well, I hear his position on seals could be a bit of a problem," Vastel told Bélanger. When journalists were talking about potential issues with Jack's most important staff appointment just hours after his victory, it was a sign of trouble.

When Smith began his rounds of meetings with caucus members and staff in the days after Jack's victory, he detected some of the same opposition. The situation was quickly becoming an early test for the new leader, and it was increasingly difficult to contain it as an internal spat. At the time, Jack didn't have a lot of tools at his disposal. He had few staff or surrogates to go to bat for him. He barely knew where the washrooms were on Parliament Hill. "Some of us said, 'Stay strong,'" recalls Cox, whom Jack called during this first week of his leadership. "But Newfoundland was Newfoundland. You couldn't have a caucus revolt on day one."

Heading into the February 5 caucus meeting, Jack had figured caucus members would air their concerns and they could take it from there. Things didn't play out like that. First, the MPs asked Smith to step out of the room. Once he had, MP after MP got on the speaker's list to insist Smith had to go. The caucus gave Jack an ultimatum: get rid of Smith or they'd ratchet up the public pressure through the press. It's either him or us, they said.

At the end of the meeting, Jack called Olivia in Toronto. Weather the storm, she advised; this will blow over. Jack proceeded to Svend Robinson's office, conveniently located next to the room where the caucus held its weekly meeting. Rick Smith, who was waiting there, asked, "How did it go?"

A shell-shocked Jack replied, "Not good, brother, not good."

Before Jack could say anything else, Smith interjected. "Look, this can't be about me," he said. "I have thrown you off in the first days as leader. This is a distraction we don't need. I'm resigning, Jack, effective immediately."

The game plan for the first days of the transition had been wall-to-wall media so that Jack could talk about his plans for the party and ideas for the country. Instead, he was facing members of the press outside of the NDP's caucus room about the staffing controversy. Reporters seldom bothered to come to the NDP "caucus outs" on Wednesdays, the designated day for political parties to hold weekly caucus meetings when the House of Commons is sitting. This week was different. Camped out down the hall, the media smelled blood. Jack didn't disappoint them with his announcement of Smith's sudden departure.

To the media, Jack either lacked judgment in appointing Smith in the first place or had no spine for failing to stand up to his critics. Either way, it was lose-lose for Jack. The reports in the press were scathing, calling it an embarrassing gaffe by a rookie leader who couldn't even make it through two weeks on the job without a serious misstep. That night, I sat with Rick Smith in his living room. We were both devastated, even though we knew his resignation was the only way out of a bad situation. When we tuned in to the CTV national news with Lloyd Robertson, we were stunned to see that Smith's departure was one of the evening's top stories. The NDP had arrived in the big leagues, it seemed, and this kind of fumble got big-league exposure. We sat in silence as we absorbed the message of the day: the incident underscored Jack's vulnerability in the eyes of critics, who said he didn't understand the country, and it was tarnishing Jack's decisive victory.

In hindsight, it's clear Jack and his campaign should have anticipated some of this blowback. That way, he could have reached out, quietly and proactively, to explain his decision ahead of time to key leaders in the party and caucus, outlining why Smith was a smart choice for the position and assuring them of the party's continued and unequivocal support for the seal hunt.

The perception that Jack didn't understand the country wasn't helpful. Neither was having a new party leader without a chief of staff. "Rick was very much part of the transition," recalls Cox. "He put together the first hundred days. Then all of a sudden you have your right-hand person knocked off. That's really hard. Now, there was no captain in the leader's office to put together a team of supporters on the Hill and build bridges with stakeholders.

There was also no Plan B. Jack and his team took a long time to recover from the setback, with no long-term permanent chief of staff appointed until after the 2006 campaign. It was a rough start for a new leader who had delivered such a great speech to staff about team building. "It was like returning to things the way they used to be: We were firm on things until we felt resistance. It was demoralizing for staff to see Rick go," recalls Kevin Dorse, who worked for NDP caucus services from 1998 to 2010.

SOME OF US SAW THE spat over Smith as a proxy for opponents in the party to attack the new leader. Caucus saw an opportunity to flex their muscles, and they took it, we thought, signalling to the urban environmentalists who surrounded Jack that they were going to be kept in check.

Jack, who always saw the good side of people, wasn't so harsh in his assessment. He quietly processed the incident, learned from it and moved on, without holding any grudges. His response was vintage Jack. Right from the beginning of his leadership, he didn't personalize politics. That was his disposition. He just got down to work.

The work started with building relationships inside caucus. For a blueprint on moving forward, he relied on the lessons of his father, who'd served as caucus chair under Mulroney's leadership from 1986 to 1993.

When Parliament was in session, Robert Layton would sit down with the prime minister weekly at 24 Sussex, before the party's Wednesday morning caucus meetings. The elder Layton reported on the general mood of the caucus and advised Mulroney of any issues brewing that he felt the leader needed to know about.

Jack often said his dad had taught him that the most important thing for a leader was the caucus. Without those MPs, the leader had nothing. After he became NDP leader, Jack thought of his week as running not from Monday to Friday but from Wednesday to Wednesday—from caucus meeting to caucus meeting. (Years later, leading a caucus of 103, he would still relay this sentiment to new caucus members.)

Jack would need good caucus relationships. Over the years, the NDP caucus had morphed into a group that had become focussed on winning debates in Parliament, not elections. But like Ed Broadbent before him, Jack wanted power, not the crown of the debating club. "That's what Tommy was about," explains Broadbent today. "That's what J.S. Woodsworth was about. It wasn't about winning debates in Parliament—it was getting power, so you could really make change."

Jack began by building a strong working relationship with Bill Blaikie, a crucial step in developing a cohesive caucus. Jack didn't want to have Blaikie as a thorn in his side. Blaikie had no interest in playing that role, either. The two didn't know each other well. They had met only once before the leadership race began, when Jack made a presentation to the NDP caucus in 2002 as head of the FCM. But both invested time to build a solid relationship. Scotch helped.

A few weeks after Jack had lost his chief of staff, he and Blaikie had a long and very productive session in Blaikie's parliamentary office on the second floor of the West Block. It would be the first of many throughout Jack's early years as leader. They bonded over their shared United Church upbringings, and Jack, in a good-natured way, walked Blaikie through how he had won the leadership. Blaikie, in turn, provided some frank advice to Jack: not all cameras are created equal, and some microphones are worth walking by. Jack took it in stride, and nearly crawled out of the office that night, after polishing off the bottle of Lagavulin with ice and water.

His relationships with Blaikie and others inside caucus were tested often during the early days of Jack's leadership as he worked to get ready to fight his first federal election. Libby Davies, an early supporter of Jack's, was appointed as House Leader. She accepted the post reluctantly because she was not a procedural expert, but she learned the ropes quickly and emerged as a calm, steady presence, a role she played throughout Jack's leadership.

Managing his relationship with Svend Robinson was trickier for Jack. The polarizing MP from B.C. wanted to serve as foreign affairs critic, but there was no way that was going to happen, given his vocal position on the Middle East. Jack assigned Robinson the health portfolio instead. Robinson accepted his post, but that didn't stop him from ruffling feathers. The first time Robinson acted out during a caucus meeting, Jack immediately shut things down. When Robinson stormed out of the room, Jack made him come back in and apologize to caucus. Although Robinson had done this many times before, it was the first time the leader had ever called him on it. The incident gave Jack a lot of credibility in the eyes of caucus, Bill Blaikie remembers.

Robinson would eventually step down as an MP in April 2004 after admitting to stealing an expensive ring at an auction house. Jack talked to Blaikie before Robinson made the announcement: "We have a man down. It's Svend." After Jack got through his own separate and difficult press conference on April 15, Blaikie told him, "You got lucky." That might have sounded harsh, because Jack and Robinson were friends and political allies. But Robinson had created political headaches for every NDP leader since he'd first been elected in 1979. So this development, though embarrassing for Robinson and awkward for Jack and the party in the short term, would be beneficial from the perspective of caucus management. (During the 2004 election, Robinson's long-time assistant Bill Siksay would win the seat, keeping the NDP's hold on the Burnaby–Douglas riding.)

When it came to caucus business, Jack made mistakes, too. His orientation to organizing was in his blood. At Toronto city hall, that had meant he reached out to activists and organizations on any file he was working on. As NDP leader, he organized the caucus into advocacy teams. Franz Hartmann, his former executive assistant in Toronto who had joined Jack's office in Ottawa after the leadership win, was tapped to coordinate outreach.

The idea of linking the NDP caucus with various advocacy groups made sense on paper. The caucus would find out from these groups how the NDP could help advance their interests in Parliament, and these groups would mobilize for the NDP when the time came, right? The initiative failed for a very simple reason. At city hall, Jack had been in power, just like every other shrewd councillor who knew how to advance a file. In Ottawa, the NDP was in opposition, stuck in the far corner of the chamber as the fourth party in Parliament. The best the party could do was table a private member's bill, which would likely go nowhere, or ask a few questions during Question Period.

The NDP really couldn't help progressive groups, but the governing Liberals could. And even though they had failed most of those groups, repeatedly, the power dynamic meant progressive groups continued to play ball with the Liberals. Many of them voted that way, or pleaded with people to "vote strategically"—code for voting Liberal as the best governing option when up against Conservatives. To crack strategic voting, we needed to find a new way to engage civil society.

There were stumbles out of the gate, but Jack made some good moves on the parliamentary side to build on the groundwork he had laid during the leadership race. Framing the Liberals as wavering on important issues was part of that. During the leadership race, Jack had spoken often about his position: Canada should say yes to the United Nations search for weapons of mass destruction in Iraq and no to Bush's invasion. In his speech the morning after his victory, he spoke with clarity about whether Canada should support Bush's unilateral doctrine of pre-emptive strikes.

Canadians had been demonstrating their opposition to Bush's plan, and Jack and members of the caucus participated in rallies across the country. NDP MPs asked questions in the House of Commons and continued to apply pressure. Chrétien, evasive as usual about the Liberal position, mocked the party at one point, saying, "They think a good singsong would solve all of the problems."

Tactically, our strategy worked for us, because it helped segment the population: if you were opposed to the war in Iraq, you were likely predisposed to voting NDP, but you may not have been doing so in 2003. We wanted to speak to these voters. If the prime minister announced support for Bush's plan, the NDP would become the only national party on the side of the majority of Canadians. If the prime minister decided to keep Canada out of Iraq, he would legitimize our position and give us credibility as a force that couldn't be ignored.

On March 17, Chrétien announced in the House of Commons that Canada would not be participating in the invasion of Iraq. The government's decision not to join the "coalition of the willing" was incredibly popular. Chrétien got a bump in the polls. But the announcement also emboldened the NDP and the anti-war movement. (In May 2011, a classified U.S. document leaked to WikiLeaks would reveal that on the same day as the Chrétien announcement, Canadian diplomats privately told the U.S. they wanted to "emphasize" that Canadian naval and air forces could be "discreetly" put to use during the U.S.-led attack. Vintage Liberal Party: say one thing, do another.) Chrétien's decision legitimized Jack's position and solidified his leadership in the eyes of the caucus. It also helped in our long rebranding effort to put to rest the image of Jack as a glib politician who preferred slogans to substance.

This was a welcome shot in the arm for us in spring 2003, but it was now time to double down on our strategy to corner the Liberals. Phase two was the NDP's clear, and early, opposition to the U.S. ballistic missile defence scheme. Seeing two steps ahead in the game, we'd begun to ramp up the profile on Bush's Star Wars campaign, positioning that would later put Chrétien's successor, Paul Martin, in a tough spot.

We kept looking for smaller ways to reinforce the narrative, too. Some of them worked, some didn't. Bill Blaikie was an outstanding orator in Parliament and an excellent performer in Question Period, but he didn't readily take messaging advice or embrace the pithy quotes Jamey Heath sometimes provided.

In May, Liberal Justice Minister Martin Cauchon travelled to Washington to brief the U.S. government on Canada's proposed marijuana decriminalization bill. Vetting by the Bush administration delayed the tabling of the bill, and the Liberals never passed the bill. Following Cauchon's disastrous trip, Heath saw another opening to hammer the Liberals as weak-kneed when it came to standing up to the Americans. In this instance, it was about the softwood lumber dispute.

Heath came up with a line for Blaikie to deliver during Question Period: "Mr. Speaker, we are talking about supporting Canadian sovereignty and we certainly hope that on the softwood lumber file the Liberals have more luck than they did when Mr. Spliff went to Washington." The play on the famous Jimmy Stewart movie, *Mr. Smith Goes to Washington,* in reference to Cauchon's recent trip to the U.S. capital, ended up making Jane Taber's quote of the week in the *Globe and Mail*'s weekly political wrap.

The comment almost hadn't made it to the floor, though. Blaikie didn't know what a spliff was, and he wasn't convinced other people would get it. With Question Period approaching, Heath proposed a deal: they'd ask three pages if they knew what the word meant, and if they did, Blaikie would deliver the line. Blaikie agreed. All three pages got the joke.

ON JACK'S FIRST NIGHT IN Ottawa after his leadership victory, he'd taken Jamey Heath and Franz Hartmann to the legendary Rainbow blues bar in the Byward Market for an end-of-day drink. When the conversation turned to the next federal campaign, Jack and Heath got into it, for the first time, about what would be a realistic goal for the NDP. The sponsorship scandal had not yet destabilized the governing Liberals, and Paul Martin's team was musing about a super majority, with talk of 250 seats. Heath predicted 25 seats for the NDP, almost twice as many as we held at the time. He figured that was ambitious.

Jack made it crystal clear Heath's target was not ambitious enough. "Think bigger," he challenged. Setting his sights on winning a few extra seats was not what he had in mind. He understood it was going to take a lot of work to change the NDP's fourth-party status. "Politics is like water polo. Stay calm on the surface, work underwater where they can't see you, and then kick hard," Jack told Heath.

Jack wasn't advocating attack politics—he was talking about modernizing the NDP to make a viable alternative for Canadians. In the immediate sense, that meant changing how the party operated so that it would be election-ready. We figured the next federal election could come anytime after the coronation of Martin as Liberal leader in November. That meant we had about nine months to get ready.

Alexa McDonough had established a committee in May 2002 to assess the performances of the NDP's past campaigns. The group presented its findings to Jack and party officials the following February, just weeks after Jack was elected leader. The proposal was to start preparations as early as possible; run a truly national campaign focussed on growth, not saving the furniture; allow for regional messaging flexibility, in recognition of the varied opponents in different parts of the country; and undertake a vigorous fundraising effort.

Jack created an Election Planning Committee (EPC) to oversee the huge task before us. We were up and running by March and held our first meeting in April. A group composed of key campaign staff based in Ottawa began meeting weekly to support the work of the EPC. Party staff, meanwhile, started overhauling our online work and fundraising infrastructure. Jack was at the forefront of each ambitious goal, and wherever possible we linked the work of the House with the work of the party to present a coherent, consistent message.

By June, Bruce Cox had come on board full time as national campaign director. Shortly after, we appointed our ad agency, NOW Communications in Vancouver, and our polling firm, Strategic Communications, for the upcoming campaign. NOW had served as the NDP's ad agency in 1997 and had participated in many of our successful provincial campaigns, most notably in Saskatchewan and Manitoba. Strategic Communications, our polling firm for Jack's leadership campaign, had just come off an impressive victory for the Coalition of Progressive Electors (COPE) in the 2002 civic election in Vancouver.

We knew we needed to do some research on our target audience. Traditional NDP voters hadn't been voting NDP for at least three election cycles, and we wanted to talk to this group to figure out why. Before the end of the summer, we had set up our first focus groups, held in Vancouver, Winnipeg, Toronto, Montreal and Halifax. These swing voters hadn't ruled out voting NDP but were not ready to commit to casting a ballot for us. This was our first time in the field since the 2000 election. We were starting with a blank slate—a new leader in an ever-changing political landscape, and we wanted some empirical data to guide our campaign decision making.

The good news from our focus groups was that people generally liked the NDP. In most cases, they liked our values and felt we had a positive contribution to make to shaping the country, based on our past history. That wasn't enough to make them vote for us, though. We had a lot more work to do.

We were up against some negatives, too. First, the NDP was largely invisible, and that was costing us support. To counter that, Jack and the team seized media opportunities under the mantra of saying no to nobody. Karl Bélanger executed an aggressive scrum management strategy after Question Period that pissed off the other opposition parties. Jack would head out to face reporters before the Liberal and the Bloc Québécois leaders, jumping the queue before they were finished in Question Period. Sometimes, we stationed him behind a minister so that Jack could try to sneak in after to the awaiting media. We saw a direct correlation between our visibility and our vote. If we could remind a portion of the population that we were out there, our vote would go up.

When it came to Jack, our target universe in the focus groups didn't know a lot about him, particularly those outside Toronto. And what they did know about him wasn't always positive. The Toronto group was split. In Montreal, one participant said that he would vote for the NDP if they ever decided to run candidates again in federal elections.

Second, we also learned from the focus groups that the Liberal voters in the room were, by and large, unsatisfied customers. "There is no alternative" pretty much summed up what they told us. When we probed them about Paul Martin's record as finance minister, people were not upset that he had cut billions from health and social programs. There was little traction in going after Martin's slash-and-burn record, we learned. We needed another angle.

We tested another line of attack. How did people feel about Martin removing the Canadian flag from his steamships when he was head of Canada Steamship Lines (CSL) as a way to avoid paying taxes in Canada? Even though Canadian Alliance finance critic Monte Solberg had repeatedly questioned Martin about his tax dodging during Question Period, our focus groups reacted at first with disbelief, then outright hostility. "Paul Martin would never do that," they told us. Once people absorbed the information, it began to stick as a significant negative. But they took some convincing, so if we wanted to use this issue to tarnish Martin's brand, we needed to undertake a massive education process—and fast.

By the fall, we had a two-track plan: introduce Jack to Canadians and try to redefine Martin. On track one, the imminent arrival of a new prime minister and the pending merger of the Progressive Conservative Party and the Canadian Alliance meant the national media scene was a little too crowded for us. Instead, we put Jack, unencumbered by the House of Commons calendar, into community after community to raise his profile. We even planted a story in the *Ottawa Citizen* about asking our focus groups whether Jack should shave off his moustache. The issue had actually come up in one of them, though from a participant, not us. But the pitch worked. A nice big picture of Jack, alongside a rendition of what he would look like without his moustache, accompanied the story. What counted was getting his face in the news and reminding people that the NDP was still around.

We knew redefining Martin would be a daunting task. The Liberals were riding high in the polls with a commanding majority government and had millions of dollars in the bank as they geared up to fete a new leader. We'd have to be creative to educate the country about Martin's corporate record and capture the attention of our target audience. Standing up in Question Period wasn't going to cut it. The NDP was broke, so our initiative had to cost virtually nothing. But we managed to come up with a creative idea.

We launched flyourflag.ca on Thanksgiving Monday, October 13. It was a cheeky but engaging website that served as our platform to define Martin. Visitors to the website were asked to vote for which Third World country's flag Martin should fly from the Peace Tower when he became prime minister. "As a shipping magnate, Paul Martin consistently refused to fly our flag—because flying another country's flag helped him avoid Canadian taxes, Canadian wages and Canadian environmental standards," Jack said on the site, showing the different flags of convenience. "So which flag will he fly when he becomes prime minister?"

The campaign, conceived and developed by director of communications Jamey Heath, was pitch perfect and Jack loved it. It was also the first online campaign in Canadian politics, and we garnered a tremendous amount of media for being pioneers. We collected thousands of new email addresses and sowed doubt in people's minds as to just who Paul Martin really was. In the first week alone, the site had fifty-two thousand visitors and more than two thousand of them signed up to join our email newsletter distribution list. More people joined the NDP that week than in the entire month of September. It wasn't bad for a project that had just one expense: registering the domain name.

A few weeks later, on November 14, Liberals gathered in Toronto's Air Canada Centre to crown Martin as their leader. Jack sat up in a skybox with Karl Bélanger to observe the proceedings. The event was impressive: thousands of partisans packed into the arena to watch U2's Bono endorse Martin. The narrative was less than helpful for us. Given Martin's organizational and financial strength, along with his personal popularity, some commentators mused that the Liberals could wipe Jack and the NDP right off the map. Jamey Heath called me from the floor that night to lament the size of the crowd and how young and diverse the delegates were. The Liberals were confident and acted like winners. We agreed we had to do the same.

The Martin machine, branded as a juggernaut by the media, was one thing. The historic merger of the conservative movement was another. After signing an agreement in principle on October 15, the members of the Progressive Conservative and the Canadian Alliance parties made it official on December 6: they would end the vote splitting of their shared universe and combine the best organizational and fundraising capacities of both parties. The first leader of the new Conservative Party would be elected the following March.

Being a British Columbian, I was keenly aware that fundraising and the ground strength of the Canadian Alliance meant new challenges for us west of Ontario, where the fights were mostly NDP-Conservative. The merger presented possibilities for the NDP among red Tories who didn't like the Alliance and could never bring themselves to vote Liberal.

As if all of this wasn't enough to keep us up at night, there was another ominous threat bearing down on us. In a matter of weeks, the future financial security of the party would be challenged.

TOMMY DOUGLAS, THE PRAIRIE PREACHER and party icon, used to say that all things come in trinities. Jack's first year as leader was no exception. After the apparent Martin juggernaut and the merger of the conservative parties, a new financing law for political parties, which came into effect on January 1, 2004, rounded out a difficult twelve months.

In the days following Jack's leadership victory, Chrétien had signalled his intention to bring in a new law to limit drastically the amount individuals, corporations and unions could give to registered federal political parties. It was the Liberal Party's response to early rumblings of the sponsorship scandal.

We knew the proposed law, C-24, would affect the Liberals more dramatically than it would the NDP. Since our party's founding in 1961, we had relied mostly on small donations from individuals. But we also counted on union donations to help finance our campaigns and, equally important, to provide collateral for election loans. The Liberal Party, in contrast, had grown to rely on corporate Canada to fund their operations. For example, in 2000, the NDP depended on unions for only 33 per cent of its revenues, whereas corporate donations accounted for 60 per cent of Liberal Party revenues.

Chrétien didn't seem bothered by the fact that the new legislation might be crippling his own party, perhaps because he saw Paul Martin amassing a giant war chest to wrestle the leadership from him. The NDP supported the idea of removing big money from federal politics, even though we knew we'd take a hit. We knew we'd have to shift our fund-raising culture, and by the summer of 2003, the clock was ticking.

Jack's optimistic outlook meant he saw opportunities in difficult situations. This was no exception. He figured if national unions could donate no more than $1,000 in total to local riding associations every year, as of January 1, 2004, why not ask them to donate what they had been planning to give us over the next few years now, while it was still legal? The cash would be a nice little nest egg heading into the next election campaign. But then Jack got a better idea. One day in August 2003, Jack got a call from André Foucault, who was secretary-treasurer of the Communications, Energy and Paperworkers Union of Canada (CEP) and co-chair of our election planning committee. Foucault had an election finance meeting coming up, and he wanted to talk with the leader ahead of time.

"André, I can't talk right now; I have a flight to catch," Jack told Foucault.

"No problem," he replied. "I'll drive you to the airport, and we can chat on the way."

Just before Foucault turned in to the terminal's drop-off area, their discussion turned to the CEP's recent purchase of a building at the corner of Bank and Laurier in downtown Ottawa. Foucault had been the lead for the union on the purchase, and an intrigued Jack probed him about how the deal had come together. He'd started thinking that a nest egg was small compared with an asset that would appreciate over time and could be used as collateral to secure campaign loans.

"We gotta buy a building," Jack told Foucault, before darting off to catch his flight. The two shook on it. We are going to do this, they agreed.

Later that afternoon, Foucault walked into the election finance meeting with party officials. "We need to put a new item on the agenda," he announced.

"What is it?" asked federal secretary Chris Watson.

"The purchase of a building," Foucault said.

"What are you, nuts?" chimed in Éric Hébert-Daly, who was the party's money guy as assistant federal secretary.

"This is serious," Foucault said. "I met with Jack this morning, and he is adamant that we put together a game plan so the party can buy a building before C-24 comes into law."

When word got around the office, most of us thought it was a crazy idea—another crazy Jack idea. Here we were, only a year away from an election, without two sticks to rub together, and Jack wanted us to buy a building in cash in a matter of months. For Foucault, the idea wasn't such a stretch. He was confident the union movement would step up. Plus, he had just gone through the process.

The next morning, Foucault phoned the CEP's real estate agent, Wayne Benedict of Colliers International. "We need another building. Explore the possibilities," he instructed Benedict. Foucault alerted the CEP's lawyers to be on standby for a quick sale, because the time was incredibly tight. Jack had gone from concept to execution in forty-eight hours.

Soon after, Foucault was sitting in his CEP office when he noticed a "For Rent" sign on a three-storey building across the street. He knew the third floor had been empty for a while. Shoppers Drug Mart occupied the ground floor, and a federal government agency had a short-term lease on the second floor. Foucault asked Benedict to look into whether the owner would be willing to sell the building.

When it turned out the owner was interested, Benedict asked Foucault who the buyer would be. Before answering, Foucault hesitated. "Who is the current owner?" he asked.

"Great-West Life, a subsidiary of Power Corp.," Benedict responded.

"For now, it's the CEP looking into it," Foucault replied.

Power Corp.'s co-chief executive officer André Desmarais was married to Jean Chrétien's daughter. The company was mammoth, so the chances of those making real estate decisions at one of its subsidiaries having any connection to the guy running the corporation was unlikely. But, just in case, Foucault decided to keep the NDP out of it.

Internally, we dubbed the effort "Project X," and only a handful of people in the party knew what was going on.

The federal NDP was no stranger to real estate in the nation's capital. Back in the late 1980s, the party had owned a building at the corner of Metcalfe and Somerset, not far from Parliament Hill. They had a mortgage on it, though, and since the building was single occupancy, there was no revenue from tenants. When the party got into financial trouble after the 1993 election debacle, they couldn't afford it any longer. They had to sell it.

The Great-West building across from CEP's headquarters had two sizable units to rent out, including a retail unit on the ground floor with high foot traffic. If we could raise enough money to buy it outright—that was Jack's goal—the party would secure stable revenue from the other tenants and live rent-free during the good times and bad. It was a smart model and a testament to Jack's big thinking. The tricky part would be raising $3.5 million in cash over the next 120 days.

Jack's strategy was simple. Go first to the most sympathetic unions, secure their support, then use their commitment to convince others. To help us figure out how much to request, Jack asked Hébert-Daly to put together a spreadsheet showing what each of the large affiliated unions had contributed to the party over the past ten years.

The pitch, to come from Jack himself, would be straightforward: in four months, you won't be able to donate anything substantial to the party, so give us up front what you would have given over the next ten years, before the deadline of December 31. Jack's starting point was the CEP, which, under the stewardship of Foucault and CEP president Brian Payne, got things rolling at their September council meeting. The council voted unanimously to allocate $500,000 to the party's building fund. Even the Quebec members of the board, who supported the Bloc Québécois, got behind the project.

With his first major contribution in hand, Jack worked the phones. He first turned to the Canadian Auto Workers (CAW). Despite Buzz Hargrove's high-profile clashes with the NDP over the years, he immediately took up Jack's challenge and pledged $500,000. The United Food and Commercial Workers (UFCW), the International Association of Machinists and Aerospace Workers (IAMAW), the Canadian Union of

Public Employees (CUPE) and the United Steelworkers jumped on board with $500,000 each. Once the first domino had fallen, Project X picked up tremendous momentum. Capitalizing on the excitement around his leadership, Jack raised the remaining $500,000 from labour federations and smaller unions, allowing the party to buy the building outright.

Jack's cash offer was accepted, and the New Democratic Party became the proud owner of its own building. Renamed the Jack Layton Building after Jack's death, it is now worth a lot more than the purchase price, and it remains vital to the party's financial well-being a decade later.

Jack's move was audacious. It was also exactly what the party needed. He had won over the skeptics and taught us an early lesson. With big thinking, you can seize the impossible. Jack had given the NDP a huge financial boost, but that wasn't all. He'd also enhanced his own stock among caucus and staff as a guy who could both think big and deliver. With a federal election only months away, Jack would soon get a shot at proving he could deliver on the campaign trail.

CHAPTER 4:
A KICK TO THE GROIN

After months of election planning, we were all set to go—when Paul Martin visited Governor General Adrienne Clarkson on May 23, 2004, to ask that Parliament be dissolved for a June 28 election. Or at least we thought we were ready to go.

War room director Brian Topp, heading up the rapid response and media unit, had arrived about a week earlier to join the rest of the team. Topp, who had served in the same capacity during the 1997 campaign and worked on other provincial and municipal campaigns as well, brought bench strength to the campaign headquarters in Ottawa. Most of us in senior positions had never run a federal campaign, and Jack was about to head out on the hustings for the first time as NDP leader.

Jack had cold-called Topp a few months earlier after seeing him in a documentary about David Miller's successful campaign for mayor of Toronto in November 2003. Topp, executive director of the Toronto branch of the Alliance of Canadian Cinema, Television and Radio Artists at the time, had served as one of Miller's campaign advisors. Topp had spent from 1993 to 2000 in Saskatchewan, much of the time as NDP premier Roy Romanow's deputy chief of staff. He had initially supported Bill Blaikie for NDP leader but switched to Jack after a call from Romanow caused him to reconsider. "I think you're backing the wrong guy," Romanow had told him. "The mayors in Saskatchewan are lining up behind this Layton guy."

When Topp arrived in Ottawa, he was direct about his approach. His clarity of purpose represented a clean break with the past, and people appreciated it.

"Here's how these days are going to unfold. We're going to work hard. We're going to hit them where it hurts. We're going to support our own team. And we're going to have a lot of fun. We'll start our days at 6 AM. Take fifteen minutes to review the papers and then pitch your best ideas for the day. The nightly news will be on at 11 PM. I'll be watching it, and I expect not to be alone," Topp told his rapid response team, a smart group that specialized in opposition research, an area beefed up under Jack's leadership.

Next, Topp did the rounds with members of the senior campaign team, asking each of us a key question. He knew that the first question any effective campaign must be able to answer convincingly is: "What is this election all about?" You could tell a lot about how ready a team was by how sharp and consistent their answers to this question were.

Under campaign director Bruce Cox, our senior team had been meeting regularly for nearly a year. Sue Milling, from United Steelworkers, was our deputy campaign director. Her job was logistics, to make sure the trains ran on time. Chris Watson, NDP federal secretary (a position now known as national director), was in charge of assisting candidates with Elections Act compliance, and assistant federal secretary Éric Hébert-Daly handled the money. Heather Fraser was director of organization, overseeing the ground operations and candidate recruitment. My job was director of communications, which meant I was in charge of all printed materials, such as leaflets, lawn signs and buttons, as well as all websites and online campaign efforts. I was also in charge of managing the relationship with our ad and polling agencies. David Mackenzie, Jack's interim chief of staff after he lost Rick Smith, was assigned to the campaign plane as the lead political advisor. Jamey Heath, also set to go out on tour, would be the key communications advisor there. Donne Flanagan, Gary Doer's former director of communications who replaced Mackenzie as chief of staff, served in the war room and wrote speeches for Jack.

None of us could answer Topp's vital question. We didn't agree on what the campaign was about or who our main opponent was. Topp turned to Cox. "We have a fundamental problem here," he said.

In the months leading up to the election call, the campaign working group had spent its time getting the logistics of the campaign in place and putting together a list of campaign commitments. Now, with the writ set to be dropped in a few days, we couldn't answer the key question of what the election was about. We'd soon discover we hadn't done a very good job of crafting the campaign commitments, either.

The Manitoba NDP had just come off a successful campaign, re-electing Gary Doer as premier with an even greater majority. Doer's five-point plan in the 2003 campaign had played very well with voters, but despite objections from a few of us, many were convinced that our list of commitments needed to be exhaustive. Narrowing these down to a concise, memorable list of priorities was an exercise in discipline we weren't ready for.

On the eve of the election, we had eight commitments, each with sub-points. Jack would later admit that even he couldn't remember them all. It was a problem that would plague our campaign for the next five weeks: a campaign by committee tends to focus on satisfying internal interests, not appealing to voters.

This wasn't an ideal situation for a party about to embark on the NDP's most resource-rich campaign to date. In September 2003, we had put together a campaign budget of $8.8 million. We upped it to $11.6 million just before the writ was dropped. A significant chunk of that—$4.7 million—was earmarked for media, the biggest amount in party history. By contrast, the 2000 campaign ad media budget had been $1.8 million.

We had already spent an additional $700,000 on pre-election TV ads that ran in February and March. One English spot introduced Jack to Canadians; the other criticized Paul Martin. It's hard to measure the effectiveness of pre-election ads, but we thought they were a crucial investment. The idea was to energize the base, impress the media and increase Jack's profile. If anyone thought the NDP was down, we'd remind them otherwise.

The plan seemed to work. Just as the Conservative Party selected Stephen Harper as its first leader in March, the NDP hit 20 per cent in popular support in a Compass poll. That was more than twice what we'd earned in the 2000 election, and Jack's goal had been to get to 20 per cent before his first federal campaign. So the benchmark was important to us.

The EPC had identified that step one along our road to building the NDP as a national alternative was to reassemble the people who used to support us. In 1988, under Broadbent, the NDP had garnered 20.38 per cent of the popular vote (2,685,263 votes) to form the party's largest-ever caucus, with forty-three members. We believed the selection of Harper as Conservative leader would help us win back our Western populist voter base: he was polarizing and was not well known in most of Canada. Then, in January, Broadbent jumped back into politics, winning the nomination as the NDP candidate for the Ottawa Centre riding. Just before getting ousted by Paul Martin the previous fall, Chrétien had appointed long-time loyalist and MP for the riding, Mac Harb, to the Senate. This opened up an opportunity for the NDP in the long-held Liberal riding, now being contested by Martin insider Richard Mahoney. Broadbent's job was to bring home the NDP votes lost in Ottawa Centre and elsewhere over the previous fifteen years.

Armed with a poll commissioned by the party showing that Broadbent could win the downtown Ottawa riding, which included Parliament Hill, Jack began to lobby the former leader. Broadbent didn't take much convincing, he says today, though he "hadn't even thought of it" before Jack approached him. "There was a rebuilding going on. Having supported Jack in the leadership I felt I could carry that on. Besides, I could be competitive in the campaign, I could help Jack and I could walk to work to boot."

The downward trajectory of Liberal support in all regions, and the Conservative-NDP fight in many places west of Ontario, meant opportunities for the NDP. Our internal polling from December 2003 showed that New Democrats under Jack had significant support all over the country. The campaign team opted to spread our ground resources accordingly. At the outset, in addition to our fourteen incumbents, we invested people, time and money in dozens of additional seats.

The Quebec riding of Manicouagan, where former leadership candidate Pierre Ducasse was carrying the NDP banner, made the list. Most of the campaign team knew that it was a long shot, but we needed targeted ridings in Quebec and this was likely the shortest of the long shots. In 2000, the NDP had received a paltry 2 per cent of the popular vote in the riding, matching the provincial average in Quebec. Under the leadership of McDonough, who had struggled in the French-language debate, the party had no ground game or money to spend on ads in the province. Instead, the party had mostly write-in candidates—known as "names on ballots" in English and *"poteaux"* in French.

Party activity had increased in Quebec during the last leadership race, so we had several credible candidates besides Ducasse lined up for the 2004 campaign. Still, the amount of resources devoted to the province was a testy issue for the campaign team. Some thought we should devote our resources to areas of traditional strength and work from there. Jack, Bruce Cox and I, among others, disagreed with that position. Jack, from very early on, had been convinced we needed to make a breakthrough in Quebec. He was born and raised there, and it was very important to him to try to tap into the province's social democratic history. That's why he'd continued to work so hard at improving his French with weekly tutoring sessions, despite his gruelling schedule. A quip from someone about Stephen Harper's French had really stuck with him. "Harper's French is better than my French," Jack told us.

Low polling numbers in Quebec would keep the party down nationally and help make the case for strategic voting arguments, particularly in Toronto. I didn't think we'd win a seat in Quebec in the 2004 campaign, but I knew we had to increase our votes there—and that meant spending time and money in the province. If we didn't raise our support in areas of non-traditional strength, the three of us argued, then we wouldn't regain the areas where we used to be strong. Quebec served as a proxy for that debate, and the leader prevailed.

It was showtime. By now, it was too late to address the basic problem that Topp had flagged. With no clear answer on what the campaign was about, every decision became a drawn-out debate without any grounding. What flowed from this process were poor decisions—or no decision at all.

Jack kicked off the campaign on Parliament Hill on May 23 flanked by local candidates Ed Broadbent and Monia Mazigh. Mazigh had worked tirelessly to free her husband, Maher Arar, from a Syrian prison after the U.S., in a case of extraordinary rendition, deported him there in September 2002 despite his Canadian citizenship. Alexa McDonough and the NDP had advocated for their cause, and over the years, Mazigh and McDonough had become close. McDonough, with the enthusiastic approval of Jack, had approached Mazigh to see if she would be interested in channelling her tenacity and energy as a Member of Parliament. After the launch, Jack promptly boarded the leader's plane and headed to Vancouver's Chinatown with Olivia to signal that the West held promise for the NDP. There, he announced our eight commitments.

It was the beginning of the party's most ambitious tour on record. Additional resources, along with Jack's high energy, meant we could go wherever the votes were, or might be. But the first week would also include a lot of self-inflicted wounds caused by an inexperienced team.

We were committed to learning from the mistakes of the 2000 election campaign, so we wanted to make sure both local campaigns and the media on tour had the necessary materials. These included a series of fact sheets that highlighted particular issues, summarized the failure of the Liberals and the other parties to address those issues, and outlined what the NDP would do to solve them. Eager to court the media and impress them with our preparations, the media team on the leader's plane distributed all of the fact sheets at once, instead of giving them out day by day. That meant we'd effectively handed the media our platform in the opening hours of the campaign.

It was always going to be hard to get heat on our upcoming policy announcements, given that reporters like to file off-script, especially when covering a fourth party that doesn't shape the debates. Now, our announcements were old news, and reporters were still looking to file copy. It wasn't long before the devil found work for these idle hands. The next few days were a trifecta of trouble.

Jack released our platform in Toronto on Wednesday, May 26. The document, stick-handled by Franz Hartmann, was fiscally aggressive in outlining how we'd pay for our promises. Before the campaign launch, Brian Topp had asked to have a look at the platform. When Hartmann refused, Topp persisted. Soon Topp was told to let it go, part of a pattern of leaving internal conflicts unresolved. "I shouldn't have backed off. I should have threatened to resign," Topp told me years later, saying it was one of his biggest regrets in the campaign.

Topp's concerns were warranted. Among other things, the platform called for an inheritance tax, as had the NDP's platforms in 1997 and 2000. In those earlier campaigns, the proposal hadn't generated any trouble, likely because of the NDP's irrelevant stature in the world of Canadian politics. This time, it was different, and the tax on the sale of a house following a person's death became the central media story about our platform launch. We were finally getting coverage, but we'd handed our opponents a heavy stick to beat us with.

The inheritance tax hurt us everywhere but especially in urban markets, where we were hoping to make breakthroughs. NDP policy people could argue with anyone on the proposal's merits: it was progressive because it affected only the top tier of the wealthiest homeowners in Canada. But all the public heard was that we were thwarting their ambition to build a better life for themselves and their children. And in cities like Vancouver and Toronto, where real estate values were very high, it wasn't hard for middle-class homeowners to imagine a hefty tax bill for their children after their deaths. The reaction on the doorsteps in ridings across the country was so negative that the campaign would drop the policy from our platform a week before voting day.

The night of his platform launch in Toronto, Jack was scheduled to headline Olivia's nomination meeting for the Trinity–Spadina riding at the historic Church of the Holy Trinity. The event had been purposefully left until then to create momentum for her local race. Jack was anxious that everything go well. In an attempt to calm things down, Karl Bélanger suggested that after Jack's speech, he hold the post-nomination scrum outside the church. Jack was distracted, though, making it difficult to brief him, and he had a special connection to the place. The church did outreach with Toronto's homeless community, and a plaque in the church square commemorated homeless people who had died on the streets.

During the scrum, a reporter picked up on a theme raised during Jack's speech at Olivia's nomination—Paul Martin's cancellation of the federal social housing program—and asked whether Jack felt the prime minister was personally responsible for the deaths of homeless people. The question was an obvious trap, and Jack was experienced enough to avoid it. He didn't. Flanked by Olivia and Marilyn Churley, the candidate in Beaches–East York, another NDP target riding in Toronto, he started ranting. Pressed again by the reporter, Jack agreed it would be fair to say Martin was personally responsible for deaths of homeless people because of federal cuts to affordable housing. "I believe that when Paul Martin cancelled affordable housing across this country, it produced a dramatic rise in homelessness and death due to homelessness, and I have always said that I hold him responsible for that," Jack said. "He chose to give the money in tax cuts to his corporate friends, and I will not forgive him for that."

Initially, Heath and Bélanger disagreed about how much damage had been done. At least people would be talking about the NDP campaign and thinking about homelessness, an issue on which only the NDP had credibility, Heath figured. But the reporting was brutal. Jack's comments made front pages and the top of newscasts. News outlets held online polls asking whether he should apologize. Reporters started quizzing NDP MPs on what they thought of Jack's remarks, generating negative stories about unease and a split within the ranks. Some reporters even approached dial-a-quote political scientists to criticize the idea of personal responsibility in the arena of public policy. That's when we knew the story wasn't going away.

Our campaign's first attempt to diffuse the homeless bomb, at a scrum in Montreal on Friday, May 28, didn't go well. Jack understood that he had screwed up, but the reaction to his comments frazzled him. He knew there was a relationship between public policy decisions and people's lives. The scrum with assembled reporters was cut short when a visibly upset Jack turned and headed to a waiting RCMP vehicle, where he climbed into the back seat and put his face in his hands, a move captured on camera. The media were dead silent as he walked away.

Since Jack hadn't apologized explicitly, just tempered his language, the resulting headlines kept the story alive, with variations on "Layton Keeps Swinging at Homeless Issue" and "Layton Unwavering in Criticizing PM: NDP Leader Gets Dissident MPs On Side." It wouldn't be until the following Tuesday, when Jack did two interviews with the CBC while in Vancouver, that our campaign was able to pivot from the issue. Even so, the resulting stories carried an unhelpful frame. The CBC's Peter Mansbridge asked Jack if he believed Martin was a killer. "No, not at all," Jack replied. "Martin Not a Killer of Homeless, Layton Says," read the headline afterwards. Another, "Blame for Homeless Deaths Belongs to All Canadians, Layton Now Says," played up Jack's comment that blame should be shared "collectively" by "Canada as a whole." He couldn't relinquish the idea that government decisions have concrete effects on people's lives. "The consequence of the action is we've had an explosion of homelessness, we've had more deaths in the street and Canadians want something done about that," he had told the CBC. "I know the remark jarred some people, but you know, what jars me is that, in a country as rich as this, we have people dying in the streets."

In her Ottawa Notebook in the Saturday, May 29, edition of the *Globe and Mail,* Jane Taber created a new "Super-Not-Hot" category for Jack that week, in addition to her usual "Hot" and "Not Hot" political players of the week. The campaign's third misstep had occurred too late in the day on Friday to make it into Taber's column, but it did hit the front page of the Saturday *Globe* under the headline, "Layton Would Axe Clarity Act."

The campaign had made a point of going to Quebec during our first week out to signal to Quebecers—and the rest of the country—that Canada's second-largest province mattered to Jack and the NDP. Jack hadn't travelled with Pierre Ducasse to the remote community of Sept-Îles, Ducasse's hometown, to talk about the Clarity Act, legislation passed by Parliament in 2000 that outlined some of the conditions by which a province might secede from Canada. But when a reporter asked him about the law during a scrum, he was knocked off message and gave a clunky answer: "If there was a proposal to withdraw it, I don't believe that it contributed to the promotion of Canadian unity." He also said he'd recognize a declaration of Quebec independence if sovereigntists there won a referendum.

The campaign moved quickly to try to contain the damage with a declaration from Jack on May 29. He clarified he would not push for Parliament to repeal the Clarity Act; the issue was not a priority, and he was only expressing a personal view. We got the headlines we needed—"Layton Backs Off Repeal of Clarity Act"—but our opponents made sure the story didn't die there. The Liberals trotted out Stéphane Dion, who had introduced the Clarity Act when he was intergovernmental affairs minister. "A lot of [Layton's] MPs in his caucus must be very embarrassed," Dion told reporters. "The mystery to me is how come a committed Canadian like Mr. Layton is so irresponsible and ambiguous and confused about the unity of his country."

Reporters also asked Bill Blaikie and Ed Broadbent about Jack's comments. Both were astute politicians, and they knew they couldn't dodge the issue. "It was difficult," Blaikie says now. "The last thing you want to do is disagree with your leader in the middle of the campaign. When the media phoned me and said, 'Jack Layton just said that he would repeal the Clarity Act. What do you think of that?' I wouldn't agree with that."

Broadbent also answered the best way he could, telling reporters that Jack "gave his personal view that he thought [the act] was a bad idea. He took the same position as Mr. Lapierre." It was a clever pivot to refer to Paul Martin's Quebec lieutenant, nationalist Jean Lapierre, who had said publicly he considered the Clarity Act "useless." But Broadbent also had to state the obvious. "My own position is that I support the Clarity Act. I appeared before the committee as an expert witness."

"Our party has had discussions of this issue over the years. I'm sure that will continue, but let's hope that in fact what we can do is look forward to the building process of a flexible and cooperative federalism,"

Jack told reporters in the northern Ontario town of Timmins, where he had hoped to talk about something else. "It's a debate really from the past because what we're all agreed on is we want to build for the future and build that positive relationship with Quebecers."

These three incidents, all occurring within a day of each other during the first week out on the hustings, came to define the NDP campaign. This rocky start also caused an already uneasy relationship between headquarters and the tour to worsen.

Federal campaigns are huge undertakings, and the most important relationship in a campaign is the one between the central campaign office and the team on tour. The conditions under which each operates are unique, and the perspectives are very different. If you are part of the leader's tour, you see a completely different campaign than you do from headquarters in Ottawa. The team on the plane deal with the travelling media all day and spend most of their time in the air and in hotels. Their day is made up of logistical considerations. Staff in headquarters feed the plane daily and see none of that. They are consumed with the messaging and coverage of the campaign. These two entities must work in lockstep, or there's trouble. There must also be absolute mutual trust.

If you lose that trust, your entire campaign can break down. The plane can "go rogue," meaning the tour team begins to rewrite speeches and press releases. And that's what started to happen during the 2004 campaign. The plane began to improvise. Sometimes, it was because they were operating in a vacuum. Other times, they disagreed with headquarters.

The fourth party in Parliament doesn't get onto the front pages of newspapers with innovative policy ideas. You do get coverage if you screw up or say something outrageous. So the balance is tricky to achieve. After our horrendous start, we kept trying for coverage, but we often failed. The fourth party talking about the dangers of private health care or the need for investment in infrastructure hardly merits a news story when the governing party and the one nipping at its heels in the polls release key planks and bicker back and forth about the issue of the day. One headline captured the situation: "Layton Drops from Radar."

That dynamic played out until debate week, the fourth week of the campaign. This would be Jack's opportunity to stand alongside the prime minister and the Official Opposition leader and get noticed. Our debate prep, though, became a microcosm of the troubles of the campaign: no one was really in charge. Ron Johnson from NOW Communications was pegged as the lead, and Franz Hartmann also had a major presence, drilling details into Jack about every policy area that might come up. But the prep sessions involved too many people with too many opinions, many of them ineffective. During one session, Jacques Thériault, a communications staffer from Quebec, left the room crying. That's how well things were going. We did all agree on style, though. The other leaders would have an interest in pushing Jack out of the debate, so our plan was simple: don't let them. Fight to get in and be noticed. Our mantra, invisibility is death, applied in spades here.

In the French-language debate on June 13 at Ottawa's National Arts Centre, Jack held his own with his populist French, clearly the best of any NDP leader since the party's founding in 1961. This was an important introduction for Jack to French-speaking Canadians, and he used the opportunity to tie the policies of the NDP in with the progressive impulses of Quebecers. At this stage in the campaign, the Bloc was surging, and we were a mere blip on the radar. The debate didn't put much of a dent in that dynamic.

It was vital for Jack to make a good first impression in French, but it was a dress rehearsal of sorts for the bigger audience the next night in the English-language debate.

Just before showtime, Olivia, in Ottawa to support her husband, handed Jack a water bottle with a little whisky in it. Backstage, he took a sip for courage. This was the biggest night of his political career, and he was nervous.

Once the debate got underway, Jack stuck with the plan. Paul Martin came up with a good line meant to cut him down. "Did your handlers tell you to not stop talking?" he asked Jack. It was a cutting rebuke, but Jack had little choice. If he stood by passively and didn't interrupt, he

71

would be invisible. Engage too much, and he would look overeager. It was the classic fourth-party conundrum.

There was another dynamic at play during the debate that didn't help. Unbeknownst to any of us, Donne Flanagan and Jack had cooked up a signal system. Jack would leave his BlackBerry on so that it would vibrate on his hip every time Flanagan sent a message to remind him to smile. Jack's smiling persona was in contrast to that of Harper and Martin, so he wanted to use that to his advantage. The problem, of course, was that many people across Canada had Jack's PIN, which makes your device vibrate when someone sends you a note. Messages kept coming in from all over the country, and Jack's BlackBerry buzzed throughout the debate. Jack thought it was Flanagan telling him to smile more. He followed the directive and smiled way too much. According to a Compass poll released June 16 on the public perception of the leaders' performances, Jack had come third in the English debate and dead last in the French-language debate. This was not the boost we'd been hoping the debates would give our less-than-inspired campaign heading into the final stretch. The endgame had arrived, and we weren't feeling confident.

IN ANY CAMPAIGN, IT IS difficult to pinpoint exactly when an election is either won or lost, because there are so many variables. But there are events that are turning points. During the 2004 campaign, something that would change the race dramatically occurred on June 18. It became a lesson the NDP war room would never forget.

We weren't riding any momentum by June 18, but we were still holding steady. The Liberals were floundering, and the Conservatives were seeing an uptick in support. Trying to build on that, the Conservative war room issued two press releases, one headlined "Paul Martin Supports Child Pornography?" and the other "The NDP Caucus Supports Child Pornography?" The Conservatives were referring to a debate in Parliament in which the other parties had opposed Tory proposals to close a loophole exempting some art from anti-pornography legislation on the grounds of "artistic merit." Our position, and that of the other parties, was that judges could distinguish between nude angels in ecclesiastical art, for example, and images of sexual assaults on children.

Stephen Harper, blindsided by his war room's charge, quickly convened a conference call with his advisors. Harper decided against apologizing and went on the offensive instead. But the explosive charge against his opponents hurt his party. The Conservative momentum stalled.

This wasn't the first bozo moment for the Tories. Earlier in the campaign, the party's official languages critic, Scott Reid, had questioned bilingualism. Ontario Conservative MP Cheryl Gallant had compared abortion to beheading, and a video of B.C. Conservative MP Randy White had surfaced in which he talked about wanting to restrict the Charter. The child porn screw-up, on the heels of these other missteps, reinforced people's discomfort with the new party's perceived radical edge on social policy. It was a cumulative effect that finally seemed to affect the Conservative numbers.

More lucky than smart, the Liberals pounced, and the tide began to turn. They'd always planned that their endgame message would be to tell NDP voters they needed to rally around the Liberals to make sure Harper was defeated. This turn of events fit perfectly into that narrative.

During the final week of the campaign, Paul Martin, the country's most conservative Liberal prime minister in history—he initially opposed gay marriage, supported his pro-life MPs and slashed social spending in favour of huge corporate tax cuts—went from riding to riding repeating his disingenuous endgame stump speech. "There are differences between ourselves and the NDP, and we shouldn't try to hide them, but we share the same values. They spring from the same well. In an election race as close as this one... with the stakes as high as they are, the simple fact is that a vote for the NDP on Monday could very well make Stephen Harper prime minister on Tuesday."

Martin's claim was not only desperate but also untrue. In fact, his plea would help to elect *more* Conservative MPs, because the Liberal Party had little chance of winning many seats west of the Ontario-Manitoba border. But try to convince the media establishment of that, let alone voters.

Our senior team hadn't settled on the best way to combat strategic voting, and ten days before election day, we landed on a compromised message: the NDP was looking for a central role in Parliament. We sharpened that message as we entered the last week: Jack wants a minority Parliament and wants to hold the balance of power. But that didn't address the basic argument the Liberal campaign was peddling, that NDP voters must vote Liberal to stop the Conservatives. All we could say was "that's not true" when faced, over and over again, with Martin's claim that the Liberals and the NDP sprang from the same well. We had not thought through the third period of the campaign, and it hurt us badly. What we were learning would inform how we approached the issue during the next federal campaign and throughout the rest of Jack's leadership. But first, we had to get through election night on June 28, 2004.

When Jack stepped onstage that evening, the numbers indicated the NDP would hold the balance of power in a minority Liberal government. His speech was framed around this projection. Reporters filed their stories and headed to the bars.

Jack's press secretary, Karl Bélanger, and some other staff and party activists had gathered back at the hotel for a few drinks. The TV was on, and Karl was watching the numbers roll in from B.C. They kept going down. At twenty seats, Bélanger punched the screen. "We just lost the balance of power," he muttered.

A few floors up, in my hotel room, I was watching the final results from tight races out west between the Tories and the NDP. Earlier in the evening, there were as many as 26 seats in which we had won or were leading. It was now early morning, and it seemed every few minutes another NDP seat moved over to the Conservative column. I thought if I shut the TV off, maybe our slide would stop. It did. At 19 seats. The Liberals had won 135 seats, the Conservatives 99 and the Bloc Québécois 54, with 1 independent elected as well. We'd fallen 2 seats short of holding the balance of power in a minority Parliament.

In the end, the NDP received 2.1 million votes and nearly doubled its share of the national vote, capturing 16 per cent of the popular vote. Yet, despite this strong growth, the party had gained only five new seats. We lost both our seats in Saskatchewan, and Olivia Chow lost in the Trinity–Spadina riding. Despite Jack's pitch to urban voters, we had failed to win a batch of urban seats. Other than Jack's own seat in Toronto–Danforth, the pickups were largely traditional NDP seats from the industrial heartland or rural Canada: Hamilton, Sault Ste. Marie, Timmins and northwestern B.C.

JACK HAD INSISTED THAT WE ensure Olivia's campaign had everything it needed for her to win. We had. So what had gone wrong? Every riding has its own distinct characteristics, so what happened in Trinity–Spadina during the 2004 election helps to explain, in part, what happened right across Canada.

Internal polling at the start of the 2004 campaign had Olivia ahead with a nineteen-point lead: 48 per cent for her and 29 per cent for Liberal incumbent Tony Ianno. The news came as a relief. But then we got overconfident.

Jack, recognizing that Olivia would be an asset for other NDP candidates running in ridings with large Chinese-Canadian communities, directed the campaign to put together a "B" tour that would take her around the country. We had a full-time staffperson dedicated to coordinating her events. In the NDP, it was common to establish "B" tours for surrogates—political stars who can raise the profiles of candidates or stand in their place—but it was unprecedented to send a yet-to-be-elected candidate on the road when she was in a tough local fight of her own at home.

By week four, the race was tightening. With ten days to go, internal polling had Olivia holding at 48 per cent, but Ianno had inched up to 35 per cent. The Liberals were following a two-pronged strategy in an effort to close the gap. The first was to persuade Olivia's supporters that if they sent her to Ottawa, they would lose a great city councillor. Like other city councillors who ran for federal office in the 2004 campaign, Olivia had not stepped down from her civic seat. Ethics officials at city hall had informed her in writing that there were no problems with her running for Member of Parliament while sitting as a councillor. But even though she was perfectly within the guidelines, we had left ourselves open to the Liberal gambit.

The second tactic was strategic voting. The line being peddled was, "only the Liberals can defeat the Conservatives in this riding, so you must vote for us." In Trinity–Spadina and across the country, the argument worked by demonizing Harper, downplaying the chances of the NDP winning and blurring the policy lines between them and us.

On the weekend before election day, canvassing on Bloor Street, Olivia knew something was up. People wouldn't look her in the eye. Her heart sank, because she sensed what it meant. That Monday, Liberal MP Ianno bested Olivia 23,202 votes to 22,397; the Conservative candidate received just 4,605 votes.

Jack had known that strategic voting was a challenge for us across the country, but seeing it play out in Olivia's riding had made it personal. He was devastated by the loss. The couple were supposed to be heading to Ottawa together. On Tuesday morning, as Jack and Jamey Heath were on their way to the Toronto airport for their flight to Ottawa, it was all he could talk about. He committed right there to focussing our time and resources on finding ways to combat strategic voting—in Trinity–Spadina and across the country. "I want a full debrief on why we lost, and I want a plan on how we win it next time," Jack told Heath.

To be effective, we would have to do two things: show that the NDP had the strength to beat the Conservatives and shine a light on the differences between us and the Liberals. During the 2004 campaign, we had failed at both.

Winning only nineteen seats in the election was devastating. Our publicly stated goal had been to capture more than 20 per cent of the vote and beat Broadbent's record of forty-three seats. We fell well short. The 2004 results were a kick to the groin—and that was exactly what we needed. Our campaign team had made a lot of mistakes, and we committed to learn from every one of them.

Internally, we had two problems going into the 2004 election. First, those with the titular authority hadn't actually been in charge.

Campaigns are not democracies, we'd been reminded. You do need to hunt and gather, but then you need to reach a decision point.

Second, we'd had a fundamental disagreement over what the campaign should be about. Members of the senior team were not like-minded, and we'd been thrown together for the first time, making it harder for the group to gel. But identifying your opponent is perhaps the most important thing to do in a multi-party campaign, and we'd failed in that respect. Our message was too complicated for voters.

Analyzing the campaign showed us we'd spread our resources too thin on the ground, encouraged by poll numbers taken before the campaign that suggested we could win in ridings all over the country. We didn't have the air war figured out, and our missteps throughout the campaign had us drowning in crisis management that knocked us off message. Our platform, too unfocussed and too expensive, had been more about satisfying internal interests than about appealing to voters. And in the absence of a compelling message, both the leader and the campaign were forced to improvise, staying one day ahead of events, if that. As Brian Topp put it, "The first two-thirds of the campaign were self-sabotage."

Still, in the post-campaign debrief, we found three reasons to be optimistic. We had increased our vote count by 1 million; we'd come in second in fifty-one ridings; and we had lost eleven seats by fewer than a thousand votes, giving us leads for growth in the next campaign.

We were facing a more immediate opportunity, too. For the first time since 1979, Canada had a minority Parliament. And although the NDP did not hold the clear balance of power, we did have a chance to steer the direction in Parliament and get things done. If we managed that, our MPs would not only be fulfilling their duties as parliamentarians, but we would be giving our leader and candidates in the next election something that very few opposition parties have: a record of accomplishment. The question was, could Jack pull it off?

CHAPTER 5:

TWO SEATS SHORT

Immediately after the election, Jack instructed his new critics to reach out to their government counterparts to explore areas of common concern. A student of our party's past, he knew that some of the finest initiatives in Canada had been done in minority Parliaments.

Tommy Douglas, the father of medicare, worked with Lester B. Pearson to get the Medical Care Act passed in 1966. The Canada Pension Plan and the Quebec Pension Plan were also products of Pearson's minority government. Under the 1972 Pierre Trudeau minority government, NDP leader David Lewis helped bring in national social housing, changes to the political financing laws and steps to ensure greater domestic ownership of Canadian energy resources.

New Democrats had also been successful in minority Parliaments at the provincial level. In the late 1970s, Stephen Lewis, head of the Ontario NDP, worked with Progressive Conservative premier Bill Davis to pass a series of progressive laws. In Saskatchewan, when NDP premier Roy Romanow was re-elected to a third term with a minority government in 1999, he listened to the message sent by the electorate and created a governing coalition, appointing Liberal MLAs to the Cabinet. What followed was stable progressive governance for the people of Saskatchewan, for which the NDP was rewarded with an outright majority win in 2003. It was a sensible approach and a smart political calculation.

The Liberals under Paul Martin had another approach in mind. Only a couple of ministers bothered to respond to the outreach from our critics. After a decade of majority rule, it appeared the Liberals meant to hold on to their power as tightly as they could. "The rhythm of the [2004] campaign was one of having clouds of shit rain on us from the opening day for weeks on end, and so to come out of that campaign holding on to the reins of government felt pretty good," Martin's chief of staff, Tim Murphy, would later explain.

The Liberals had to figure out how to get a Throne Speech passed when the House of Commons reconvened in the fall. To get through that confidence vote, they had two options. They could open up a dialogue with the opposition, or they could draft a Throne Speech on the assumption that one of the opposition parties would let it pass.

When Martin finally invited Jack to 24 Sussex Drive on August 23, 2004, Jack had high hopes for the meeting. "I was particularly aware of the real possibilities that existed because, after all, that's why we were here. At least, that's what I thought," Jack wrote later in *Speaking Out Louder,* referring to moving forward on a series of initiatives for families. "As I would hear over the next hour, and amplified over the next several months, this, however, was not a Liberal prime minister or a Liberal Party prepared—or even inclined—to work with New Democrats in the way prime ministers Pearson and Trudeau had."

Martin even joked at their meeting that the "wellspring of common values between the Liberals and the New Democrats' that he so successfully explained in the campaign might run dry pretty quickly," Jack recalled. He left the meeting thinking, "Is that all there is?"

As Tim Murphy would later admit, the Liberal strategy was to build up public support for the content of their first Throne Speech. The Prime Minister's Office believed the NDP would be forced to vote with the government if the speech included issues that the NDP had run on in the 2004 campaign, such as new funding for cities and helping aboriginal communities. According to Murphy, the Liberals were not interested in "opening the kimono" from the get-go.

Events didn't roll out the way Martin's team planned, and the shenanigans in the weeks leading up to the vote on the Throne Speech sowed seeds of mistrust among all parties that would come to define the minority Parliament. Not long after his disappointing meeting with Martin, Jack met jointly with Conservative leader Stephen Harper and Bloc leader Gilles Duceppe in Montreal. The informal affair, organized by Duceppe, produced a package of joint amendments for the upcoming Throne Speech. Jack didn't think the passage of the speech merited a showdown. He just wanted a nod from Martin about his willingness to give a little. Duceppe and Harper, though, decided to ratchet up the rhetoric. Martin responded to their brinkmanship by freezing out the NDP and striking a deal with the other two parties just an hour before the confidence vote. Jack learned about the deal from news reports.

It was an inauspicious start to a political season that played out on two tracks. Inside Parliament, the prime minister had a barren legislative agenda and couldn't decide whether he was going to stand up to George Bush on missile defence. In February 2005, *The Economist* would dub Martin "Mr. Dithers." Outside Parliament, the Gomery Commission looking into the sponsorship scandal was doing severe damage to the Liberal brand.

Justice John Gomery's inquiry sucked up all the political oxygen in the media. Jack had trouble getting attention, despite the NDP's smart and strategic campaign against missile defence leading up to and following Bush's keynote speech in Halifax on December 1. During the trip, Bush said he hoped Canada and the U.S. would move forward together on the issue. But the daily coverage about Liberal corruption considerably weakened Martin, especially after appearances before the commission by Chrétien and Martin himself. This new dynamic would play to Jack's advantage during the budget negotiations.

Paul Martin certainly hadn't planned to engage with Jack in any negotiations. In January, Jack was on board a special flight with the prime minister and the opposition leaders en route to Phuket, Thailand, to tour the devastation after a Boxing Day tsunami. Jack was disappointed with Martin's approach to governing in a minority Parliament, the first in twenty-five years in Canada, so he took the opportunity on the long flight to talk to Martin, knowing the federal budget was coming up. Martin didn't mince his words. "Jack, you're two votes short," he said.

By February 2005, the government's budget was at the printer, but the Liberals still had no dance partner. They were gambling that one of the opposition parties would vote for it, part of the explicit Liberal strategy to govern on a vote-by-vote basis. "It wasn't clear at that point that either the NDP or the Conservatives were going to bring us down [on the budget]," recalls Tim Murphy. But the Liberals figured all along that there would be a confidence motion before the budget could be voted on. The government was in survival mode, and everything they did was about positioning the Liberals for the next election, thinking it was coming soon. Murphy talked to the Liberal campaign director once a week during this period, in case the government fell. "These were tense days," he remembers.

Ralph Goodale, the Liberal finance minister, tabled the budget in the House of Commons on February 23. In a throw to gain Harper's support, the Liberals pledged to reduce the general corporate tax rate from 21 per cent to 20.5 per cent in 2008, 20 per cent in 2009 and 19 per cent in 2010, at a cost to Ottawa of slightly more than $3 billion. Goodale also committed $12.8 billion over the next five years for the Canadian military, the biggest increase in more than twenty years.

Harper responded immediately by declaring that the Conservatives would support the budget. Calling it "better than expected," he added, "I'm a lot happier than I thought I'd be. The major priorities in this budget are Conservative priorities... I certainly don't see anything in this budget that would warrant two elections in a year."

Jack agreed with Harper: it was a conservative budget, so the NDP wouldn't be supporting it. We knew our nineteen votes would be irrelevant, though, since Harper had committed his caucus's ninety-nine votes to get the budget passed. This was not where we wanted to be during the spring budget season: completely shut out.

But things were about to change. On April 7, Justice Gomery lifted a publication ban on most of Jean Brault's testimony before the inquiry. Brault, the former head of the Montreal advertising company Groupaction, told the inquiry that he was repeatedly asked to make cash donations to the Liberal Party of Canada in Quebec and to put election workers on his payroll in exchange for federal sponsorship contracts. Public money had been funnelled to the Quebec wing of the federal Liberal Party to help pay campaign costs in recent federal elections, Brault testified.

The political sands shifted immediately. Public opinion polls showed Liberal support evaporating, while support for both the Conservatives and the NDP was increasing. Some members of the NDP caucus saw this as a good window for an election. We were all ready to go under the leadership of campaign manager Brian Topp, who had been appointed immediately after the 2004 election. Jack wanted to make sure our decisions wouldn't be dictated by being unprepared to wage a campaign.

After the Brault bombshell, Stephen Harper announced the Conservatives no longer planned to support the budget. Jack met with Harper on April 18. The meeting was brief, thirty minutes in all. Harper informed Jack he was planning a motion of non-confidence, because he was concerned about the impact of the explosive testimony on the country. Despite the lack of trust between them in the wake of the Throne Speech incident, they emerged from the meeting with a deal: Jack agreed to support a Conservative motion to change the order of opposition-day motions. Under the current parliamentary schedule, the Bloc was slotted as the next opposition party to table a motion, but neither Harper nor Jack was prepared to get behind a Bloc motion of non-confidence.

The Liberals caught wind of this, though, and Tony Valeri, the government House Leader in charge of the parliamentary agenda, moved all the opposition days to a later date. The opposition parties went ballistic, and the House descended into complete chaos.

Martin responded by taking to the airwaves in a television address to Canadians on April 21. Desperate to avoid an election in the shadow of Brault's testimony, he effectively stamped the current Parliament with a best-before date of February 2006. After detailing all the steps he had taken regarding the sponsorship program and apologizing for what had happened, he laid out a timeline. "I commit to you tonight that I will call a general election within thirty days of the publication of the commission's final report and recommendations. Let Judge Gomery do his work. Let the facts come out. And then the people of Canada will have their say."

All the party leaders were in the lobby of the House of Commons to have their say after Martin's address to the nation. Harper started things off by speaking to Quebecers, saying the sponsorship scandal wasn't a black mark on them or on Canada but rather on the Liberals. The crux of his statement was a justification for why the Conservatives wanted to bring the government down immediately. Gomery's final report was scheduled for release on February 1, 2006. "But how can we continue—politically, ethically or morally—to prop up a government that is under criminal investigation and accusation of criminal conspiracy?" asked Duceppe.

Duceppe's comments aligned with those of the Conservative leader. The Bloc had been on the ropes, and Gomery had saved them. It was now clear that both parties were softening up the public for a non-confidence vote in the House of Commons. The two parties needed the NDP, though.

Since the election, Jack had been trying to figure out how the NDP could actually affect government decisions. He had mastered this approach to politics during his long run at Toronto's city hall. This was his first chance in Ottawa.

Jack too began his speech with an appeal to Quebecers, saying the scandal wasn't about them. Then he did something that no other leader had dared and nobody expected: he pivoted from the scandal and issued a direct invitation to Martin to try to make Parliament work. We thought his message would resonate, but it was a risk to say the NDP was willing to work with—and prop up—a corrupt government and party.

"I know you care deeply about your family, your community... our environment. I share the hopes you have for them," Jack said in his televised address. "I also share your disappointment. The corruption scandal is not a national crisis. It's of deep concern, but it is a Liberal crisis, not a national one.

"I believe people are tired of this corruption and tired of asking for respect but receiving none... At the same time, we have a Parliament teetering on the brink. We can't condone corruption, and are losing confidence in this prime minister.

"But education, training for workers, and the environment are more important than this scandal... But this also provides a chance for the dithering to end and action to begin. We want to help get a balanced budget passed. So I say to Paul Martin: Bring the budget to a vote, take out the surprise corporate tax cuts and invest that money in things people want.

"The NDP is in no rush to judge the scandal. But we are in a rush to get something done through getting a better budget passed, to show politics can be about you," Jack concluded, looking straight into the camera set up in the foyer of the House of Commons as Martin's senior staff watched from the corridor of the prime minister's third-floor office above.

It was a political judo move, using the weight and power of your opponent against him. If Martin wanted to let Gomery do his work and have Parliament function in the meantime, then let's call him out on it. Let's take him up on the offer he had just made in front of millions of Canadians. We knew the Conservatives and the Bloc would be livid at us, but we didn't care. The effort was underway to brand Jack Layton's NDP as the party committed to getting things done for Canadians.

The next morning, on April 22, the Prime Minister's Office called, asking for a face-to-face meeting to discuss Jack's offer. The meeting between Jack and Martin would take place the evening of April 24 at the Royal York Hotel in Toronto. Both leaders were going to be in town that afternoon to address the annual Sikh Vaisakhi festival. Both sides agreed to keep the timing and location of the meeting confidential. In the meantime, our gamble was playing out well in the press. Martin got the initial headlines he wanted from his mea culpa speech. The day two story and beyond, though, would be all about Jack's offer.

If Martin had needed reminding that things weren't going his way, he would just have had to tune in to CBC Radio's *The House* that Saturday morning. Irish rock star Bono, who had a year and a half before spoken glowingly of Paul Martin at the Liberal leadership convention, was now lashing out at the prime minister for not fulfilling his promises to increase foreign aid. It only strengthened Jack's hand.

After delivering his speech at Vaisakhi, Jack headed to Olivia's city hall office to meet with Olivia, Jamey Heath, NDP House Leader Libby Davies and Bob Gallagher, Jack's new chief of staff. (Donne Flanagan had left after the 2004 campaign.) The group wanted to hammer out the NDP's formal proposal for the meeting with Martin and his staff later that evening.

Throughout the weekend, Jack had already telegraphed pretty clearly what he was looking for: despite what he called a "stench of corruption," he said the NDP would support the budget if Martin agreed to shift billions earmarked for corporate tax cuts to environmental and social programs.

He was in good company. Phil Fontaine, national chief of the Assembly of First Nations, had called out Martin for his hollow talk about transformative change, saying the original Liberal budget would "condemn our people to last place for a lot longer." René Daoust, president of the Co-operative Housing Federation of Canada, had questioned where "the $1.5 billion promised in the last election for affordable housing" had gone. Paul Muldoon, executive director of the Canadian Environmental Law Association, had said the budget did not "create confidence in Canada's ability to take effective legislative action to implement a Kyoto plan."

The details of what would later become the first NDP federal budget were hashed out in Olivia's city hall office. The proposal was straightforward: forgo the $4.6 billion in corporate tax cuts and use the money to fund education and training; create affordable housing, including for aboriginal people living in third world conditions; fight pollution; build transit; protect workers; and help keep Canada's commitment to reduce global poverty. In return, the NDP caucus would agree to vote confidence in the government until the revised budget received royal assent.

Jack, Davies and Gallagher met the prime minister, who was joined by his chief of staff, Tim Murphy, and Liberal House Leader Tony Valeri in Martin's suite at the Royal York.

"There wasn't a lot of chemistry between Paul Martin and Jack Layton. It is fair to say that we didn't trust you, the NDP," Murphy would tell me years later. Jack's take on Martin wasn't positive either. Writing not long afterwards, Jack explained that, in the handful of meetings with Martin, "I always found it difficult to have a 'let's get down to business' kind of conversation with him. His subtle condescension, bred of accustomed power, seemed to get in the way."

The Liberals had run out of options. They knew the minute they agreed to a sit-down with Jack, they would be doing so from a position of weakness. The Conservative Party was enjoying a surge in support in Ontario, putting Harper in a strong position heading into an election if Martin's government fell. Still, as the meeting got underway, there was an instant feeling things weren't going well. Jack laid out the NDP's proposals. Martin and Valeri countered with procedural issues to explain why what the NDP was asking for couldn't work. Neither side could tell whether the other was setting them up for failure.

The meeting didn't last long. The Liberals left the meeting with low expectations. At best, they figured the talks would allow them to survive another week or so. Jack, Davies and Gallagher left skeptical about whether the Liberals were serious about making Parliament work.

Nonetheless, both parties agreed to keep the conversation going. They also agreed that future talks would be better served if neither leader participated, so a meeting between the two parties' house leaders and chiefs of staff was set up for the next day. Davies had worked with Valeri in the House, and they had a cordial and respectful relationship. Gallagher and Murphy knew and respected each other from the same-sex benefits fights waged at the Ontario legislature in the 1990s, and they got along.

Jamey Heath was waiting for Jack, Davies and Gallagher at a pub near the Royal York to debrief and map out the next steps. "How did it go?" Heath asked them.

"Not great," said Jack.

"Is there a deal?" asked Heath.

"We don't know," Jack replied.

Heath needed something more concrete. Prior to the meeting, he and Martin's director of communications, Scott Reid, had worked out a media protocol. If it looked as though a deal was possible following the meeting, both teams would adhere to radio silence. Nobody wanted any surprises during this delicate process. If there was no chance for a deal, it would be open season in the media.

Heath stepped outside to call Reid. "Scott, is it radio silence or not? There seems to be some confusion here."

"What do you mean? It's radio silence," Reid told Heath.

"Scott thinks a budget deal is quite possible, so it's radio silence," Heath told Jack back at the table.

The protocol was for Sunday night only and did not extend into Monday's media cycles. The deal held firm. Some of the press had reported on Sunday that a private meeting was being held that day between Martin and Jack, but nothing from the actual meeting was leaked. It was a modest confidence-building measure between the two teams. If we could trust each other on the media protocol, perhaps there would be enough trust to make a deal.

The next morning, April 25, Jack held a press conference at his constituency office in Toronto's east end. The small office was overflowing with journalists. Jack reiterated his straightforward demands of forgoing the $4.6 billion in corporate taxes and investing the money instead in targeted social spending. Then he added a key element: a deadline of 5 PM the following day for a response from the prime minister. There would be no dragging this out, no dithering.

Empowered by their leaders to negotiate a deal, Davies, Gallagher, Valeri and Murphy began to work in earnest in Ottawa. We took solace in the fact that, no matter the outcome, Jack had positioned the party well. If there was a deal, good things would happen for Canadians and there wouldn't be an election the country did not want. If we didn't get a deal, Jack would still be the guy who had tried to make Parliament work for the people.

On the morning of deadline day, April 26, we called a press conference for 5:30 PM at Ottawa's National Press Theatre, across the street from Parliament Hill. By 4 PM, Jack had two statements ready to go: one if there was a deal, one if there wasn't. As the clock ticked down, we learned the sticking points for the negotiators were not on the budget details but on process. Just after 5 PM, Jack left his Centre Block office to head to the press conference, both statements in hand.

As Jack and Jamey Heath were walking across the lawn on Parliament Hill, Heath's phone rang. It was less than thirty-six hours since Jack had issued the deadline. "We have a deal," Bob Gallagher told Heath. The imminent press conference had pressured the Liberals to close the deal.

A few moments before Jack's press conference got underway, Heath called me at party headquarters. My heart sank when I heard there was a deal. Earlier that spring, I had cancelled plans to work on the provincial NDP's campaign in B.C. just hours before my flight to Vancouver was set to take off. The threat of a federal election had made it too risky to leave. By now, I had also spent months working with the NDP's campaign team. At the time the budget crisis erupted, Brian Topp was already based in Ottawa, working full time on the campaign. The war room was set up, our campaign plane was booked, our literature and signs were printed, and a tour plan and platform were in play. Now we would have to throw a lot of it into the recycling bin. I was happy there was a deal, of course, but it's impossible to work so hard on preparing for a campaign and not want to see it through.

When Jack arrived at the National Press Theatre, the place was brimming with media. The assembled scribes fell silent as the NDP leader took his seat and pulled out the speech marked "Deal." The huge grin on his face relayed the news he was about to announce. This, after all, was what politics was about for Jack, the way Parliament should work.

"This budget isn't perfect. But it's better. It's balanced, and it includes tax reductions for small business," Jack told reporters. "It also invests in people and our environment." Then, he revealed the details: $1.6 billion for affordable housing construction, including aboriginal housing; a $1.5 billion increase in transfers to the provinces for training and tuition fee reductions; $900 million for the environment, with one more cent of the federal gas tax going to public transit; $500 million for foreign aid to bring Canada closer to the long unfulfilled Liberal promise of allocating

0.7 per cent of GDP to overseas development; and $100 million for a pension protection fund for workers.

It was gutsy: Jack, the leader of the country's fourth party, not the government's finance minister, was announcing the details of a federal budget. But this was an NDP budget. Jack wanted to mark the first time since the early 1970s that the NDP had a direct say in public policy. Predictably, Martin and the Liberals were furious. But they also knew $4.6 billion was a bargain for getting to stay in power, and it was a tiny fraction of the government of Canada's $220 billion budget.

The morning after the announcement, Jack got a standing ovation at campaign headquarters. He also saw our long faces. We knew getting this money was better for the country, and we could use the extra time to prepare, but we'd had the pillars for an election campaign in place. We'd even had "Campaign 2005" T-shirts made. (They're now a collector's item for New Democrats.) But now we would need to refocus a lot of our positioning to include the budget proposals and our role in securing it in a minority Parliament.

Outmanoeuvred, Stephen Harper hammered us in the House and the media, saying the NDP budget was the "price to make corruption go away." Some of our supporters also attacked us for getting into bed with the corrupt Liberals. The Conservatives and the Bloc were gunning to kill Jack's budget to trigger an election. And, as Paul Martin had said, we were still two votes short. There were three independent MPs sitting in the House by now, and we needed two of them to back our budget. By convention, a tie would be broken in our favour by the Liberal speaker of the House of Commons. We were heading for a showdown in Parliament, and we didn't know how the vote would go.

Then Paul Martin surprised us—and everyone else. On May 17, I was on a morning panel for CBC News Network's daily politics program with Don Newman, arguing with my Conservative counterpart about the budget, when Newman interrupted us. "I'm just getting word that the prime minister has an announcement at the National Press Theatre. Let's go live," Newman said. Down the hall from the studio, Brian Topp was with David Mackenzie, Jack's former interim chief of staff and senior advisor at the time, in a CBC boardroom, attending a meeting with officials from the other parties and representatives from the country's broadcasters to discuss the details of the national leader's TV debates in the event of an election.

When we saw Belinda Stronach, a Conservative MP and former Conservative leadership candidate just fourteen months earlier, walk in to the National Press Theatre alongside Martin on the studio monitor, a collective gasp went up. Newman yelped "Holy mackerel" on live TV. Stronach, who moved directly into Martin's Cabinet, claimed that she had grown uneasy with Stephen Harper's leadership, his focus on Western Canadian alienation and his desire to bring down the government with the help of the Bloc Québécois.

At the front door of the CBC building, their meeting abruptly adjourned by news of Stronach's defection, Topp and Mackenzie hovered outside, said goodbye to their counterparts and watched as the two Conservative reps headed down the street. Once the Conservatives thought they were out of earshot of Topp and Mackenzie, one of them turned to the other. "What the fuck was that? Holy fuuuuck!" Topp and Mackenzie exchanged grins as they headed back to the office.

Stronach's defection changed the math, but the vote still wasn't settled. One of the independent MPs had declared he would be voting against the NDP budget, another announced that she would be voting for it. So it would all come to down to one person who had yet to declare his intentions: Chuck Cadman, a former Reform MP who was now the independent MP for Surrey North.

Two days after Stronach's stunning defection, the Liberals invoked time allocation, triggering two key confidence motions on the night of May 19. The first was on the original Goodale budget. The second was on the NDP budget amendments. It was showtime.

ON THE WAY TO HIS seat in the House of Commons, Jack stopped by Cadman's seat to say hello. "You have an important decision resting on your shoulders, Chuck. Best wishes," he said. Moments later, Cadman stood to cast his vote for the NDP budget. Speaker

Peter Milliken broke the tie to make the final vote 153 to 152. The first NDP federal budget in Canadian history had passed. By the time the budget received royal assent on June 28, Jack was already thinking about the fall agenda. "What's next? What could we accomplish?" he asked his team. Jack was now firmly in charge. His high-wire budget play had worked, earning him support to push further.

His leadership style as the happy warrior—someone Broadbent described as "intolerant of intolerance"—had also helped build cohesion and trust in caucus. Jack's way was to reach out and listen to his colleagues, then persuade, not lecture. His approach made people feel comfortable and positive. All the same, the caucus was still nervous about the budget gambit. The Liberals were seen as toxic, and the Conservatives and the Bloc were furious at the NDP. There was no clear path ahead for us, making this among the most difficult and defining times for Jack's leadership. Martin had announced he would pull the plug on his own government and head out on the campaign trail early in the new year. If the opposition parties didn't team up to end things earlier, that would allow for about twelve weeks of sitting days in Parliament—not much time to get things done.

The question in the spring had been whether an election could be averted. The question now was when the campaign would formally begin. The parliamentary math had also gotten worse for us. On July 9, Cadman had died of cancer at the age of fifty-seven. The NDP had also lost a caucus member over the same-sex marriage issue.

By allowing Parliament to continue, Jack's budget move had secured the passage of Canada's marriage equality law. In fact, the same-sex marriage bill passed third reading in the House of Commons on the same day the NDP budget bill received royal assent. First introduced in February, the marriage equality bill would have died if the budget had been voted down, along with all the other legislation before Parliament.

Jack, a supporter of marriage equality long before most people, felt in his bones that it was a matter of human rights. That's why he insisted all NDP MPs vote for the bill. MP Bev Desjarlais from Churchill, Manitoba, defied him and voted against it. Martin had left it as a free vote for the

Liberals, and thirty-two members of the Liberal caucus opposed it. The bill passed with the support of the NDP and the Bloc, whose combined numbers were enough to defeat the social conservatives in the Liberal and Tory caucuses.

Jack stripped Desjarlais of her critic portfolios and moved her into the back row. In October, after she lost the NDP nomination in her riding, she resigned from the NDP caucus to sit as an independent. "It's not okay in our party to have loosey-goosey views on human rights," Jack had said at the time of the vote. "This isn't a question of personal views or personal morality. It's an issue of moral rights."

The Liberal strategy in the fall of 2005 did not include working with the NDP. But we had some inside information. Back in the spring, when everyone thought an election was imminent, a senior communications advisor to the Martin team had sat down for lunch with Brian Topp and outlined in great detail what the Liberals had in store. The Martin advisor had told Topp that the Liberals felt there was little threat to them from the right but plenty from the left flank. For that reason, their plan was to tack left in the run-up to the next election and try to occupy the political terrain usually owned by Jack. If they could crowd us out, they figured our voting base might jump to them. That fall, Liberal national director Steve MacKinnon and party president Mike Eizenga would travel to London for discussions with key advisors to Tony Blair about how the Liberals could use the levers of government to appeal to progressive voters.

This information was helpful as we developed our strategy for the fall session. The caucus was split. Some believed we should keep working with the Liberals in an attempt to get things done, regardless of the math. They thought it was better to try and fail than not to try at all. Others argued it was time to get a little distance from the Liberals, who were taking a beating in the public opinion polls in the wake of the sponsorship scandal. This second group was mindful of what had happened in 1974. NDP leader David Lewis had worked closely with Trudeau in the minority Parliament after the 1972 election. When his government fell two years later, Trudeau co-opted the NDP vote to win a majority. Our seat count fell from thirty-one to sixteen. We couldn't let that happen again.

Jack listened to both groups in the caucus. He knew where the Conservatives and the Bloc stood: they wanted an election as soon as possible. Harper was still enjoying a lead in national polls, and Duceppe was dominating in Quebec since the sponsorship scandal. But Jack also knew Harper wouldn't pull the trigger without the NDP, even though the Bloc and the Conservatives had enough combined votes. It would look really bad for Harper to be siding with the Bloc to bring the government down. Harper needed the NDP as moral cover on any confidence vote. This was a huge advantage for us: the smallest party in the House was once again in the driver's seat.

Each of the NDP's options had pitfalls, and either path would be tricky. But Jack was in politics to get things done. We'd been told our budget idea would never work, and it had. "Isn't it worth at least trying again?" Jack asked the caucus.

The Supreme Court's Chaoulli decision, released on June 9, gave us an opening to approach the Liberals: Canada's top court had ruled that the Quebec government could not prevent people from paying for private insurance for health care procedures covered under medicare.

The issue of preserving medicare was in Jack's DNA, as it is for every New Democrat. Universal health care is one of the things that defines us as Canadians, and it is the NDP's greatest accomplishment. The Supreme Court ruling was a threat to that legacy, so it was an easy policy area on which to move. Besides, Jack and the caucus figured Martin would be open to striking a deal. His father, Paul Martin Sr., had sat in the Cabinet that oversaw the expansion of federal hospital insurance in the 1960s, and the prime minister had claimed during the 2004 campaign that medicare was the "fight of his life."

Jack turned to NDP health critic Jean Crowder to draft a proposal for closing the door on privatization. Roy Romanow, who had led the Commission on the Future of Health Care in Canada in 2002, agreed to help us craft our position. Jack met with Paul Martin at 24 Sussex on October 25 to outline our proposal's key elements. These included preserving a single-payer system and making future federal transfer funds conditional on provinces ensuring that public money not go to for-profit medicine.

When Martin punted the file over to his health minister, Ujjal Dosanjh, a former NDP MLA and B.C. premier, Jack knew the Liberals weren't serious about striking a deal. Otherwise, Martin's office would have stick-handled the issue, just as it had with the budget process. "It felt that we were being specifically set up to fail," Martin's chief of staff would tell me years later about Jack's health care pitch. "As time went on, it felt that it was a negotiation to give Jack a talking point for the election."

There's no doubt Martin's refusal to stand firm against the privatization of medicare served the NDP well politically. But Jack actually wanted a deal. Hope died when Dosanjh would only accept one piece of our proposal—forbidding doctors to work both inside and outside the public system at the same time.

On November 1, this tap dance with the Liberals around health care was interrupted by the release of the first report of the Gomery Commission. It was such big news that it was treated like a budget. That meant a lock-up at Ottawa's old city hall, just down the street from Parliament Hill, for reporters and opposition parties. The lead researcher in the NDP caucus services, Kevin Dorse, was sent to the lock-up on our behalf. (The second report was scheduled to be released on February 1, 2006—Martin's trigger to start an election.)

Dorse didn't need to dig deep to get a flavour of what was to come. Under the "major findings" section in the report, titled "Who is Responsible?" Justice Gomery stated in plain language that the Commission of Inquiry found "clear evidence of political involvement in the administration of the Sponsorship Program" and "found the existence of a culture of entitlement among political officials and bureaucrats involved with the Sponsorship Program, including the receipt of monetary and non-monetary benefits." It was now official: the judge had found evidence of an orchestrated plan to funnel taxpayer dollars illegally to the Quebec wing of the Liberal Party of Canada. Martin was fully exonerated and Chrétien was not directly involved in the scheme, Gomery's report said, but as the former prime minister, Chrétien must bear much of the responsibility, because the sponsorship program was run out of the Prime Minister's Office.

When the doors opened, Dorse raced back to Jack's office in Centre Block to brief Jack, Jamey Heath and me. Dorse had prepared a one-page summary for us and also gave us an oral briefing using direct quotes from the report. The report was an indictment of the Liberal Party for "illegal campaign financing," "kickbacks," "greed and venality" and "clear evidence of political involvement" involving $147 million, Dorse reported. Contrary to what the Liberals had argued before the commission, public servants "were not the sole cause of the 'sponsorship scandal' nor were they its principal beneficiaries." The Liberals had "disregarded the relevant laws governing donations to political parties, and contributed to the all too common perception that [politicians] are dishonest and disreputable persons." They were responsible for "inappropriate political interference... excessive concentration of power in the Prime Minister's Office... blatant disregard of Treasury Board policies."

Gomery's report also blamed the Liberals' "culture of entitlement" that led to their "refusal... to acknowledge their responsibility for the problems of mismanagement that occurred," Dorse told us. Jack stopped Dorse there. "Show me where he said that, where he talks about their culture of entitlement," he asked. Dorse opened the report to the appropriate page so that Jack could see it in black and white. This was a bombshell.

Jack now had a decision to make. The Liberals appeared no longer interested in cooperating with us in this minority Parliament. The fall session had become dysfunctional and unproductive. What was the point of keeping it going, now that Justice Gomery had made such a definitive finding of corruption?

On November 2, Jack notified the Liberal government that continued NDP support would require a move against the growth of private health care. The Liberals refused, and Jack announced the collapse of the medicare negotiations on November 7. Jack had a plan for what should come next, but he would need to confer with Bill Blaikie, the dean of the House of Commons and someone widely respected as a procedural expert.

"We knew that our job was not to prop up any party that refused to work together to get things done for Canadians while insisting on its own predetermined election timetable. Our job in Parliament was to work, not twiddle our thumbs while the clock kept ticking on health care," Jack would later write.

Jack's idea was to table a motion on the NDP's next opposition day, scheduled for later in November, calling on Martin to dissolve Parliament in January, for a vote in February. That would move the election up by about a month but avoid a campaign spread out over the Christmas holidays. Jack and the team knew the Liberals would use their last few months in office to go on a pre-election spending spree, and he wanted to shut down that possibility.

Jamey Heath called Blaikie on Jack's behalf. "If you say this can't work, we won't do it. If, in your opinion, it could, we'll do it," Heath told Blaikie. Blaikie informed him there was nothing in the rules that prohibited it.

Jack outlined the NDP plan to the public on November 9. The pitch was simple: his motion would allow the House to pass a few more pieces of legislation in what little time was left on the parliamentary calendar. A scheduled First Nations/First Ministers meeting could also proceed on November 24 and 25. Technically, it would not be a non-confidence vote and the motion was not binding on the government, but it would carry the weight of the majority of the House on the preferred timing for the next election.

In public statements, both Harper and Duceppe responded favourably to Jack's pitch. "I think it's an innovative proposal. It's trying to address things that concern us all," Harper said. Duceppe added: "I do think we've made an important step forward."

The three leaders agreed to meet in person on Sunday, November 13, in Harper's Centre Block office. Before then, Jack had some figuring out to do. He wanted to get some outstanding legislation passed before

Parliament dissolved, including an element of the NDP budget, the wage protection bill. The Conservatives opposed that bill, so he'd have to come up with an idea to get Harper to switch his vote.

He decided to use Harper and Duceppe's desire to trigger an election against them. The NDP would only support a non-confidence vote ahead of Martin's timetable of February 2006 if the Conservatives and the Bloc helped the NDP pass the wage protection bill and the First Nations summit went ahead as planned. Before his meeting with Harper and Duceppe, Jack needed to get a sense of whether his idea would fly.

On the Friday night, Heath called Tom Flanagan, one of Harper's advisors. "I need to get a message to Harper. Can you do that for me?" Heath asked. "Yes, I think I can make that happen," Flanagan responded. Heath outlined the plan. "If the Liberals say no to our motion, you vote for our legislation and we'll second your motion of non-confidence. Do you think that has a reasonable chance of success?" Flanagan didn't waver. "Yes," he replied.

Jack was feeling confident as he headed into the boardroom of the Opposition leader's office on Sunday. But the atmosphere was tense. This was the first time the three leaders had met since their Throne Speech discussion, and that arrangement hadn't ended well. Despite the bad blood, they agreed on a strategy: offer the Liberals one more chance to avoid a pre-Christmas non-confidence vote backed by a united opposition. They'd give Martin ten days to accept the NDP motion, which would call on him to prorogue Parliament in January, making way for a February election. This would bring an orderly end to the session. If Martin refused, the government would face a non-confidence motion by the end of November, triggering an immediate election. The second piece of the agreement stipulated the Conservatives would vote for the NDP budget initiative to protect workers' wages, and the NDP would back a crime bill the Conservatives wanted passed.

Before finalizing the deal, Jack still needed to consult his caucus and get complete buy-in. Jack had already asked a lot of the caucus when he'd negotiated the NDP budget, and there was no guarantee they'd go along this time; sometimes, they saw danger, not opportunity. Because the caucus was so small when he became leader, he'd inherited a consultation dynamic in which everyone had a say. Jack and Bob Gallagher split up the calls, and the two made the pitch to caucus members. Everyone signed off on the plan.

On Monday, Paul Martin rejected the proposal, arguing the other parties couldn't choose a "confidence light" option: they either had confidence in the government or not. Jack would decide on the "not" option, but the Liberals hadn't yet unleashed the last of their gunfire—a plan that combined arrogance and a gross misreading of how parliamentary democracy should work.

As it turned out, the Liberals weren't interested in an orderly conclusion to the session in January. They had already planned a three-month spending spree of taxpayer dollars in the run-up to a campaign to begin by the end of February, and they wanted the time to make the NDP voter-friendly announcements as part of their pre-election positioning.

Now, facing a non-confidence vote by the end of November, the Liberals needed to accelerate their announcements. In the week before the government fell, the Liberal government unveiled commitments adding up to $40 billion in spending. In just one day, the Liberals made thirty different spending announcements.

To persuade the NDP to roll over, the Prime Minister's Office phoned non-governmental groups and requested they put pressure on the NDP through the media to keep Parliament going and bombard NDP MPs with calls and letters. In return, the Liberals said, these groups could look forward to favourable announcements in the coming days.

Our caucus had never experienced such concerted pressure from non-governmental groups. It was tough, but Jack and the caucus knew New Democrats weren't there to support unconditionally a party in service of their re-election strategy. This showed a growing maturity. The groups, though, did not show such maturity and got played. Our motion would afford exactly thirteen fewer sitting days in Parliament than Martin's own election timetable.

On November 21, Jack's motion passed the House of Commons with the backing of the other two opposition parties. It called for Martin to dissolve Parliament in January, for a February 13 election. The Liberal government ignored the vote, clearing the way for Harper's motion of non-confidence to be introduced later in the week. On November 28, following the aboriginal summit, the House voted 177 to 133 no confidence in the government.

A fifty-six-day campaign, set for a January 23 election, was about to start. We had a record of achievement and would get our chance to fix many of the mistakes from the last campaign. It would be our do-over, our mulligan. Were we ready this time?

CHAPTER 6:
THE MULLIGAN

From the outset, Brian Topp had developed a clear chain of command within the organization to avoid the pitfalls of 2004. The election planning working group, co-chaired by Topp and deputy campaign director Sue Milling, began meeting weekly by teleconference. We were a group of senior party officials, party elders and representatives from our advertising and polling firms, NOW Communications and Viewpoints Research.

There was no knowing how long Martin's minority government would last, so by February 2005, we had our campaign apparatus up and running, with most of our candidates nominated, money in the bank, and our polling and ad firms well into their work.

We had also tackled a few major issues that had arisen during the 2004 campaign. First, we had to implement a strategy that would allocate our ground resources in a more effective way. Second, we had to address strategic voting.

What we decided to do with our ground game was revolutionary and controversial inside the party. Jack, though, got behind the plan. In the 2004 election, we had allocated our resources on the ground thinly, seeking multiple breakthroughs across Canada. In most cases, our optimism wasn't warranted. If there was one statistic that reinforced the change in direction, it was this: we had lost eleven seats by less than a thousand votes in 2004. For the next campaign, we adopted a strategy known as "big air, tight ground." This meant that communications and advertising dollars would be spent to reinforce an NDP profile in all regions, regardless of the likelihood of winning, but our ground resources would be tightly allocated to ensure we would win close races.

To deliver "big air," we increased our TV ad buy to $5 million, our biggest ever. As before, we made sure every campaign had promotional materials. But instead of targeting dozens of seats, we would target only forty. This included our nineteen incumbent seats, where we would try to build a firewall around our MPs by giving their campaigns everything they needed for success. Basically, we were following a "bite and hold" strategy to ensure incremental wins. Local campaigns outside the targeted ridings and in areas of non-traditional strength felt abandoned even before the writ was dropped. That was heartbreaking, but there was no way around it. Once Martin rejected our proposal to avoid a drawn-out campaign over the Christmas holidays, we knew our campaign budget of $14.48 million wouldn't go as far as we had planned. We were now looking at a campaign that was nearly twice as long as the 2004 campaign, at a time of year when transportation costs, especially for the leader's airplane, would be higher.

We didn't suspect the Liberals would make a case for strategic voting: we knew it. They had been playing that card for years. If there was one question that I faced most often as director of communications for the NDP's 2004 and 2006 election campaigns, it was this: How are you going to stop strategic voting? The problem kept us up at night, and we were determined to find a way to beat it.

Our strategy, developed over a seventeen-month period leading up to the November 2005 campaign kickoff, was premised on Jack's belief—and that of the campaign team—that we had to solidify the social democratic vote if the NDP was ever to make a breakthrough. That meant we needed to make voting for the Liberals untenable.

During the 2004 campaign, we hadn't landed on who our opponent was. We battled with Conservatives for seats in the West, with the Bloc in Quebec and with the Liberals in Ontario and Atlantic Canada. We were going to fix that this time and go straight at the Liberals from day one. After all, they were the government, and it was their jobs we wanted.

There were plenty of critics in the party who argued that our strategy of going hard on the Liberals could make the Harper Conservatives the net beneficiaries. But what these people refused to acknowledge was that our job was to elect New Democrats. Our pioneers had not built a movement so that the NDP could help elect Liberals. Our job was to defeat them—along with Conservatives and Bloc MPs.

We approached disillusioned Liberals who were now voting NDP to give testimonials in our TV ads. This would send a signal to New Democrat supporters—Liberals were abandoning the Liberal ship and finding a comfortable home within the NDP; surely New Democrats could sit tight.

The second element of our fight against strategic voting was to point out that the Liberals had the same social conservatives in their caucus as Harper's caucus. The more fear progressive groups expressed about Harper, the more likely it was that potential NDP voters would switch to the Liberals. We wouldn't do Martin's job for him. We would contrast our vision and values with Harper's, but we weren't going to go over the top to demonize the Conservative leader, like the Liberals did.

We were armed with research to pull out when Martin tried to play the fear card. We knew he would say, for example, only Liberals would protect a woman's right to choose and defend same-sex marriage. Yet some Liberal MPs were members of the parliamentary "pro-life" caucus, and thirty-two of Martin's own MPs had voted against same-sex marriage legislation; it became law only because there were enough NDP and Bloc MPs in the House of Commons to back the bill.

Our strategy to undermine strategic voting got even tighter after Jack's successful manoeuvre to rewrite the 2005 budget. We had always planned to pitch him as the leader committed to making Parliament work and getting results for Canadian families. When he actually pulled it off with the budget, we sharpened our message to run on our record, the first time the NDP could do so since 1974. Our slogan was "Getting Results for People."

We used the opening days of the campaign to remind voters that in 2004 they had elected nineteen NDP MPs to get things done. We had delivered some significant measures, despite the fact that we were the smallest party and lacked the balance of power. We also reminded people that the NDP attempted to work with the government to stop the creeping privatization of health care, the top-of-mind issue for voters, but Martin's Liberals had refused.

We highlighted this in the first part of the campaign by travelling to Saskatchewan, the birthplace of medicare, after the campaign kickoff in Toronto on November 29. With Tommy Douglas's daughter, Shirley Douglas, by his side, Jack held up his credit card to decry the ongoing privatization of health care under the Liberals. If Canadians wanted results for medicare and in other areas, our pitch was, they needed to send more NDP MPs to Ottawa.

The Liberals had executed their plan to pick off New Democrat voters far earlier than usual in this campaign. On Friday, December 2, Martin popped up at the annual meeting of the Canadian Auto Workers to deliver a keynote address and received a warm welcome from then union president Buzz Hargrove. Hargrove and others had been publicly critical of Jack for his support of the non-confidence motion that had brought down Martin's government a few days earlier.

We watched the spectacle of Hargrove handing Martin a CAW jacket on live television from our war room in campaign headquarters. Then, we had to watch it at the top of the hour on cable news throughout the day.

The development was far from ideal. Here we were, not one week into the campaign, and a former NDP stalwart was publicly signalling support for the Liberals. Saying "We're out to stop the Tories," Hargrove declared that the Liberal government who had chosen corporate tax cuts over social investments until the NDP forced it to rewrite its budget "deserves to go back to Ottawa with even bigger numbers."

Strategic voting, as a concept, is pitched by its proponents as backing the candidate in a particular riding who is seen as having the best chance of defeating the Conservative nominee. The nuance never works, though. News coverage of the strategy usually reduces it to a variation of what CBC News produced that day: "Liberal Leader Paul Martin urged members of the Canadian Auto Workers to abandon the

New Democrats, a pitch that won qualified support from the head of the union."

Our campaign decided not to go after Hargrove personally. Jack, in particular, wasn't interested in a public squabble with the CAW leader. He was disappointed by this turn of events, of course, but it only strengthened his resolve. Then Hargrove hit us again, this time in Windsor, Ontario, where incumbent NDP MPs Brian Masse and Joe Comartin were seeking re-election in the city's two ridings. Hargrove had said he supported voting for NDP candidates except where the Liberal candidate had a better chance of winning the riding. Yet there he was on December 9, standing next to the campaigning Liberal leader in NDP territory as Martin re-announced a promise to spend $46 million to help DaimlerChrysler upgrade its Windsor and Brampton facilities.

While the Liberals were busy using Hargrove to try to pick off NDP voters, the Conservatives were implementing their strategy to grow their base in a disciplined, methodical way. Doable and tangible policy nuggets, including a promise to lower the GST from 7 per cent to 5 per cent and to replace child care spaces with a monthly cheque for parents, appealed directly to their emerging voting coalition of middle-class suburbanites, immigrant communities and older Canadians. Promising these small goodies also helped to inoculate them against the Liberal charge of a Conservative hidden agenda.

The Conservative approach tripped up the Martin campaign. Appearing on a television network on Sunday, December 11, Martin's director of communications, Scott Reid, attacked Harper's proposed Universal Child Care Benefit—$100 monthly payment per child until the age of six—as "beer and popcorn money." Despite a quick apology from Reid, the Harper campaign pounced, attacking the Liberals for a mindset that said big government knew better than parents. The incident folded brilliantly into Conservative messaging. The spat between the two parties destabilized Martin's campaign just as we were heading into the first set of televised leaders' debates. It also marginalized the NDP.

Because the campaign was drawn out over the Christmas holiday, the consortium of broadcasters had opted for two sets of debates: one in French and English in Vancouver before the holidays and the other in Montreal in the new year.

Brian Topp had fixed the problems with our debate prep by putting Ron Johnson of NOW Communications firmly in change. With the help of media coaching guru Barry McLaughlin, the focus was on improving Jack's technical debating skills. This was a marked departure from 2004, when twelve people had been involved in debate practice. Now, we cleared the room to let Johnson and McLaughlin do their job. The streamlined effort served Jack much better, but he still wouldn't break through to make a significant mark.

Our campaign used the first English-language debate on December 16 as an opportunity to have a little fun with Martin, already branded as Mr. Dithers by *The Economist*. In an effort to highlight the Liberal leader's vacuousness and inability to set priorities, I stole a tactic the U.S. Democrats had used during the 2004 presidential debate and created bingo cards full of Martinisms: overused lines and platitudes such as "let me be clear," "my number one priority," "let Justice Gomery do his work."

We thought our irreverent "Give 'Em the Boot Bingo" would be the most effective way to undercut Martin's credibility, part of our overall goal to make him unattractive to NDP voters. Thousands of bingo cards were downloaded from our website by viewers, and when Martin started repeating lines from the cards during the debate, our point was made. The media noticed and gave us overwhelmingly favourable coverage.

Like the Conservatives, our strategy was to go hard in both the pre-Christmas and post-Christmas halves of the campaign. The Liberals planned to keep their powder dry until after the Christmas break and spend the bulk of their advertising dollars in the last three weeks of the campaign. But they had to decide how much to invest in Quebec in the wake of the devastating Gomery report. Just before the Christmas break, the Liberals' senior campaign team decided to pull $2 million in advertising money out of English Canada and put it into Quebec. There had been little movement in public polls, and the Liberals' internal polls still had them ahead. But they also knew things were unstable in the wake of

Justice Gomery's findings. "The biggest worry we had was the credibility challenge for [Martin] in Quebec," recalls Tim Murphy, then Martin's chief of staff. He paraphrased the sentiment in Quebec: "You Liberals have made us in Quebec look stupid. Second, Paul Martin was now seen as an anglo."

In the slow days between Christmas and New Year's Eve, with little movement in the polls, we caught a break. All hell was about to break loose.

Wednesday, December 28, was supposed to be a relatively low-key day on the campaign trail. Things were starting to slow down again after the fatal Boxing Day shooting of fifteen-year-old Jane Creba. The teenager had been one of Jack's constituents in the east end of Toronto, and her shooting just steps from Toronto's Eaton Centre had made for a frenzied few days for Jack. The killing of an innocent bystander in Canada's largest city was a personal tragedy for the Creba family. Jack also thought it was the right time to talk about gun violence.

With Jack's national tour on hiatus during the holidays, some staffers in our war room in Ottawa had taken a few days off to be with family, a rare reprieve from an extended winter campaign. People were starting to stumble back into the office on Wednesday morning when things got very busy. Just as the Liberals were about to step up their game, we cut them off at the knees.

It began with a phone call from the RCMP to the receptionist at NDP Caucus Services on Parliament Hill. Most staffers were on leave from their parliamentary jobs to work on the campaign. During the election, the receptionist was holding down the fort.

The RCMP was calling to let the NDP know it had faxed a letter to the parliamentary office of our finance critic, Judy Wasylycia-Leis. The receptionist called campaign media officer Ian Capstick to pass on the message.

A month earlier, Wasylycia-Leis had asked the RCMP to look into whether there had been a leak of the federal government's income-trust announcement on November 23. In the hours before the announcement, trading had been heavy in trusts and dividend-paying stocks. Respected forensic accountant Al Rosen had spoken out publicly, saying it looked as though some traders on Bay Street appeared to know the details of the announcement before Liberal Finance Minister Ralph Goodale made it—after the markets had closed.

Capstick and his colleagues in the war room assumed the letter from the RCMP was a document to acknowledge receipt of Wasylycia-Leis's request. Just to make sure, the team dispatched Chuck Brabazon, an assistant to Wasylycia-Leis, to dig out the letter from the stack of faxes that had been collecting dust since the office closed down for the campaign. Brabazon scanned the letter from RCMP commissioner Giuliano Zaccardelli dated December 23. He called the war room to read it to Elliott Anderson, the campaign staffer who had kick-started the whole process a month earlier. "We would like to advise you that a review of this matter has been completed. Based on the information obtained during the review, the RCMP will be commencing a criminal investigation," the commissioner's letter said.

"Holy fucking shit," responded Anderson, who immediately went to war room director Raymond Guardia's desk to brief him and other war room staffers. It was around 2 PM, and we had to decide whether to release the letter the next morning or push it out late in the news cycle that afternoon.

"No, we can't hold on to this any longer. It will look like we are holding on to it even longer than we already have. We need to go with it today. Call Judy," directed Guardia.

Capstick reached Wasylycia-Leis, who was in a Toronto suburb visiting relatives during the holiday week. "Can you get downtown now?" he asked.

"Yes," she said. "Tell me where?"

Anderson suggested the steps of the Ontario legislature.

The late afternoon press conference didn't last long, but it shook things up in a dramatic way. It was cold and dark, as Wasylycia-Leis handed out copies of the letter. The press raced to file their stories.

This event would have a significant effect on the outcome of the campaign. But the RCMP investigation into a possible leak at the Department of Finance—one of the most effective war room efforts for the New Democrats to date—almost didn't happen. It was a lesson in how the art of politics is practised.

We had learned a lot from the 2004 campaign, and beefing up our opposition research and our war room capability was a priority. We'd watched carefully to see how the other parties did their opposition research. In the 2006 campaign, we set up a more aggressive war room under the direction of Guardia. We brought in staff who performed the day-to-day opposition research function on the Hill and imported key people from other provinces. This included Ciara Shattuck, a political staffer from the Manitoba government; Marcella Munro, who was active in the civil organization Vision Vancouver; and Elliott Anderson, the director of research for the Ontario NDP at Queen's Park.

The unit, up and running before the campaign officially began so that people could get their sea legs, assembled each morning at six after scanning the papers and reviewing the lineup of the evening news the night before. At the daily meeting, each member of the unit pitched their best ideas for how we should attack our opponents that day. Elliott had noticed a CBC story that featured Al Rosen, well known for his reform work at the Ontario Securities Commission. Rosen was emphatic that something had been amiss on the day Goodale announced the Liberal government's policy on income trusts. "Clearly, there was a leak between 2 and 4 PM," Rosen told the CBC, citing an abnormal spike in activity on the Toronto Stock Exchange in the hours before markets closed.

Elliott knew from his time at Queen's Park that complaining to the Ontario Securities Commission probably wouldn't pay dividends, but he recalled Liberal Finance Minister Greg Sorbara having been served with a warrant by the RCMP's Commercial Crime Unit in another case.

Guardia liked the idea of pushing the issue hard, and Topp green-lit the effort. The House of Commons was still in session, so Judy Wasylycia-Leis stood up in Question Period on Monday, November 28, to ask Goodale if he would launch an investigation into the issue.

Goodale misplayed his hand terribly. He said he was absolutely sure that nobody in his department had leaked any information, calling the line of questioning a drive-by smear. "I have made inquiries within my office and within the department, and I'm satisfied that all of the proper rules were followed appropriately," Goodale told reporters after a raucous Question Period. The next day, Wasylycia-Leis fired off her letter to the RCMP.

Goodale is an honest person with the reputation of being a straight shooter, but he received bad advice. He said categorically that nobody in his department had done anything wrong. In the absence of an internal investigation, no minister could know that. It just wasn't plausible.

There had certainly been no expectation that the RCMP would respond to Wasylycia-Leis's letter during the campaign, but Guardia and Topp knew that asking for an investigation would keep the issue going in the medium term. They also remembered how another incident had played out eighteen years earlier. Back in 1988, when Guardia and Topp were working for NDP candidate Phil Edmonston in Chambly, Quebec, there were rumours that Richard Grisé, the local PC candidate, was getting kickbacks on local contracts. Others shopped the story around to media outlets, but reporters made it clear that they weren't touching it in the absence of a police investigation. Unbeknownst to anyone, RCMP was investigating the matter. After Grisé was elected, the RCMP arrested him, and he eventually resigned from the House of Commons following a fraud and breach of trust conviction.

Fast-forward nearly two decades, and the income-trust investigation hung over every campaign stop for Martin, who reiterated he wasn't going to fire Goodale as finance minister. Goodale himself kept repeating that he was cooperating with the RCMP but wasn't going to step aside during the probe.

It didn't take long for public opinion polls to move. By week six of the campaign, the first week of January, the Liberals had slipped into second place in national polls. Harper, who had run a competent first half, pulled ahead for the first time.

The Liberal campaign floundered. As they panicked, they began to improvise. The most glaring example was on display on January 9, during the second English-language debate. In an awkward segue, Martin announced that the Liberals would get rid of the constitution's notwithstanding clause if they were re-elected.

Just a few days earlier, Martin had released his party's platform, and the plank was not in it. His comment was a Hail Mary pass, and reaction inside the media room at the CBC building in Montreal where the debate took place was not good for the red team. Heath and Bélanger watched as operatives for the Conservatives and the Bloc burst out laughing. *Toronto Star* columnist Chantal Hébert, a specialist in Quebec affairs, ran out of the room, looking gobsmacked. As we watched Martin's declaration from the war room in Ottawa, we let out a collective groan. We knew—and they knew—they were in trouble.

Our own platform launch would come a few days later, on January 12 in Hamilton, Ontario. The launch in the 2004 campaign had gone very badly. This time around, we kept it simple and decided to release it late, just eleven days before election day. We also had party officials conduct the technical briefing, allowing Jack to focus on the overall message of the platform at a later press conference. He stuck to our main points: our commitment to continue to get results, clean up corruption in Ottawa and stop the privatization of medicare.

Our opponents had done their part to scuttle the launch by shopping around an old story to the media about Jack's hernia treatment at the Shouldice Hospital in Toronto. The spin was easy: Jack was a hypocrite as the great defender of public medicare since he had visited a private clinic years earlier. We knew the attack would be coming at some point in the campaign, so our war room was ready with the facts about the clinic's history. Shirley Douglas was on standby and jumped in to explain. The family-run, non-profit Shouldice Hospital was founded in 1945. When medicare was introduced in Ontario in 1971, facilities such as the Shouldice were grandfathered. The vast majority of men in Toronto went to the clinic for hernia treatment that was covered by Ontario's medicare regime. This all took time to explain. When you're doing that, you're losing ground. It was a minor knock against us, but because of our preparation and aggressive push back, it didn't overtake the campaign.

Throughout the campaign, we'd been focussed on another issue: strategic voting. On January 13, just ten days before voting day, Buzz Hargrove and the leaders of other unions and social advocacy groups held a press conference in Toronto to announce the creation of the "Think Twice Coalition." In November, these groups had criticized Jack for teaming up with the Conservatives and the Bloc Québécois to bring down the Liberal government. They now were back, warning Canadians about the dangers of electing a Conservative government. The group listed developments to fear in the event of a Harper victory, including deregulation, more greenhouse gas emissions and big tax cuts for corporations. The Liberals had made these same policy choices, but the coalition overlooked their record to pinch-hit for them.

Our mission remained the same: to defeat the Liberals and replace them in government. Although Jack personally respected the individuals behind the coalition, those of us whose job it was to elect New Democrats were furious at their shortsighted and simplistic political tactics: they were helping the very people who stood in the way of real progressive change in Canada. And soon the "think twice" message would suffer a well-deserved blow to its credibility.

On January 18, less than a week before election day, Martin dragged out Buzz Hargrove one more time to appeal to people to vote Liberal. This time, Hargrove popped up in the town of Strathroy in the Lambton–Kent–Middlesex riding in southwestern Ontario, where the Liberals had won the seat by fewer than two hundred votes in 2004.

This is where their strategy with Hargrove began to unravel. The policy of the CAW was confusing and contradictory. By a vote of its members at a convention, the union was encouraging people to do several different things. The union called on people to vote Liberal in ridings where a Liberal candidate held the seat or had a chance to defeat a Conservative. If the NDP candidate in the riding had a chance of beating the Conservative, people should vote NDP, even as Hargrove campaigned for the Liberals in NDP-held ridings. The CAW's Quebec section was pro-Bloc, so the union was also encouraging voters in Quebec to vote for the separatist party to defeat Conservative candidates there.

When a journalist travelling with the Liberal tour asked Hargrove in Strathroy what voters should do in Quebec, he told them they should vote Bloc to stop Harper. This comment shouldn't have surprised the

Liberals, because the Quebec CAW policy was public, but it would send the party into a tailspin, later forcing Martin to stand in front of reporters to distance himself from his chief surrogate. (Hargrove's pitch also didn't work in Strathroy, where the NDP support went up by about two thousand votes while the Liberals lost over twenty-six hundred votes, losing the seat to the Conservative candidate by more than eight thousand.)

In our war room, you could hear a pin drop during the joint Hargrove-Martin press conference in Strathroy, carried live on the all-news channels. As things continued to spiral downward, we just smiled. Many people in the party had ties to the CAW and to Hargrove personally, and neither Jack nor the central campaign uttered a dismissive remark against him. But Hargrove had ended up being a net negative to the Liberals, and he'd made Paul Martin look like a fool. "Back to work, everyone," Topp said to the campaign crew when it ended. By then, we had already pivoted to our own endgame strategy. We had one overall goal: to stem so-called strategic voting. To do that, we had developed a two-track plan. Paul Martin had designed his campaign as an appeal to progressive values, yet his party harboured many candidates who didn't share them. We decided to point that out. Martin had signed off personally on each candidate, so whenever he campaigned with a local Liberal candidate who opposed abortion rights or same-sex marriage, we called him on it. Our war room had the information in the can. All we needed to do was see where Martin was going that day, call up the file with the candidate's position and voting record, and then email or phone every reporter on the Liberal tour to share this information. By the time Martin was scrummed that day, the journalists had fodder to go after him on his hypocrisy. During the final days of the campaign, our message was driven home when the media got footage of a Liberal candidate running down the hall. He was trying to escape from reporters who were asking why he held values his leader was warning the country they would get if they elected the Conservatives.

We had also developed a message to close the deal with our voter base in the final days of the campaign. We went on the offensive and made a direct appeal for Liberal voters to vote NDP. Topp, in seeking a way for us to strike the right balance, recalled the successful appeal made by Liberal leader Ross Thatcher to Progressive Conservative voters in the 1964 Saskatchewan election to defeat CCF premier Woodrow Lloyd. The pitch was simple: "Lend us your vote." The offer was not marriage, but a date: just this once, just this election, vote for us. If you aren't satisfied, you can go back to your old party in the next election campaign.

Jack started using the line on January 16, seven days before voting day, and repeated it over and over again. "Lend us your vote while the party you have supported in the past cleans itself up," he would say. By the last days of the campaign, Liberal voters knew the party was likely heading for defeat, which would trigger a long drawn-out leadership race. Our message worked as a good insurance policy: New Democrats would be in the House to keep Harper's feet in the fire.

Some in the Parliamentary Press Gallery snickered, but they weren't our target. Our message struck the right chord with Liberal voters and penetrated in enough places. It was a good fit in the era of the consumer voter, rather than the old tribal one. It also helped that the Liberals didn't mount an effective response. They later admitted they had never seen this tactic before. We weren't asking people to abandon their heritage, just to support us in this election, in this context. That was a much easier decision for them to make. Our appeal to Liberal voters simultaneously reassured our base that they should stay with us, while getting Liberal voters into the habit of voting New Democrat.

IN THE END, WE WERE able to build a firewall against strategic voting. The NDP picked up an additional 400,000 votes, for a total of 2.5 million votes nationwide. Our caucus grew from nineteen to twenty-nine seats, though our percentage of the popular vote increased only from 16 to 17.5 per cent. Still, our "tight ground" strategy worked: we won most ridings that we had lost by a whisker in 2004, including Trinity–Spadina, where Olivia was running for us again. We also came in second place in fifty-three ridings—a natural place from which to build our next campaign. Jack had been more disciplined on the campaign trail, and we had worked out some of the bugs in the campaign infrastructure. We had performed more strongly in the debates, and we'd focussed our messaging on our main Liberal rivals, along with mounting a more sophisticated e-campaign and boldly rejecting the Think Twice Coalition.

It was far from mission accomplished, though. As Topp put it, "It was the necessary, but not the sufficient. We achieved the minimum we needed to." We were still the fourth-place party. The Bloc managed to hang on to 51 seats. They had gotten a reprieve because of the sponsorship scandal. The Conservatives had won 10 seats in Quebec on their way to a 124-seat Conservative government, ending a thirteen-year run for the Liberals.

Our reaction to the Conservative win was mixed. We opposed vehemently the direction Harper wanted to take the country, but, with a minority, we knew that Parliament would keep him in check, even though we were a few seats short—again—of holding the balance of power. The battle lines were also clearer. Our new opponent in government meant we wouldn't pull any punches. This would set up an opportunity for the NDP to offer a clear alternative to the Conservatives.

We had to contend with Liberals and their surrogates who blamed us for the Conservative victory. But in a democracy, it's up to the public to decide who they want to govern. If you want to win, you have to earn it. Part of the Liberal downfall was their inability to recognize that an election campaign is a competition for votes among political parties. In the end, the public decides. The Liberals and their allies in the Think Twice Coalition had lost sight of that when they blamed Jack for killing a national child care program, as though it fell to the NDP to advance the political aims and objectives of the Liberal Party.

In the case of child care, the money that the Liberals had handed out to the provinces was contained in the budget in the spring of 2005, which the NDP saved. The Liberal government had signed bilateral arrangements on child care with all ten provinces by November 2005, just days before Parliament fell. There was no legislation to enshrine the agreements in law. The NDP would have supported the quick passage of such legislation, but no child care bill was ever tabled, either in that Parliament or during the Liberals' long majority rule from 1993 to 2004.

In the end, the party that promised to scrap the Liberal child care plan won the most votes and seats. The Conservatives had a mandate from the people to carry through with their promises. That is the way the democratic system works. Yet the Liberals never blamed themselves for the loss of the election. They blamed Jack for voting non-confidence in a Liberal government that had already committed to a February election.

The Liberals, by losing 30 seats, had cemented themselves as a party in decline, with a caucus that had shrunk to 103. In just over two years, Team Martin had kicked out Jean Chrétien after three majority wins, run off every other opponent, convinced the media of the coming juggernaut—and then driven the party into the ditch. Martin announced his retirement on election night.

Jack was on a different course. He was strengthening our foundation, and after the 2006 vote, it was clear there was one major section that needed work: Jack's home province of Quebec.

CHAPTER 7:

COURTING QUEBEC

At the time of the NDP's founding in August 1961, Quebec's Quiet Revolution was well underway. Premier Jean Lesage, the popular leader of a progressive Liberal government, activated the province's fiscal and legal authority after his election in 1960 to accelerate the process of francophone Quebecers becoming masters of their own house. The move to nationalize hydroelectricity assets, create investment funds for local businesses and expand social programs produced a sense of confidence and opportunity in Quebec. This lent credibility to the state as a vehicle for positive change, and it went hand in hand with a rising nationalist sentiment. By the late 1960s, most of the left in Quebec was wrapped up in the burgeoning sovereignty movement. They were fighting for a sovereign Quebec, not a social democratic Canada.

The NDP recognized Quebec as a nation within Canada at its founding meeting, and its first leader, Tommy Douglas, embraced asymmetrical federalism. Douglas held up the creation of the Canada and Quebec pension plans in the 1960s as a way for national programs to be established while recognizing Quebec's distinct status. Jack and his mentor at McGill University, Charles Taylor, would later argue that flexible federalism was an approach that could work for Canada and satisfy the aims of social democracy alongside the needs of Quebec.

A series of events foiled the federal NDP's attempts to make inroads in Quebec over the next four decades: Trudeaumania in 1968; the constitutional wrangling throughout the 1970s and early 1980s; Brian Mulroney's Conservative sweep in 1984, his free trade offer in 1988, the collapse of the Meech Lake Accord in 1990; and the rise and domination of the Bloc Québécois over the next twenty years.

There were glimmers of hope for us in each of these developments, but they proved fleeting.

In the 1960s, Tommy Douglas had made a strong push towards Quebec. Douglas recruited charismatic lawyer Robert Cliche, who became associate president of the federal NDP and leader of the Quebec NDP. Cliche ran in the Beauce riding in 1965, losing by only three thousand votes. Charles Taylor also ran a strong campaign in the same election in Mount Royal against a young Pierre Trudeau, capturing 30 per cent of the vote and garnering national attention. In 1968, Cliche took another run at an NDP breakthrough in the Duvernay riding near Montreal and fell just short; he captured 44 per cent of the vote, losing by fewer than twenty-five hundred votes.

(At the provincial level, labour activist David Côté won the CCF's first and only provincial seat in the Quebec National Assembly in 1944. The Quebec NDP ran a small number of candidates in the 1970s and 1980s but never garnered more than 2.5 per cent of the popular vote in a provincial election. The provincial NDP in Quebec disbanded in 1989.)

In the mid-1980s, NDP leader Ed Broadbent, despite his weak French, invested resources and time into the federal party's Quebec organization and reached out to the Quebec labour movement. Broadbent was popular, and the party was credible enough at the time for former Progressive Conservative MP Robert Toupin, who had recently become an independent representing the Terrebonne riding in suburban Montreal, to cross the floor to join the NDP caucus in 1986. (Toupin returned to being an independent within a year and would subsequently lose as an independent candidate in the 1988 general election.) In 1987, the NDP held its first-ever policy convention in Montreal, where the reception was warm.

Momentum appeared to be on the party's side heading into the 1988 election. Membership in Quebec totalled twenty thousand. But Quebecers embraced free trade and stuck with Mulroney. Broadbent did manage to increase the party's support to 14 per cent of the vote in Quebec, cracking double digits for the first time and securing three times as much support as during his first campaign as leader in 1979. But despite a strong team of star candidates, including Rémy Trudel, François Beaulne and Paul "The Butcher" Vachon, the NDP failed to elect a single Quebec MP and came second in only seven ridings, including Témiscamingue (38 per cent of the vote), Chambly (32 per cent) and Abitibi (26 per cent). The party was not strong in any part of Montreal, though we had pockets of support in Montérégie, Mauricie, around Quebec City and in the sovereigntist heartland, the Saguenay.

"Not winning a seat in 1988 in Quebec was a huge setback," recalls Broadbent, who resigned shortly after the election. The results in Quebec were a key motivating factor in his decision. "We did well in B.C. and Ontario," Broadbent remembers, "but we didn't do as well as a lot of people hoped, and certainly I was down. It was the first time ever I was down—because we didn't get the breakthrough."

In 1990, under federal leader Audrey McLaughlin, consumer advocate Phil Edmonston became the first New Democrat elected in Quebec. Edmonston had placed a strong second behind the PC candidate in the francophone Chambly riding, southeast of Montreal, in 1988, and he agreed to carry the NDP banner there again when a by-election arose.

Edmonston won the by-election by twenty thousand votes, capturing 68 per cent of the vote. Many party activists thought that after thirty years, the NDP was finally on its way to establishing a strong presence in Quebec. The victory was short lived, however. The party failed to do the necessary outreach and policy work to build on the by-election win, and McLaughlin neglected to appoint Edmonston to a senior critic position, which would have shown Quebec voters that they mattered.

Edmonston and many New Democrats across Canada were devastated when the Meech Lake Accord, a set of constitutional amendments including the recognition of Quebec as a distinct society, died in June 1990. Edmonston's own constituency staff became full-time organizers for the upstart Bloc Québécois, founded by sitting Liberal and Progressive Conservative Quebec MPs under the leadership of former Mulroney cabinet minister Lucien Bouchard. The new caucus of Bloc MPs in Parliament became the vehicle to articulate Quebec frustrations with Ottawa. In the summer of 1990, the Bloc announced it would contest a by-election in the Laurier–Sainte-Marie riding, with Gilles Duceppe as their candidate. Overnight, NDP candidate Louise O'Neill, who was until then favoured to win the by-election over the Liberals, finished a distant third.

By the time of the 1993 general election on October 25, just one year after the second attempt at constitutional amendments through the Charlottetown Accord had failed, support for independence in Quebec was way up. Edmonston decided not to run again, and the NDP's fortunes tanked in Quebec. Province-wide, the party's vote dropped to below 2 per cent, helping to create our worst-ever showing in a national campaign: the NDP captured less than 7 per cent of the popular vote in Canada. In the Chambly riding, the NDP lost sixty-five percentage points, garnering just 3 per cent of the popular vote in the riding.

The Bloc, a party dedicated to breaking up the country, became Her Majesty's Loyal Opposition, winning fifty-four of Quebec's seventy-five seats and sweeping nearly all the province's francophone ridings. After a short run that looked so promising, the NDP returned to its traditional spot in Quebec politics—completely off the radar.

JACK KNEW THIS HISTORY WELL, but he was undeterred. Jack thought it was the wrong approach to force Quebecers to choose between being Canadians and being Quebecers. They were Canadians by virtue of being Quebecers, and Quebec was part of Canada. Their route to citizenship was through their collective identity. He also recognized that Quebec nationalists weren't automatically separatists: to think so was to ignore an important—and volatile—segment of the voting population. Mulroney had courted nationalists. So had Paul Martin.

Leaving Quebec nationalist voters to the Bloc was a real risk to national unity, Jack believed. He wanted to reach these Quebecers along with the large number of disaffected Quebec Liberal voters who over the years had lost faith in their party. These two disparate groups of voters would become part of Jack's coalition in Quebec, but there would be a long way to go before we could get them to look at us seriously. That had become painfully clear in September 2003, when we assembled a focus group of francophone Liberal and Bloc voters to probe what they thought of the NDP and Jack, still new to his role as party leader.

A few of us from party headquarters in Ottawa drove to Montreal to listen in. Focus groups don't give you quantitative data like polling does. But a few hours of probing more deeply into what voters are thinking, and testing your arguments, is valuable qualitative research. We sat quietly to observe behind the two-way mirror.

There were a few tidbits of good news. We could sense a desire in the focus group for an alternative to the Bloc and the federal Liberals. People liked our values. But to them, the NDP was a party of "elsewhere in Canada" that they didn't really trust—a Prairie party, an Ontario party or a B.C. party. Another key message was that people wouldn't support us until we ran credible candidates who could win. One of the focus group participants thought the NDP had actually stopped running candidates in Quebec; he recommended we start up again if we wanted to earn his vote. One woman said the NDP reminded her of a little ant: the party worked hard and was determined, but it was small and easily squished. As frustrating as it was to hear, we knew she was right: the NDP at the time was easy to dismiss and even easier to step on without anybody ever noticing.

Back in Ottawa, we began a fight inside the party to invest more time and money in Quebec. Jack and his inner circle pushed back when some in the party argued forcefully that it was a waste of time and money. They wanted to focus on Quebec after we had made gains in the traditional areas of support like Ontario, B.C. and the Prairies. Jack's side argued that gains in our traditional areas of support would fully return only if we could show we were making gains in Quebec. So far, the best we'd been able to do was make small incremental gains. We'd increased our popular vote from 4.6 per cent in the 2004 election to 7.5 per cent in 2006. That was better than the 1.8 per cent we got in 2000, but it also bolstered the naysayers, inside the party and beyond, who said that history was stacked against Jack and Quebec wasn't worth our efforts. We disagreed, but we knew Jack's Clarity Act misstep in 2004 had pointed to a larger problem.

The party couldn't improvise on fundamental issues like national unity in the middle of an election campaign, which is how Jack's comments came across to the public in Quebec and across Canada.

Our team in Quebec was devastated with the 2004 results. With Jack as leader and some better-calibre candidates, the team had hoped to pick up one or two seats, including the Manicouagan riding, where leadership candidate Pierre Ducasse was running. Ducasse did increase the NDP vote five-fold, but coming from such a weak starting position meant he came in third with 10 per cent of the vote.

The Quebec membership went through some soul-searching. The NDP had been a follower in Quebec since the time of the Quiet Revolution. When the Parti Québécois held a referendum on sovereignty association in 1980, we opposed it. When the federal Liberals repatriated the constitution in 1982, we supported them. When the Progressive Conservatives rolled the dice with the Meech Lake Accord, and later the Charlottetown Accord, we followed. In response to the 1995 referendum, the Liberal Party had drafted the Clarity Act to spell out the conditions under which the federal government would enter into negotiations with a province to separate. We supported the legislation.

We'd been bystanders to the initiatives of the real Quebec political actors. It was time for us to become proactive, to go on the offensive. After the 1997 election, McDonough had tried to tackle the Quebec puzzle when she commissioned the Social Democratic Forum on Canada's Future. The panel included prominent Quebecers such as Charles Taylor, Nycole Turmel, vice-president of the Public Service Alliance of Canada at the time, and social activist Marianne Roy. Its mandate involved recognizing and respecting the Quebec people in a meaningful way. But when the panel completed its work in 1999, McDonough, who struggled with French, had failed to articulate explicitly how the values of Quebecers and the New Democrats intersected and how the party saw Quebec's role within Canada.

Jack's Quebec team, under the leadership of organizer Rebecca Blaikie, continued to build on the infrastructure side. But we also had important policy work to do. It was time for the federalist social democratic party to develop a progressive modern vision for Quebec in a united Canada.

We knew the national question was not the main preoccupation for our Quebec membership, but having a cohesive answer to it was the price of admission for a party vying to form government.

In the weeks following the 2004 campaign, NDP activists in Quebec met to discuss how the party could articulate positions on a variety of issues, from the recognition of Quebec's national character to cooperative federalism. Pierre Ducasse, associate vice-president of the party at the time, proposed that, instead of a series of policy statements, the NDP should draft a declaration that threaded together a coherent, comprehensive social democratic position on Quebec's role within the federation.

The team agreed, and Jack tapped a group led by Ducasse to begin drafting the declaration. In January 2005, Jack hired Ducasse to work in his leader's office on Parliament Hill. As someone who had both the ear of the leader and the trust of the Quebec membership, Ducasse's job was to complete the draft and present it to Jack for review.

That spring, Jack circulated the draft among the members of the caucus for feedback. Not surprisingly, the issue of what constituted a clear outcome in a referendum was a sticking point. But these discussions were happening in private now, not on the campaign trail during a federal election.

"The paper has been circulated," Jack wrote to Ducasse in an email on April 19. "Bill Blaikie raised concerns about the second-to-last paragraph in the section dealing with any referendum vote. The paragraph discusses the NDP's position should there be a 50% +1 vote etc. You should try to speak with him before the meeting tomorrow if you can. Perhaps including some of the wording from the Supreme Court decision itself. We're going to have some work to do here. It won't be easy. But the paper gives us a great opportunity to move this forward."

Ducasse understood that bridging the gap would be a challenge. "I'll try to set up something with him," he responded by email. "But ultimately, reworking the writing will not necessarily be enough. We all know there is a very real difference of opinion. I'm sure you understand that we can't dilute the policy to a point where it doesn't say anything. But I'll do all that I can."

Jack knew he was walking a tightrope, but he remained positive. "Our goal is to do the hard work needed to forge a consensus if this is possible," Jack replied to Ducasse. "The easiest steps (!) were securing agreement to this point. Now we have Ed Broadbent and Bill Blaikie who were literally in the House through the two decades (in Ed's case three decades) where these matters were discussed. Do not get discouraged. Be constantly optimistic. There is no other way. Words can be nuanced and language adjusted to find solutions. Rely on the specifics of the Supreme Court ruling to help."

The caucus discussions continued, as did conversations with Brian Topp. Topp spoke at length with Jack about the Supreme Court ruling. Before drafting the Clarity Act, the Liberal government under Jean Chrétien had sent a reference to the top court in 1998 to clarify the legality of a unilateral declaration of independence. The ruling would later inform the Clarity Act, which passed in Parliament with the support of the NDP in 2000.

The Court said that if Quebecers voted on a clear question with a clear majority, then the federal government would have an obligation to open the negotiation process. But neither the court nor the Clarity Act outlined precisely what the threshold for triggering negotiations was. The policy being proposed stated that the "NDP would recognize a majority decision (50% + 1) of the Quebec people in the event of a referendum on the political status."

For Jack it was unacceptable to have Quebec outside of the constitutional family forever. Bringing them in, he believed, was a two-step process: first, you relentlessly present your case for a strong, progressive Canada that respects the people of Quebec, and second, you only secure the signature when you are guaranteed success.

Using this perspective to inform their thinking, Topp and Jack, along with Karl Bélanger, talked through language around Quebec for the NDP to use in the upcoming campaign and beyond. They settled on "Winning conditions for Canada in Quebec." Karl pushed for this phrase because he felt it summarized the NDP's vision and wouldn't get Jack bogged down in legal details.

It was a play on a famous Lucien Bouchard statement: he had said he wouldn't hold a referendum unless he was able to put together the winning conditions. Jack tested out the line sporadically in interviews and scrums before the election campaign got underway at the end of November 2005, but he first used it with meaningful impact in the leaders' debates in Montreal in January. The line has remained in the NDP's toolbox ever since.

Jack talked through these themes with the caucus, and in the end, he was able to get buy-in. The draft document, dubbed the Sherbrooke Declaration, was presented to the general council of the Quebec section of the party in Sherbrooke, Quebec, on May 7, 2005. The declaration cleared its first hurdle when the group voted overwhelmingly to adopt it.

In speaking to reporters at the time, Jack was careful to emphasize the NDP's support for asymmetrical federalism. "I know that the Quebec wing is in the middle of adopting an interesting proposition on the place of the Quebec nation in an asymmetric, cooperative and flexible Canada," he told the media. "I very much like this approach that is being developed and that confirms and reaffirms the principles we have already upheld."

The declaration was an important element of our Quebec strategy. If it was adopted by the federal membership at the party's next policy convention, the NDP would have, for the first time, a comprehensive policy on Quebec's role within Canada.

IT WAS NO FLUKE THAT we decided to hold our convention in Quebec City in September 2006. It was part of our campaign to court Quebecers and show them how much they mattered to Jack and the NDP. We couldn't screw it up.

As director of communications in the leader's office at the time, my job was to showcase the party as a serious player vying for the support of Quebecers. Jack's ground rules were clear: all staffers dealing with delegates, the media and the public were to be francophones or bilingual.

Our keynote speakers would be Quebec headliners, and our panel chairs and moderators would speak for equal amounts of time in French and English. We would ensure that French was spoken on the floor from the microphones during policy debates, and these debates would highlight issues that showcased how the party's values were in sync with those of Quebecers.

Making sure the Sherbrooke Declaration, already endorsed by the Quebec section of the party, became NDP policy was also vital; otherwise, the NDP would fall flat on its face in front of the whole province. The stakes were high—and Jack would wear the defeat if we failed.

In the run-up to the convention, members of the party's Quebec council called riding associations across the country to garner support. They asked members to read the declaration, talk about it and get back with any questions they might have. By the time the Quebec City convention opened, the Quebec team had reached out to more than half of all the riding associations, the first time such a comprehensive internal outreach had been done within the federal party.

Jack had been doing his own outreach campaign in Quebec. In the months leading up to our Quebec City convention, there were a lot of quiet conversations. There was also public speculation about Tom Mulcair's political career.

On February 27, just weeks after the 2006 federal election, Mulcair had quit Quebec premier Jean Charest's Cabinet in a very public dispute. Mulcair had been serving as the province's environment minister, and he refused to support a project to transfer lands in the Mont-Orford provincial park to condo developers. He decided to leave the Cabinet table and sit as a backbencher rather than accept a demotion to minister of government services.

After he left Charest's Cabinet, Mulcair politely turned down overtures from the Green Party. He also talked to the federal Conservatives. During this period, he also considered hanging up his skates and walking away from politics, perhaps joining a law firm or doing environmental consultant work.

Mulcair and Jack didn't know each other, though they had met briefly years earlier. In 2002, when Jack was serving as president of the Federation of Canadian Municipalities, he was in Laval, Quebec, for a meeting. At the time, Mulcair represented the Laval riding of Chomedey in the National Assembly as a member of the Opposition Liberals. The FCM had called Charest's office, requesting a meeting with a provincial representative while Jack was in town. Charest's office sent Mulcair.

Jack and Mulcair met at the Cosmodome, Laval's space and science centre. The meeting was straightforward and uneventful. Neither man had a handler with him and neither had any idea who the other was, even though Mulcair had met Jack's father, Robert Layton, years earlier. In 1984, the elder Layton, a newly appointed cabinet minister in Mulroney's government, was looking for a chief of staff and interviewed Mulcair at his Beaconsfield home. At the time, Mulcair was the director of legal affairs for the English-speaking rights group Alliance Quebec, which wanted to get plugged in to the new government in Ottawa. (Years later, when Mulcair recounted this story to Jack, Jack replied, "Yeah, but I got you.")

Not long after Mulcair's resignation from Charest's Cabinet in 2006, Pierre Ducasse struck up a relationship with Graham Carpenter, Mulcair's assistant in his Chomedy riding office. Each knew his boss wanted to meet with the other's, and it was their job to help set things up.

Jack knew it would be a real catch if Mulcair were to deliver a keynote address on sustainable development at the forthcoming convention in Quebec City. He asked, and Mulcair, who was weighing his political options, said yes.

"I've just talked with Thomas Mulcair about speaking at convention," Jack told convention coordinator Ira Dubinsky over the phone a few weeks before the event. Dubinsky put the phone on his shoulder and googled Mulcair while Jack was talking. "Oh, this is a big deal," Ira thought to himself.

"When it was announced Tom would be a speaker, no one knew where it would lead," recalls Rebecca Blaikie, whose job it was to get as many Quebecers to attend the convention as possible. She had begun using the draft Sherbrooke Declaration as an organizing tool to entice people in Quebec to come to the convention and join the party. Having the document helped, but people expressed lingering doubts. *"Oui, mais,"* Blaikie often heard.

The convention lineup already featured high-profile party stalwarts such as Shirley Douglas and Stephen Lewis, and the last-minute addition required some last-minute juggling, but it was well worth the short-term chaos.

Jack had made a commitment to professionalize the party, and we put on a slick show at the convention with strong visuals for the cameras. It was part of our effort to build a refreshed NDP brand around Jack, whom our polling and focus groups had consistently shown was more popular than the party itself. "That attracted me," Mulcair explained later of the quality of the people in the organization.

Tom spoke about sustainable development and how the federal government under the Liberals had let Canada down. After he left the podium, a group of Quebec media scrummed him. Jack's plan—to show the Quebec media and political establishment that the NDP was serious about makings gains in the province—appeared to be working.

For NDP veteran Raymond Guardia, who had spent years toiling away in Quebec on behalf of the party, the convention was electrifying. Guardia chaired most of the proceedings, and he could sense the energy in the room, especially when delegates endorsed the Sherbrooke Declaration as party policy.

"You'd have to go back nearly twenty years, to the 1987 convention in Montreal, for the last time Quebec New Democrats felt this good. The feeling among those from Quebec was amazing," he recalls. Following the passage of the declaration, thousands of delegates broke into spontaneous chanting of the French version of the party's name: "NPD! NPD!"

This was Jack's coming-out party, too. After a disappointing first election as leader in 2004 and an effort in the winter campaign of 2005–06 that failed to see the promised breakthrough in key urban areas, Jack had a lot riding on the convention. His gamble with Mulcair and his determination to pass the Sherbrooke Declaration were part of his larger effort to put his stamp on the party.

At each federal convention of the NDP, delegates are asked whether they want to trigger a leadership contest. It is a public litmus test of how much support the leader has inside the party and an important number over which the media obsess. Every leader knows that anything lower than 75 per cent support in this vote of confidence will be cited by political opponents and the press as evidence you've lost the party's grassroots. Jack was preoccupied with the vote all weekend.

The referendum on Jack's leadership took place on the morning of the final day of convention, before his address to delegates. He nervously awaited the results in the green room backstage with his chief of staff, Bob Gallagher. After party officials counted the ballots, they gave me the numbers so that I could convey them to Jack before he headed to the stage.

"We got the results. Ready?" I asked.

Jack, reviewing the speech he was about to deliver, looked up and replied. "Yeah, go."

"Congratulations—92 per cent," I said.

A big smile crossed his face. Jack knew what it meant. Delegates from across the country, including a sizable group from Quebec, had endorsed his leadership in convincing numbers. Despite the disappointing results from his two election campaigns, he had a mandate to take the party from one satisfied to sit on the sidelines to one that wanted to govern.

Five years earlier, his party had been going through a full-blown midlife crisis. Now, it was united, focussed and laying the foundations for a breakthrough.

Making inroads in Quebec was vital to make the party into a viable player for power, and the successful convention in Quebec City was a critical step in this process. We now had the Sherbrooke Declaration and had shown Quebec that someone of Tom Mulcair's stature didn't think of the NDP as an ant. Now, Jack had to close the deal with Mulcair.

IT WAS NOVEMBER 7, 2006, and Jack had been courting Mulcair for a few months to join the NDP and become his Quebec lieutenant. He figured the atmosphere of the historic Mon Village restaurant, located just off the Trans-Canada Highway near his hometown of Hudson, Quebec, was the perfect spot for Jack and Olivia to enjoy a nice meal with Mulcair and his wife, Catherine. The restaurant's stone fireplaces and wood panelling made it comfortable but not too fancy or stuffy, and on this quiet Tuesday night the four of them had a section all to themselves, so they could speak freely without worrying about being overheard.

The couple hit it off over prime rib and red wine. The conversation was easy, bouncing around from kids and travel to policy and politics. Olivia was charming and Jack was his easygoing self, recalls Mulcair. "The dinner was the turning point," he says.

Catherine was vital in making the decision about her husband's next steps. The couple had been together since they were teenagers, and they always made decisions together. "Catherine was strongly impressed by Jack as a person and the vision he talked about with us that night, and he continued afterwards to show a soft touch," says Mulcair.

A few days later, on November 10, Jack followed up with a thank-you email to Mulcair: *"Merci à Catherine pour s'être joint à nous! J'espère qu'il y aura encore souvent des occasions dans le futur."* (Thank you to Catherine for joining us! I hope there will be many such occasions in the future.)

Over the next little while, Mulcair and his wife "thought about it quite a bit," he recalls.

"Are you convinced that you don't want to do politics anymore?" Catherine asked her husband, who had an offer from a law firm in hand.

"Of course I'm not done with politics. I like it too much," he replied.

"So, what's your best fit?" she asked.

"I really like Layton. I like the vision," said Mulcair.

Shortly after the dinner in Hudson in November, the NDP put down another marker on Quebec. The Bloc, attempting to box in the other parties in the House of Commons, tabled a motion: "That this House recognize that Quebecers form a nation." The NDP had held that position for decades, and there seemed to be broad support within caucus to support the motion. The Bloc quickly amended the motion on November 22 to include the words "currently within Canada."

Caucus member Charlie Angus, the popular MP from northern Ontario, laid out the problem about the Bloc's curveball in an email to

Jack. "Now that the Bloc have amended their motion to a 'nation within Canada, now, for the time being, until something better comes along, etc...' it has to change our response. No amount of internal NDP gymnastics can erase the cynicism... I look forward to us standing as a unified caucus to give these guys the thumbs down," Angus wrote to the NDP leader.

"The Bloc carries the tone of a casual date... I'm with him [Canada] at the moment 'wink wink.' Something fundamentally insincere," agreed Jack in his email reply.

In response to the Bloc, Stephen Harper introduced his own motion. "That this House recognize that the Québécois form a nation within a united Canada," it read.

Jack confirmed the NDP would support the Conservative motion. "Mr. Speaker, I am proud to represent a party that, for decades, has supported recognition of Quebecers' nationhood," Jack said in the House of Commons on November 22.

"Quebecers are an important people within Canada, a people with an amazing four-hundred-year history, an extraordinary people, proud of their values, proud of their history, an important people not only here in Canada, but around the world and in La Francophonie.

"We are proud of Quebec. I am proud to have been born in Quebec and to have grown up there, proud that my grandfather was a minister in the Government of Quebec. I am proud, like anyone who lives or has lived in Quebec and who knows that Quebecers form a nation.

"We have long supported this concept, because it is a question of respect for our fellow citizens who live in Quebec."

Forty-five years after the NDP had recognized the people of Quebec as a nation, the House of Commons followed suit. The motion passed on November 27 with the backing of the entire NDP caucus. Whether the Bloc had been laying a trap for Parliament as a whole, for Harper's Conservatives or for the NDP, it was the Liberal Party that was divided on this fundamental question. Liberal MPs represented fifteen of the sixteen "no" votes; the sixteenth was independent MP Garth Turner.

The following weekend, the federal Liberal Party, divided on the question of the Québécois forming a nation, held its leadership

CHAPTER 7: COURTING QUEBEC

convention in Montreal. The hotly contested race had been getting plenty of media coverage: the country was watching closely to see who would succeed Paul Martin. But ground zero for the sponsorship scandal wasn't the smartest choice for the struggling Liberals. It was another example of how the party was becoming tone deaf. We were there on December 2, the day of their leadership vote, to remind them of that.

"Welcome to Montreal," beamed the headline of the red pamphlet we'd produced to hand out to delegates and the media. Inside, readers would find a tour itinerary: a "Map to the Scars."

Locations to visit included the site of the inquiry led by Justice John Gomery and Restaurant Frank, where various Liberal operatives had received envelopes full of cash.

I was at the convention to do some media commentary and to spin for the NDP, along with Olivia and Karl Bélanger, Jack's press secretary. It was fun to watch delegates read our pamphlet and to generally make trouble for our opponents. It was less fun when the outcome of the leadership vote was not what we had predicted.

Our war room back in Ottawa, headed by Kathleen Monk, deputy director of Strategic Communications who joined the leader's office in August 2006, had come up with a few scenarios and drafted well-developed responses for each of them. Our research team had put together extensive notes on both Michael Ignatieff and Bob Rae, because we assumed one of these two men would win the leadership. We didn't have much of an angle on Stéphane Dion, only that he was an out-of-touch intellectual, a divisive and aloof figure in his home province.

Just before the results of the final ballot were announced, George Heyman, now an NDP MLA in the B.C. legislature for the Vancouver–Fairview riding, had emailed Jack to ask how he thought the race was going to play out. "I'm waiting for the final Lib vote and it looks like Dion (I know you wanted Iggy for the match-up) and wonder what you think of this potential match-up and who you think will actually take it?" wrote Heyman, president of the B.C. Government and Service Employees' Union at the time.

Jack replied that he was now "betting on Dion" and sensed an opening for the NDP: "I believe that we have potential to do well with Dion." Not long after this email exchange, Dion bested Ignatieff on the final ballot. As Dion stumbled through his victory speech, Karl Bélanger was at the back of the convention hall, standing with his Bloc counterpart Frédéric Lepage. The two high-fived each other. "We both thought, for very different reasons, that this was the best result that could happen to our respective parties," Bélanger explained years later.

The following morning, Jack directed caucus researcher Kevin Dorse to pull together a report on Dion's weak record as environment minister. "Someone also needs to sit me down and interview me on my work in/ on environment. It goes way back and consists of many, many actions. We should develop a record of them so that we can do a 'compare and contrast' exercise. People just don't know and we need to set the record straight," Jack wrote to Dorse on December 3.

The wall-to-wall media coverage of the Liberal convention, nearly unanimously positive, created a surge in the party's support, and it was costing us dearly. Just five days after Dion was elected leader, the Liberals had surged to 38 per cent of national support, a six-point lead over the Conservatives according to an Ipsos-Reid poll. Jack and the NDP were at 13 per cent. Two days later, EKOS Research had the Liberals ahead by seven points, at 40 per cent compared with 33 per cent for the Conservatives. We were at 10 per cent.

Dion was a sympathetic character to NDP voters, we would learn. He was a well-meaning, heart-in-the-right place academic, portrayed as an environmentalist, and our supporters didn't like it when we attacked him. In the weeks following his selection as leader, a significant number of NDP donors cancelled their automatic monthly contributions. (Months later, after seeing Dion in action, they had returned.)

Other national polls in the weeks that followed, including polls by Decima and the Strategic Counsel, showed the honeymoon continuing. The Liberals were firmly in the lead, and we were stuck in the low teens. We had seen honeymoons before, and as students of history, we knew this was to be expected. The eastern-based media has always been obsessed with the Liberals, and this becomes even more pronounced during a leadership race. But we were still concerned, nonetheless.

Of course, the Liberal record on the environment was deplorable. Dion had sat around the Liberal Cabinet table for years, part of the team that promised to meet the Kyoto target to cut greenhouse gas emissions by 20 per cent, then oversaw a 30 per cent increase—a worse record than even the U.S. had under George W. Bush. After being appointed environment minister by Martin in 2004, Dion had joined the Conservatives in voting against mandatory fuel efficiency for all cars in February 2005. A few months later, when he set up a Chemicals Sector Sustainability Table to consult on pollution issue, Dion named the vice-president of Imperial Oil's Chemicals Division as one of its co-chairs. In December 2005, Dion had won accolades for chairing the international conference to extend the Kyoto Protocol. We had seen this Liberal play before: support an agreement, then fail to act on it. But when Dion made the environment the central plank of his leadership campaign, his actual record hadn't seemed to matter.

In an email to Jack on December 10, long-time friend Peter Tabuns, former head of Greenpeace Canada and currently an NDP member of the Ontario legislature, asked if the NDP was "putting together a media strategy to promote its green cred? It makes many of us nuts to see Dion outscoring us. I know bounce is bounce but I worry about the potential for it to stick. Any thoughts?"

"We have similar concerns," Jack replied on December 11, explaining that whenever the NDP highlighted green issues, "it pushes up Dion's votes."

In mid-January of 2007, just as we were plotting how we would position Jack and the party against the new leader of the Liberal Party, I got a call from a senior staffer in the Prime Minister's Office. He asked if I could meet him on the following Sunday morning. We met in the restaurant of the Delta Hotel in downtown Ottawa.

"I wanted to give you the heads-up on a campaign we will be launching soon," the Conservative operative told me. He handed me a DVD in a case featuring a photo of a shrugging Dion. The headline "Not a Leader" was scrolled across the cover in a big chunky font. When I got home, I slapped it into my DVD player to have a look.

"What kind of leader is Stéphane Dion?" the announcer barked. The ad cut to a brutal exchange from a Liberal Party leadership debate held on October 16, 2006, between Dion and Michael Ignatieff.

IGNATIEFF: "Stéphane, we didn't get it done." [Ignatieff was referring to meeting the Liberal commitments on climate change.] "We didn't get it done and we have to get it done."

DION: "This is unfair."

IGNATIEFF: "We didn't get it done."

DION: "This is unfair... you don't know what you speak about. Do you think it's easy to set priorities?"

IGNATIEFF: "Excuse me?"

After this exchange, the narrator of the ad concluded, "Leaders set priorities. Leaders get things done. Stéphane Dion. Not a Leader. Not worth the risk."

The ad made its debut on February 4 during the Super Bowl. That was just the beginning of a massive Conservative ad buy that generated tremendous media and was devastatingly effective. Despite Dion's ten years in the House of Commons, very few Canadians outside of Quebec knew who he was. The ad let Dion do the talking. Its message was reaffirmed by Dion's weak performance and meek persona on Parliament Hill in the early days of his leadership.

Our own work in Quebec continued. Landing Tom Mulcair would have a domino effect. On January 15, Jack had emailed Rebecca Blaikie, Mulcair and high-profile civil rights lawyer Julius Grey about moving "recruitment into high gear." Jack explained he had just spoken with Cree leader Romeo Saganash about running for the NDP. "He has always felt the NDP was closest to his values," Jack wrote. "He's been approached by all parties to run, but never by us. He appreciated the approach. He said that if Tom Mulcair and Julius Grey are running, he will run for sure!! (Hear that Tom and Julius?)"

All this behind-the-scenes work was about to pay off. On February 20, Mulcair announced he would not be a Quebec Liberal candidate in the provincial election scheduled for that spring. A few weeks later, Mulcair was ready to send another strong public signal that he was serious about the NDP.

"I'll show up," Mulcair told Jack regarding Jack's upcoming speech on Afghanistan at the Université de Montréal on March 7. The two also planned to have lunch together that day, and Bélanger alerted a photographer from the Canadian Press about that. People plugged into Quebec politics would understand what it meant when they saw pictures of Tom sitting in the front row to hear Jack's speech and of the two of them lunching together that day at a nearby restaurant.

Conservative ads about Dion certainly helped the Conservatives, but they also helped Jack and the NDP. So did Dion's lacklustre performance in the House of Commons. By March, Dion's lead in the poll was gone, and the Liberals would never regain that lost ground. In every major poll conducted in March and April of 2007, the Conservatives were back on top, with gaps as high as seventeen points between them and the Liberals.

The NDP climbed out of the low teens, but we couldn't get beyond the high teens. Still, we saw some glimmers of hope. On April 17, pollster Nik Nanos published numbers that showed what Jack and his Quebec team had felt for a while: our Quebec numbers would go up dramatically if we could shake free Bloc voters. The NDP was at 13 per cent in the Nanos poll, and we would go up ten points and overtake the Liberals if the Bloc were not on the ballot. But of course they were on the ballot. That meant the challenge was distinguishing ourselves from the Bloc in just the right way. With our policy and organizational capacities now in place, we just needed the final ingredient: some strong, quality candidates to show Quebec we could win.

On April 14, Tom Mulcair called to tell Jack he had made his final decision: he was coming on board. "We can make the announcement at the end of the month or in May," Mulcair said.

"Why don't you just come up to Ottawa?" suggested Jack. "We'll meet to close the deal and we'll make the announcement tomorrow."

Things didn't come together quite that quickly, but Rebecca Blaikie had less than a week to organize the press event. She was summoned from Montreal to party headquarters in Ottawa on April 15, where she joined Bob Gallagher, Mulcair, Jack and me for a meeting in the boardroom. She went back to Montreal that evening to begin mapping out the logistics of the announcement, set for April 20 on Mont Royal.

We knew our opponents would do their best to muddy the waters by playing up Mulcair's talks with the Conservatives after he left Charest's Cabinet, but he was ready for it. "It was made clear to me, in no uncertain terms, that there was no question that they would ever change their anti-Kyoto stand," Mulcair told reporters at the press conference to announce he was Jack's new Quebec lieutenant. "So when I watch the federal Conservatives use the Liberal mismanagement of the file as an excuse to continue doing nothing, I say that people deserve better."

A week after Mulcair's announcement, Hubert Bauch of the *Montreal Gazette* wrote a weekend feature about what Mulcair's move could mean for the NDP and federal politics in Quebec. Under the headline, "NDP Plots Quebec Breakthrough," Bauch also put it in perspective: Tom was no opportunist.

"To be NDP in Quebec you gotta believe," Bauch wrote. "Not just in the standing dogma of what is the most ideological of national political parties, but believe that this time could be THE time, the first time ever the NDP doesn't get wiped off the Quebec map in a federal election."

Bauch acknowledged that Mulcair "brings to the NDP both experience in the corridors of power and street cred on the hot button issues of the day." Mulcair's move to the NDP also signalled a shift. "The Bloc was a comfortable place to park their votes... it was in large part a protest vote, but I think people are ready for a change," Mulcair told Bauch. "Quebecers are looking more for solutions than confrontation. That opens doors for us."

That thirst for change had also been evident in the provincial election held just a few weeks prior to the announcement. The right-of-centre Action démocratique du Québec had become the Official Opposition in the National Assembly in Quebec City. Some mistook these results as a turn to the right in Quebec, but we saw it as a willingness by voters to break out of the federalist/separatist divide between the established parties. This was borne out in polls showing that many ADQ voters were considering the NDP federally.

After Mulcair's announcement, our attention turned immediately to the question of whether he should run in the Outremont riding in an upcoming by-election or wait until the next general election. The Liberal MP from Outremont, Jean Lapierre, a nationalist and founder of the Bloc who'd been recruited by Paul Martin to be his Quebec lieutenant, had resigned on January 28, not long after Dion was elected leader. The prime minister had until July 28 to announce the date of the by-election.

We knew we could run a strong campaign in Outremont with Mulcair as our candidate, but it was a long-established Liberal stronghold. The Liberals had held the seat since 1935, with just one exception: 1988, when Quebec voters went along with Mulroney's free trade offer. Jack sought the advice of the working group set up under Brian Topp's leadership after the 2006 campaign to get ready for the next election.

Jack presented the group with different scenarios. Should we run Mulcair in Outremont or hold back and run him later? If he won, he would set our course in Quebec. If he lost but made gains, we could still sell ourselves as a party on the march in Quebec. But what if Mulcair lost and didn't want to run a second time?

Topp recommended forcefully that Mulcair run in Outremont. "Even if he doesn't win, it will be understandable. People there have been voting Liberal for so long, nobody could credibly claim failure. If we make it a close race, we can build on that momentum for next time," Topp told the group.

Jack also wanted to talk it through with Mulcair and Rebecca Blaikie. The three set out on a tour of the province, and during a visit to Trois-Rivières on May 24, Blaikie broached the topic. The three of them were sitting on a patio having a drink and catching up on work. Jack lifted his head from his papers, Mulcair remembers.

"I'd need some pretty convincing arguments to make me believe that I don't run my Quebec lieutenant in the first riding that opens in Quebec," he said to Mulcair. "I promise to you that we will use every resource we can to make this thing happen." Then Jack put his head back down and returned to his work.

By the time Harper announced that the by-election would be held on September 17, Jack and Mulcair had already decided to go for it. It was a huge gamble, but we decided to bet the house on Outremont.

ON THE MORNING OF SEPTEMBER 17, I picked up Jack from his Centre Block office, and we drove to Montreal together to spend voting day in Outremont. We knew from Mulcair and our local team on the ground that things were looking good, so Jack was upbeat but nervous. Outremont was a Liberal fortress, and we were in uncharted territory.

Jack spent most of the time on his phone while I drove. When Jack was nervous or apprehensive, that's what he did: he worked the phones. I was more confident and as such had made plans to stay the night in Montreal to celebrate. "I think we're going to win in Quebec, and it's going to be a late night," I'd told my wife, Sarah, the night before. I'd be leaving her alone with our two-year-old and our six-month-old baby.

The moment Jack and I began our tour of zone houses in the riding, the places volunteers gathered to pull the vote, I knew I was right to feel confident. The campaign team had built an army of 450 volunteers, mostly young people. They wanted to win, and they were revved up.

Late that afternoon, as we were walking south on Avenue du Parc near one of the campaign offices, a city bus stopped at a red light beside us. When the passengers saw Jack, they started to yell at him to come over and shake hands with them through the windows. He was a rock star, and I knew then something very different was happening.

Jack had promised Mulcair an A-plus campaign, and the party delivered. Jack had turned to Raymond Guardia to run the campaign. The veteran Quebec organizer had been in the trenches for more than two decades, and he'd been around for the NDP's only other victory in Quebec, the 1990 by-election win in Chambly.

When the party's director of organization, Heather Fraser, had first approached Guardia to serve as campaign manager, he'd said he wasn't interested. Then, Jack stepped in to ask. "I know you don't like to be pressured, but we really need to do this," Jack had said to Guardia at a party fundraiser at Julius Grey's house in Westmount.

Guardia had agreed, but he didn't want to do it alone. He reached out to Broadbent's former principal secretary George Nakitsas. Nakitsas had first joined the NDP in 1967, when he was growing up in Montreal. He had worked with Guardia and Topp in the Chambly by-election and had been Ed Broadbent's chief of staff, but now lived in Brampton, Ontario. "You have to come and do this with me," Guardia told him. "I need you to help." Nakitsas agreed to join Guardia.

The strategy was simple. Convince the media and the voters that the race was wide open, that anyone could win it. Then, make it a three-way race between the Liberals, the Bloc and us. Finally, pare it down to a race between the NDP and the Liberals. Our idea was to focus on the environment and the Afghanistan war, because we knew Quebecers lined up with the NDP on these issues. The incumbent Liberals were offside.

Mulcair had spent years in the Quebec Liberal Party, and he had never really had to fight for his seat, like New Democrats did. In his first campaign in 1994, he ran in Chomedey, a safe federalist seat, and received 68 per cent of the vote. He cracked 70 per cent in 1998 and won by twenty thousand votes in 2003. Now, Mulcair had been introduced to our campaign playbook, which he dubbed "NDP Alchemy."

Mulcair wasn't used to going door to door to canvas in his own riding. Blaikie served as translator as he waded through the dynamics of an NDP Election Planning Committee and our tracking system on voting intentions, known as "marks." Voters identified as unwavering supporters are marked as a 1, so that we make sure to pull their vote on election day. Voters who are definitely not voting for us are identified as a 5; we don't waste any time on them. Those leaning towards the NDP are either a "2 or a 3, and we reach out to try to persuade them. A voter leaning heavily against us is identified as a 4.

Outremont was not a classic NDP campaign, however. We were starting from scratch there: we had few marks from previous campaigns. We were also running a high-profile politician and a former provincial cabinet minister. Mulcair and the party were both doing something new. He was in a new political family, getting used to a new way of campaigning. The NDP had never run such a high-profile Quebec politician. It looked easy from the outside, but a lot of trust had to build through the process.

Mulcair had announced he was running in Outremont on June 21, and his campaign team was up and running by the end of that month. In contrast, the Liberals didn't have a candidate until ten days before the writ was dropped, when Dion appointed Université de Montréal professor Jocelyn Coulon.

Nakitsas had pitched the concept of an early "shock and awe" strategy. A massive sign blitz on the night of July 27 meant voters woke up on day one to a riding painted orange with thousands of signs. Nobody had seen NDP signs before, and these had two familiar faces on them: Mulcair and Jack.

This sent a strong signal to voters and Quebec pundits that something new was on offer. Volunteers from all over the island of Montreal started flooding into our two campaign offices, on Avenue du Parc and on Côte-des-Neiges. During some phone-bank nights, we had so many volunteers that we didn't have enough phones.

The campaign was also attracting notable support from some surprising quarters. A union activist from the powerful Confédération des syndicats nationaux (CSN) (Confederation of National Trade Unions) showed up to volunteer. The fellow was a seasoned organizer, and one of Mulcair's assistants, Steven Moran, chatted him up at the campaign office. "I was sent here," the activist said. The Quebec labour movement, a long-time ally of the Bloc, was quietly signalling that it wanted a presence in our campaign.

The campaign was still struggling to get media attention, though, a challenge during any summer by-election. Bélanger was sent to Montreal to generate media attention to compensate for what we assumed was a bigger Liberal machine in the riding. He used Mulcair's position as Quebec lieutenant to offer him up whenever reporters asked to interview Jack for a story. Jack stepped back from the media spotlight to give Mulcair as much exposure as possible.

Olivia Chow spent many days in the riding leading up to voting day. She focussed on the neighbourhoods in Côte-des-Neiges, where twenty-four different languages were spoken. She canvassed, and whenever she was in one of the two campaign offices, she worked the phones, calling every Chinese name on the voter's list. She also accompanied Mulcair to the doorstep in heavily ethnic neighbourhoods. Voters in the riding weren't used to that, but Mulcair was good at connecting with people. His visibility on the ground also reminded voters of a simple fact: the Liberals had been taking them for granted.

This message was reinforced by Jack's strong presence in the riding. He wasn't in the riding as often as Olivia, but he came close. The joke was that the two of them spent so much time in Outremont, they were almost eligible to vote there.

Bloc Québécois leader Gilles Duceppe certainly noticed Jack's presence. Midway through the campaign, Duceppe showed up one day to declare to the media, "Thomas Mulcair is a federalist."

Raymond Guardia, never one to take the Bloc lightly, wondered why Duceppe would feel the need to make such an obvious statement, harmless as it appeared, but that soon became clear. With three weeks left in the campaign, we were canvassing in an area of the riding that was a Bloc stronghold. The people opening their doors would identify themselves as traditional Bloc voters but said they wanted to get the Liberals out. When we asked "Can we count on your support?", increasingly the answer was yes.

The Bloc vote was causing us to hemorrhage, and Duceppe was trying to stop the bleeding by calling on sovereigntists not to vote for a federalist candidate. That was a turning point in Guardia's thinking: the Bloc, always dismissive of the NDP, had now realized we could be a threat to them in Quebec. In 2006, the Bloc had come in second in Outremont. If they fell behind this time, we would have gained momentum at their expense.

Guardia sensed it was time to switch gears. He pitched his idea to Mulcair over lunch at an African restaurant in the riding. "Tom, I want to reframe our campaign. No more policy, no more issues. The voters know where we stand. Let's make it the Tom and Jack show," he said.

"Let's do it," Mulcair replied. All policy content was henceforth stripped from the campaign, and our pitch became about the two of them, an accomplished Quebec politician and a very popular party leader. It was a perfect contrast to the Liberals' Coulon and Dion and a strong way to frame the close of our campaign.

The Liberals, meanwhile, were quiet. Mulcair and the team kept on identifying votes and blanketing the riding. The Liberal tsunami will come; never underestimate them, people said to each other. But it never did.

We sent a spy to the Liberal campaign office in the Van Horne shopping centre to collect intelligence and any available literature. "Excuse me, any leaflets on Monsieur Coulon?" our operative asked the sole worker in the office.

"Well, we don't have any pamphlets for you at this time. Monsieur Coulon is in the back writing it now," the worker replied.

With just a week to go before election day, Nakitsas and Guardia went to check out what was being billed as a big Liberal event at John Pratt Park. In attendance were a few journalists, seven MPs and another twelve people. "That's it? Where's the tsunami?" Guardia thought. A few days later, when he spotted a group of Liberal staffers from Ottawa handing out literature on a street corner, he realized the tsunami was never coming. The photocopy of a Dion profile looked amateurish. "Oh my God, the Liberals and the NDP have traded places," Guardia said to himself.

The voters also understood what it meant when *La Presse*, the influential Montreal broadsheet, published a poll three days before voting day. The poll showed the NDP ahead of the Liberals by six points, 35 per cent to 29 per cent. It wasn't an insurmountable lead, but it indicated the NDP could win, and it sent a signal to all non-Liberal voters in the riding: to end the Liberal dynasty in Outremont, vote for the NDP. The poll numbers also gave every New Democrat and progressive voter in the riding permission to vote for the party they actually wanted to.

Throughout the campaign, whenever Jack came to Outremont, he would pull Guardia aside and ask, "How many marks?"

Guardia would report: "Our goal is eight thousand, and we're getting there."

Jack would look him the eye. "Make it nine thousand. I'm serious, nine."

The evening of election day, Jack, Mulcair and I went up to the NDP's Montreal office to watch the results come in with Guardia, Nakitsas and other senior campaign workers. Mulcair's wife, Catherine, and their two sons joined us. The office was just a few doors away from the bar where our party was scheduled for later that night, Les Bobards on boulevard Saint-Laurent.

We knew from our election-day organizers that our marks were holding and turnout was brisk. Word on the street was the Conservative and Bloc voters were also turning up for Mulcair to make sure that someone other than the Liberals won.

Still, we were nervous when the numbers started coming in. The results were slow at first, but then the floodgate broke. As Guardia explained the data coming in from the zone houses throughout the riding to Mulcair, Tom's eyes teared up. We could tell from how the votes were distributed in certain polls what the overall trend would be: Mulcair was going to win big. Nakitsas had thought Mulcair was going to win, but he admitted later the margin surprised the hell out of him. After all the counting was done, Mulcair received 11,374 votes, netting 48 per cent of the popular vote. The Liberals got 6,933 votes, or 29 per cent of the vote.

It took us a good thirty minutes after Radio-Canada had announced the results to get the celebration underway. We had cracked the last nut. We had clear policy. We had a personable leader Quebecers liked. And now, we had shown Quebec that the NDP could run a strong, credible candidate with the ability to win.

Some commentators chalked up our win to Dion's failure. Granted, the Liberals had run a pathetic campaign fronted by a weak candidate. But there was a lot more going on. Outremont had set the wheels of our Quebec plan in motion, and we immediately accelerated the pace of our organizing in Quebec. We gave Mulcair the resources to tour the province with Jack, do outreach with stakeholders and find strong candidates for the next election. Jack appointed Mulcair as NDP deputy leader, along with Vancouver MP Libby Davies, and finance critic, signalling to Quebec that he would play a major role in the leadership of the caucus.

Jack was feeling great. The Liberals were on the ropes, and the NDP now had a foothold in Quebec. We just needed to keep the momentum going to win even more seats there. A breakthrough could be just around the corner, we thought.

We were wrong—very wrong.

CHAPTER 8:
APPLYING FOR THE JOB

We had begun preparing for the next federal election immediately after the 2006 vote. Jack reappointed Brian Topp as campaign director, along with Topp's deputy, Sue Milling. Both wanted another shot to see if they could crack the code and make the kind of gains that had eluded the party in the 2004 and 2006 campaigns. By the summer of 2006, our campaign working group was meeting weekly. As Jack's director of strategic communications on Parliament Hill, I would be assuming the role of chief spokesperson during the next campaign.

The campaign working group had to decide if we were going to spend the legal maximum—about $20 million—in the next campaign. The NDP had never gone to the spending limit before, because it didn't have the capacity. But after Jack put together the deal in 2003 for the party to buy a building, we were able to build equity. This made it easier to borrow money to run campaigns. By 2008, our party's fundraising capacities had also improved dramatically under the leadership of the party's director of development, Drew Anderson. So although we were still far behind the Conservatives, we were at least competitive with the Liberal Party on the fundraising front.

The working group hashed out this financing question at one of our weekly meetings in June 2008. Stakes were high, and we took the financial viability of the party very seriously. If we borrowed significantly and failed to do well in the next campaign, we risked putting the future of the party in peril. But Mulcair's victory in September 2007 had also given the party and the caucus a huge boost, so there was a real sense of optimism.

We went around the table, and I made my pitch when it was my turn. "Let's look at the terrain. We have a leader whose personal numbers are rising in the polls and a weak Liberal party under Dion. We have a united caucus and a seat in Quebec for the first time in years. We have star candidates lined up and the biggest war chest we've ever had. If we don't spend every single penny we can get our hands on in this campaign, when would we?"

We drew up a $20 million campaign budget and decided to go for it. This allowed us to go toe to toe with the Conservatives and Liberals in every aspect of the campaign, including in the emerging area of online campaigning. We were now able to invest ten times more in online campaigning with double the number of staff than the previous election. The strategy sessions over whether we should position Jack as running for prime minister were testier. Jack had experience governing during his long tenure in municipal government. Brian Topp had worked as deputy chief of staff to Saskatchewan premier Roy Romanow. I had worked in the youth office under B.C. premier Glen Clark and in the Cabinet communications office in Ujjal Dosanjh's government, as well as for the provincial ministers of finance and advanced education, training and technology. We came from government, so the idea that we were in this to govern was natural to us.

But there was an entrenched belief among some in the party, even within caucus, that it wasn't credible to think Jack would ever become prime minister. Therefore, they argued, we shouldn't campaign that way. Jack, very committed to the strategy, was consistent in his response: "I'm not in this to raise good points. I'm in this to win."

Everybody understood the risk in saying something that could be dismissed outright: Jack was making a pitch to be prime minister as leader of the fourth party, with polls showing support for the NDP in the teens. But if people were ever going to see Jack as a potential prime minister, we needed to have the confidence to say it ourselves. Taking that approach would also force our opponents to tell people why Jack shouldn't be prime minister. If they engaged us on that front, we'd be winning.

We were fighting for our share of crowded political space, and we knew it was easier to get media traction on a process story than on policy. (Even though, at the end of every election campaign, the press gallery laments how little policy there was to cover, forgetting that as a group they tend to obsess about process and usually ignore the policy parties do propose.)

We also had research on our side. In this most recent round of focus group tests, we had asked voters in our universe what they would think if Jack, while out on the campaign trail, said he was running for prime minister. One respondent had summed up the general sentiment. "Well, of course he's running to win. Why else is he running?"

This frame—electing a prime minister who would put the interests of you and your family first—helped us focus how we would attack our opponent. Jack was running for prime minister, so our main target must be the guy who currently held the position.

Identifying who we were actually running against was always a challenge for New Democrats. In the West, we competed against Conservatives, and we battled Liberals in Ontario and Atlantic Canada. Now, with a foothold in Quebec in Mulcair, we identified some Bloc and Liberal seats to target there.

Focussing on Harper didn't mean we were going to let our guard down when it came to Dion. In fact, we were nervous about the possible effects on NDP-Liberal switch voters of Harper's relentless attack on Dion and the Liberal leader's proposed "Green Shift"—introducing a national carbon tax alongside cuts in income and business taxes to offset the higher cost of consumer goods. What if Dion became a sympathetic underdog because he was getting picked on mercilessly by Harper?

In Parliament, the Liberals were in disarray, losing two sitting MPs who crossed the floor to the Conservatives. Once we'd decided on the frame for Jack's next campaign, we seized the opportunity to fight hard against the Conservatives while Dion's crew either voted with the government or abstained. By banging away at the Conservatives in the House of Commons, Jack and the NDP caucus could also hit the Liberals on the backswing. This helped tell the story we wanted Canadians to hear: it was Jack who could stand up to Harper, not Dion.

By the end of the spring parliamentary session, the Conservatives, elected just two years earlier, were girding to go to the polls, despite bringing in a law setting fixed dates for federal elections every four years. They spent the month of August laying the groundwork to trigger an early election. Harper had already cycled Jack, Gilles Duceppe and Stéphane Dion through 24 Sussex for what seemed like pro-forma meetings. He was having a hard time finding a stable dance partner in the House of Commons; if one opposition party voted with the government, the other parties jumped on them and called them collaborators. Harper also wanted to pounce on a weakened Dion, who had not recovered from the thrashing he got in the Conservative Party's "Not a Leader" ad campaign in 2007.

With the election campaign right around the corner, we needed to road-test the language we had developed for Jack. We knew it was important to get the language out there now so that people could chew on it. If the media and the public were ever to believe that Jack could be the next prime minister of Canada, we had to start saying it—directly, out loud and often.

We agreed that, as spokesperson for the campaign, I'd be the one to test drive our new strategy on *Question Period*, CTV's Sunday political show, where I'd be representing the NDP on a political panel about the upcoming election along with Liberal strategist Steve MacKinnon and Tim Powers for the Conservatives.

"So, how did it go?" Topp asked me after I got back to party headquarters from pre-taping the show in early September.

"Well, they didn't laugh," I said.

The frame, therefore, was leadership. And since Harper was seen as a strong leader himself, we decided to cast Jack as a new kind of strong in our main messaging and our advertisements in the first part of the campaign. They were all ready to go when Harper asked Governor General Michaëlle Jean to dissolve Parliament on September 7 for an election day of October 14.

For the first time since Jack had become leader, Topp opted to go with advertising agencies that didn't have experience doing political ads.

After years of working with NOW Communications, the campaign felt it was time to go in another direction. For our English ads, we went with a consortium of ad experts in Toronto who worked with our ad buyer Wills & Co. For our French ads, we hired advertising executive Carl Grenier, founder of Zoom Media and then Amen ad agency. "These guys worked hard to get into our heads, to understand our thinking. They asked, 'Where do you want to be after the next election and what would success look like?'" recalls Nammi Poorooshasb, the party's director of communications at the time.

"Stephen Harper is a strong leader," the female announcer declared in our opening ad. "With the strength to brag about billions in corporate tax cuts while one in eight children lives in poverty. Strong enough to ignore nearly 5 million Canadians who can't find a family doctor. And destroying the environment while you pay record-high gas prices. Strong leadership. We need a new kind of strong." Jack then appeared on the screen for the kicker: "The new strong is about fighting for what's right for you. I'm Jack Layton of the New Democrats."

For our campaign, we also purposely dropped "NDP" in favour of "New Democrat." First, we needed to freshen up the brand. Second, we wanted to take advantage of the rise in popularity of the Democrats in the U.S. Every night throughout the fall of 2008, Canadians would be getting an update on the U.S. presidential election, and they would be constantly hearing the term "Democrat" linked to the popular leadership of Barack Obama.

Just before the launch of the campaign, Jack and Anne McGrath had travelled to Denver to spend a day at the Democratic National Convention as guests of the National Democratic Institute (NDI). McGrath had recently come on board as Jack's director of administration on Parliament Hill and would go on to serve as Jack's chief of staff after the 2008 election. The two watched Obama's acceptance speech sitting alongside Joe and Jill Biden and other guests in the United Steelworkers of America box. Jack had a chance to speak with Biden about the upcoming election campaign in Canada and the role the economic downturn of 2008 would likely play.

Once the campaign was underway, we wanted to take advantage of this association with the Democrats under Obama. It wasn't a big thing, but this was a game of inches, and we went for everything that could give us an edge. We decided that, at the end of every ad, Jack would look straight at the camera and say, "I'm Jack Layton... of the *New* Democrats" or "I'm Jack Layton. Vote *New* Democrat."

With the global economic crisis looming, we couldn't shy away from the economy in this campaign. Besides, with Jack running to be prime minister, he couldn't shrink from the biggest policy question facing the country. The NDP had traditionally been seen as strong on social issues but weak on the economy. We wanted to kill that myth. The Conservatives, meanwhile, were branded as strong managers of the economy, and we knew they would lead with that.

We approached this challenge on two fronts. The first order of business was to set the record straight. In terms of fiscal policy, analysis from the federal government's own Department of Finance showed that the NDP had the best record of balancing the books when in government. Tommy Douglas had run seventeen consecutive balanced or surplus budgets in Saskatchewan. Roy Romanow had later brought the province back from the brink of bankruptcy after years of PC premier Grant Devine's fiscal incompetence. Manitoba's Gary Doer had run ten consecutive balanced budgets in the decade from 1998 to 2008.

Now, with a worldwide financial crisis underway, we felt we would do better focussing on microeconomics rather than macro. While Harper talked about global trends and Canada's place within them, the NDP would focus on ways to create and to protect jobs and defend Canadian households against the negative impacts of the crisis.

So that was the plan heading into our first-ever $20 million campaign: Jack was a new kind of strong; he wasn't afraid to talk about the economy; he was taking dead aim at Harper; and he was running for prime minister.

ON SEPTEMBER 7, DAY ONE of the campaign, Jack stood on the banks of the Ottawa River in Gatineau, where star candidate and former Liberal MP

Clockwise from top: Jack, whose political career at the municipal level spanned two decades, stands in front of his Metropolitan Toronto Council office in 1986. ANDREW DANSON/LAYTON-CHOW FAMILY

Jack kicks off his campaign for NDP leader on Parliament Hill on July 22, 2002. "New Energy, New Leadership" was a battle cry for those who wanted change in the party. JONATHAN HAYWARD/THE CANADIAN PRESS

Jack takes to the stage on January 25, 2003, after winning the NDP leadership on the first ballot, flanked by Olivia Chow and Ed Broadbent. CANADA'S NDP

Jack's first campaign as leader in 2004 experienced plenty of turbulence. The rebranding effort to emphasize Jack rather than the party was already underway. CANADA'S NDP

Facing reporters on election night on June 28, 2004, Jack was elated to be elected Member of Parliament for Toronto-Danforth, but he was disappointed the NDP picked up only five seats and devastated that his wife, Olivia Chow, lost her bid for a seat. CANADA'S NDP

Olivia Chow joins Jack on Parliament Hill on November 29, 2005, to kick off his second federal election campaign. He would later occupy the prestigious offices on the fourth floor as Leader of the Official Opposition. CANADA'S NDP

Jack rallies the staff at NDP campaign headquarters in Ottawa on November 29, 2005. For the party, this campaign was about fixing the mistakes of the past campaign. CANADA'S NDP

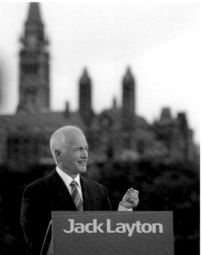

Clockwise from top left: Tom Mulcair and Jack celebrate the night of the Outremont by-election victory on September 17, 2007, at Les Bobards bar on boulevard Saint-Laurent, a win that showed Jack's efforts to build in Quebec were paying off. RYAN REMIORZ/THE CANADIAN PRESS

Applying for the job of prime minister, Jack launches the 2008 election campaign on the banks of the Ottawa River in Gatineau, Quebec, on September 7, with Parliament Hill as the carefully crafted backdrop. CANADA'S NDP

Jack campaigns to re-elect Dennis Bevington in Fort Smith, Northwest Territories, on September 8, 2008. CANADA'S NDP

September 22, 2008—Jack, with his sister, Nancy, on the campaign bus, reviews a speech before an event. Nancy travelled with Jack during the 2011 campaign as well, serving as his physical trainer. CANADA'S NDP

For the 2008 campaign, we planned carefully scripted events where visuals helped tell the story. Here, Jack is showcased as a "Strong Leader" in Edmonton on September 20, 2008.
CANADA'S NDP

Just three weeks after hip surgery, Jack faces a sea of reporters outside the House of Commons on March 25, 2011, following a non-confidence vote to bring down the Conservative government and trigger the election. JAKE WRIGHT/THE CANADIAN PRESS

Jack, framed by the Canadian flag and surrounded by supporters, launches the 2011 election campaign at the Château Laurier in Ottawa on March 26, 2011. Fresh off of hip surgery, we were relieved he could stand for the whole speech. CANADA'S NDP

Jack has a quiet moment with a great source of his inspiration, his granddaughter, Beatrice, in my office at campaign headquarters on March 26, opening day of the 2011 election.
CANADA'S NDP

Jack takes the campaign's message "Ottawa's broken and we're going to fix it" to Winnipeg on April 5, 2011. MATT JIGGINS

Jack signs a "Giving Your Family a Break" platform booklet, emphasizing the trust message, and shares it with a young supporter after the platform launch in Toronto on April 10, 2011. CANADA'S NDP

The night after the French-language debates, Jack watched the Montreal Canadiens take on the Boston Bruins on April 14, 2011, at the Bell Centre's Les Cage aux Sports bar, where he also did a little bartending. CANADA'S NDP

Flanked by NDP MP Jack Harris (right), seeking re-election, and NDP candidate Ryan Cleary (left), a relaxed Jack plays the accordion at a campaign stop on April 16, 2011, in St. John's.
JACQUES BOISSINOT/THE CANADIAN PRESS

Jack serves coffee at a local Tim Hortons in Welland, Ontario, on April 19, 2011. That day, he told voters in the manufacturing region hard hit by the recession that he would "fight like hell" for their jobs. CANADA'S NDP

With security detail in tow, Jack gets a briefing from his long-time senior press secretary, Karl Bélanger, before meeting with reporters at a campaign stop in Val-D'Or, Quebec, on April 18, 2011. MATT JIGGINS

Jack, fulfilling one of his childhood dreams, sticks around after his interview with CTV's morning show *Canada AM* on April 19, 2011, to give the weather report, a last-minute tour addition. JACQUES BOISSINOT/THE CANADIAN PRESS

Clockwise from top: Travaillons Ensemble (Let's work together) was the rallying call for Quebecers to join with progressives in the rest of Canada to replace the Conservative government. This was the largest rally in Quebec, held at the Olympia Theatre in the heart of Gilles Duceppe's riding on April 23, 2011. CANADA'S NDP

At the last rally of the campaign in Burnaby, B.C., on April 30, 2011, Jack shakes hands with supporters holding up signs with our endgame message. CANADA'S NDP

With just one more day left on the campaign trail, the leader, feeling good after the B.C. rally, swaps his cane for a putter on the Montreal-bound NDP campaign plane. CANADA'S NDP

In the final days of the 2011 campaign, supporters began to show their affinity for Jack and the NDP with the tag "Orange Crush." CANADA'S NDP

In what became an iconic image of the campaign, Jack holds up his cane, showing strength and defiance. Here, he's at the Olympia Theatre in Montreal on April 23, 2011. CANADA'S NDP

Jack talks to members of the senior campaign team on election day, May 2, 2011, at the InterContinental Hotel in Toronto. From left to right: chief of staff Anne McGrath, senior advisor Brian Topp, Jack, me and Sue Milling, deputy campaign director for the 2004, 2006 and 2008 campaigns. CANADA'S NDP

Jack and Olivia watch the election results roll in on May 2, 2011, in the family's suite at the InterContinental Hotel in Toronto. CANADA'S NDP

Jack, after the breakthrough results had come in, addresses the crowd at the NDP's election-night party at the Metro Toronto Convention Centre. "Spring is here, my friends, and a new chapter begins," he said. KEVIN VAN PASSSEN/*GLOBE AND MAIL*

Left: Jack sits in his new digs, the office of the Leader of the Official Opposition, on the fourth floor of the Centre Block of Parliament Hill on May 25, 2011. PETER BREGG/THE CANADIAN PRESS

Top: Jack waves to delegates at the NDP's convention in Vancouver on June 17, 2011, marking the fiftieth anniversary of the party, with newly elected members of the NDP's largest-ever caucus looking on. CANADA'S NDP

Above: In his last public appearance, Jack announces at a news conference in Toronto on July 25, 2011, that he's stepping down temporarily as NDP leader to fight a new cancer. NATHAN DENETTE/THE CANADIAN PRESS

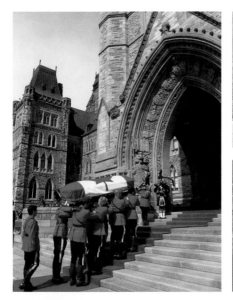

Clockwise from top left: Members of the RCMP carry the coffin containing Jack's body into the Centre Block of Parliament Hill on August 24, 2011. DEPARTMENT OF CANADIAN HERITAGE

Rarely has a politician touched the lives of so many, witnessed by the outpouring at Toronto city hall's Nathan Phillips Square on the morning of Jack's state funeral on August 27, 2011. Here, mourners read chalk messages about Jack's legacy. DARREN CALABRESE/THE CANADIAN PRESS

Reverend Brent Hawkes of the Metropolitan Community Church of Toronto officiates the funeral at Roy Thomson Hall. DEPARTMENT OF CANADIAN HERITAGE

Millions of Canadians watched the funeral on TV while thousands gathered outside Roy Thomson Hall. MICHAEL HUDSON/THE CANADIAN PRESS

Jack's granddaughter, Beatrice, attends the "I am the Layton Legacy" tribute on March 23, 2012, in Toronto. IPOLITICS/KYLE HAMILTON

Françoise Boivin would be running for us in Quebec. It was the perfect spot to kick off the campaign. Jack was gunning for power, so Parliament Hill served as our backdrop. We also wanted to send a signal to Quebecers.

"My friends, Stephen Harper announced today that he intends to quit as prime minister. And so today, I'm applying for his job. Unlike Stephen Harper, I'll put you and your family first. Unlike Stephen Harper, I'll act on the priorities of the kitchen table, not just the board-room table," said Jack, surrounded by hundreds of supporters.

The event was made for TV, and it was well planned and beautifully executed. Since we wanted Jack's opening remarks to hold for a full news cycle, we had planned no scrum. Instead, the assembled reporters filed their stories about Jack's opening statement, and then we got on our campaign plane to fly right into the belly of the beast: Stephen Harper's riding of Calgary Southwest.

Jack's tour in the opening week of the campaign was about rein-forcing our message that we were the ones to take on Harper. It included stops in several Conservative-held ridings: Vancouver Kingsway, where David Emerson had been elected as a Liberal MP in 2006 and promptly crossed the floor to the governing Conservatives; Thunder Bay, where former Liberal MP Joe Comuzzi had also switched to Harper's team; and St. John's, where Danny Williams, premier of Newfoundland and Labrador, was spearheading an ABC—Anyone But Conservative—campaign.

This time around, instead of a rising-tide campaign, we were running a beachhead campaign. Unlike in 2006, when we had identified eleven must-win seats to target after losing them by less than a thousand votes in 2004, there was no obvious grouping of seats to go after based on near misses. That meant we'd had to spend more time in the run-up to this campaign identifying which seats we should target to expand the caucus.

We identified a series of seats that would act as beachheads in their regions, allowing us to build out later. For example, the city of Edmonton had seven seats. Instead of investing in all of them, we would focus on one, Edmonton–Strathcona, and then target Edmonton East and Edmonton Centre after we'd secured our first NDP MP from the city. In

Newfoundland and Labrador, we would target St. John's East, then move to grab St. John's South–Mount Pearl. In Quebec, we would invest in the Gatineau riding to get a foothold in the region, then go after Hull–Aylmer and spread out from there. In southwestern Ontario, the Welland riding was the region's beachhead. In northern Ontario, we used Charlie Angus's Timmins–James Bay riding and Tony Martin in Sault Ste. Marie as our beachheads to target the entire region.

Before the campaign had begun, we had seeded the ground for our beachhead approach by sending caucus members to these ridings and bombarding voters there with parliamentary mailings. NDP MPs rose in the House of Commons to ask the government questions on local issues affecting these communities, such as a mill shutting down in Thunder Bay or Algoma. We complemented this by highlighting pocketbook issues of concern to voters, such as rising costs of home heating and gas.

To implement our plan, we had scheduled an ambitious tour for Jack out of the gate: in addition to our stops in Calgary, Vancouver, Thunder Bay and St. John's, we flew to Regina, Oshawa and Montreal—all in the first week. We also flew over the Athabasca tar sands and stopped in Fort Smith in the Northwest Territories.

The Liberal campaign didn't have a plane ready, so Dion spent the first few days of the campaign driving around Ottawa and Montreal, visiting safe Liberal seats. The Liberal campaign was grounded, literally, and it served as an unhelpful metaphor for Dion. But the Liberals weren't the only ones knocked off their message by a process story: we were hit with a campaign orchestrated by Green Party leader Elizabeth May.

May wanted to participate in the leaders' debates, set for October 1 and 2, so she had begun pressuring the consortium of broadcasters and building public support in the weeks leading up to the campaign. There were no written rules to guide the consortium, but the practice had been only leaders with elected MPs in the House of Commons got spots at the podium. In response to May's lobbying efforts, the consortium of broadcasters had asked each of the three main parties what they thought. Our senior team had discussed the issue at length before the campaign began. We had agreed we needed to make a decision and stick with it, especially if we opposed her participation, given the anticipated backlash from people who sided with May.

May, who had been a prominent member of the Think Twice Coalition in the 2006 election as head of an environmental organization, had also already endorsed Stéphane Dion for prime minister. Back in April 2007, she and Dion had signed an agreement not to run candidates against each party's leader during the next election campaign. In exchange for the Liberals not running against May in the Central Nova riding, she agreed not to run a Green Party candidate in Dion's Montreal riding of Saint-Laurent–Cartierville. "We recognize that a government in which Stéphane Dion served as prime minister could work well with a Green caucus of MPs, led by Elizabeth May, committed to action on climate change," their joint statement read.

May's choice for prime minister would already be at the debate, and we didn't think it was fair for Dion to have a surrogate onstage with him. We decided against supporting May's entry. We also told the consortium that Jack wanted to debate Harper, but that he could not participate if another party leader had a surrogate onstage with him. The Conservatives opposed the move on the same grounds and communicated the same message to the consortium. Duceppe also opposed May's participation. Dion was happy with the idea of having reinforcements onstage with him, naturally.

Even before the campaign began, the pressure on Jack to change his mind was immense. Some progressives claimed we were being unfair to May. Some of our own people, including some MPs, didn't like that our position put us on the same side as the Conservatives.

Jack held steady with the decision, and as chief spokesperson for the campaign, it fell to me to explain and defend it in the media. I didn't mind: it was the right decision, and I was comfortable with it. But after the campaign started, the pressure on Jack mounted. May's plan was to have supporters inundate our offices with emails and crash Jack's tour events to make news. The media would ask him at every opportunity why he wouldn't change his position. By Wednesday morning of week one, a handful of placard-waving Green Party supporters interrupted Jack while in Oshawa at the GM plant to talk about jobs and the economy. Jack was fed up that the story was overshadowing our narrative. He concluded it just wasn't worth it: he hadn't come this far to be blown off course over who was in the debate.

Jack phoned Topp to tell him he had decided to reverse the campaign decision.

"Call Brad on his cell," Topp instructed Jack before hanging up. He then called me into his office to give me a heads-up about Jack's call.

"Don't be mad, brother," Jack told me. "I just can't spend the next few days and weeks talking about her and the debates. I know this has caused you great pain, and the climb down will be even worse. Whatever you do, don't start smoking." He chuckled, knowing I'd quit when my daughter was born in 2005. It was classic Jack.

"I completely understand, Jack. Good luck out there," I said, grinning in spite of myself.

Not long after, at a tour stop at a solar panel plant in Scarborough, Ontario, Jack informed the media of his decision. Within an hour, Stephen Harper followed suit. By the end of the day, the broadcast consortium invited May to participate in the debates, which she accepted immediately.

The campaign team was disappointed and would have preferred to ride out the storm a few more days. But once Jack made up his mind, we unreservedly accepted his decision, and I went out and sold it on the TV and radio panels, facing the shitstorm that came with reversing a decision.

There was definitely criticism to be faced. Some within our campaign, and even operatives from other parties said the NDP couldn't take a punch. It was true: at the first sign of trouble, we had pushed the release valve. Jack had amazing political instincts, but at times he lacked the killer instinct that has come to serve modern leaders well.

ONE OF JACK'S MANTRAS TO the senior team had been to take the best practices from the political world and adopt them for our uses. I took this as licence to steal from the best. Parties of all stripes excel in certain areas, and Stephen Harper's team was especially good at campaign scripting, mapping out the storyboard of the campaign well in advance.

Months before the campaign started, I had begun to work with our tour and communications teams to reconceptualize how we approached the leader's tour. We needed to do a better job at telling voters what the election was about. That meant tying together every aspect: tour locations, event staging, advertising and the policies being announced. Whether people were getting their political news on television, online or in a newspaper, we'd need strong visuals to convey our story effectively. So once we settled on a scripted message, we then asked ourselves how we could add to the message or emphasize it in a visual way.

If broadcast news were to give each campaign a seven-second shot that beamed into the living rooms of the nation, what did we want that shot to be? This was especially important for the NDP as the fourth party: we had to fight even to get on the broadcast news each night. If a news producer had three shots of equal quality from each campaign, we would likely end up on the editing room floor. But if our shot was more pleasing visually and made great TV, we'd increase our chances of making the cut.

Jack was warm and personable, so we always had him surrounded by people. Throngs of enthusiastic partisans also gave our campaign a sense of momentum. If the people at home could see themselves in the people with Jack, perhaps that's where they belonged as well.

We also staged specific people to sit or stand close to Jack so that they'd be in the shot. If we wanted to emphasize a particular demographic—women, young people or new Canadians—we'd place people from that group directly behind the leader. That way, they'd be visible while Jack talked to the cameras and the assembled press.

We had a strict rule about what kinds of signs would be displayed in the shot. Our U.S.-inspired handheld signs reinforced the message we wanted to convey. In the beginning of the campaign, they said "Strong Leader." During the last week of the campaign to build momentum and inoculate against strategic voting, we switched to "United with Layton." Nothing off-script would be permitted. Nothing was done by accident or left to chance.

One of the greatest compliments we received was to have the Conservatives copy our staging. "The look and feel and style of your tour was absolutely noticed. The human background, the 'in the round' approach. It was very compatible to the strengths of your leader," recalls Kory Teneycke, Harper's former director of communications. "While we couldn't replicate it completely because Harper has a different brand, and different strengths—he'll never be Mr. Town Hall—I think it would be fair to say that there was some emulation with some of the things that you were doing."

Internally, we fielded complaints from a few corners about our strict sign policy. But we were spending millions on Jack's tour to get our message out to a national audience, and we couldn't let off-script signs confuse the message. We usually assigned the biggest guys on the tour crew to do the job of shepherding supporters with off-message signs to stand behind the news cameras, not in front of them.

Those guys couldn't help us with a problem that arose on September 17. Brian Topp and I sat in his office to watch an old online video featuring Dana Larsen, the NDP candidate of West Vancouver–Sunshine Coast–Sea to Sky Country. The footage from the defunct web channel Pot TV had been sent to media outlets from the Liberal war room and was now airing on all-news television stations.

The images from various episodes were brutal: Larsen lighting up a mouthful of joints for a "Weedy Wednesday Smokefest", dropping six hits of acid, and taking a hit of the psychedelic drug DMT before getting behind the wheel of a car. "We finished our psychedelic voyaging for the evening and now we're just driving home, smoking our very last joint that I rolled in advance," Larsen told viewers.

If the campaign didn't deal with this quickly, we risked getting knocked off our campaign script for multiple news cycles. We also didn't want to waste campaign dollars, because we were spending, on average, about $500,000 a day on the leader's tour to get our message out. After seeing the Larsen footage on the news, Topp directed the leadership of the B.C. campaign to drop him as a candidate. Topp's directive was implemented immediately. Larsen, a former Marijuana Party activist, should never have been an NDP candidate in the first place, and if Topp had had his way, he wouldn't have been.

Before the campaign had even begun, Topp had tried to get Larsen and another former Marijuana Party activist, Kirk Tousaw, dropped as NDP candidates. The federal party's director of organization, Heather Fraser, had come to Topp to warn him that the provincial party in B.C. was about to approve some inappropriate candidates.

At the time, the nomination process was largely controlled at the local riding association level and by provincial executive members. After speaking with Fraser, Topp called Gerry Scott, the B.C. campaign manager for the upcoming federal election, and asked him to urge his provincial colleagues to reconsider. "You know these guys are going to blow up in our face, don't you?" Topp said.

Soon after the call, Scott reported back to Topp that the provincial body wasn't budging. They were aware that there was some "pretty crazy stuff out there" related to drug use, recalls Scott, though nobody was aware of the footage showing Larsen driving while tripping out on DMT. The provincial executive members held the view that Larsen and Tousaw represented an important constituency for the NDP in B.C.

"There's nothing you can do," Scott told Topp.

"That's true, until the writ drops, at which time we'll revisit this matter if there are any controversies," Topp responded.

Unlike in the other parties, Jack had a clear policy against appointing people to run in specific ridings. Candidate selection occurred at the local level, and the central campaign worked with the locally elected choice— after headquarters had conducted a scan of the candidate's personal history. But the scan had missed this footage of Larsen. The best-case scenario would be to contain the issue to one day with a quick resignation and then return to our script for the week: reinforcing our economic message of affordability for families through cheaper prescription drugs, child tax benefits and more affordable care for seniors.

It's tricky for any campaign when there are calls for a candidate to resign over a bozo eruption or a damaging incident from their past. Both routes are risky. If you decide to take the hit and wait out the storm, it may not pass. If you fire one of your candidates quickly, you can look decisive and minimize the story. The risk, though, is that you allow your opponent to draw blood—and they only get thirsty for more.

On Friday, September 19, more footage from Pot TV surfaced. Recorded in 2005 but still available on Google Video, it showed Kirk Tousaw, our Vancouver Quadra candidate, smoking pot as a judge for a Pot TV competition of various strains of marijuana. Within hours, Tousaw, a civil rights lawyer and proponent of marijuana legalization, issued a statement announcing his resignation, knocking us off-script—again.

That same week, the Liberals had lost candidates for making anti-aboriginal slurs and the Green Party had lost a candidate who'd uttered anti-Semitic remarks. But there wasn't footage to go along with those bozo eruptions, so we took the biggest hit.

All campaign war rooms engage in muckraking. The work of digging up dirt on candidates from the other parties begins even before the official campaign kicks off. That way, you can use the information to throw your opponents off their message or use it as deflection if you need to change the channel to get yourself out of a tough spot. Some indiscretions or bozo eruptions from candidates are worse than others. But all campaigns toss grenades at opponents and wait to see if they explode, with the help of the media.

In the end, we lost four candidates, the Liberals lost two and the Conservatives and the Greens each lost one during the 2008 campaign. But in our case, we had a unique internal party arrangement that did not allow the national campaign team to deal effectively with candidate selections that went awry. Jack was extremely motivated to fix that before the next election.

BY THE TIME THE DEBATES rolled around on October 1 and 2, it was inconsequential that Elizabeth May was onstage along with the leaders of parties with elected MPs. The election was now all about the economy. News of the global economic meltdown was driving daily coverage, and that would continue until election day, two weeks later.

158

Jack did well in the English-language debate in a new format that saw the leaders sit at a round table. He talked to Canadians about the economic crisis through the lens of the kitchen table, just as we had planned. He attacked Harper hard, playing the role of "strong leader" we had cast for Jack. One of Jack's most effective lines against Dion reinforced this message: "If you can't do your job as Opposition leader, you can't do the job of prime minister." In the end, though, a post-debate poll found Harper had won the debate, with Jack coming in second. Expectations were so low for Dion that all he had to do was survive the night.

Jack did better in the French debate than he had in 2006, but there was nothing in the performance that outshone either Dion, who exceeded low expectations, or Duceppe. The Bloc leader, in particular, gave a very strong performance and attacked Harper hard on his cuts to arts and culture, saying they undermined "the soul of Quebec." In a battle about who could stop Harper, Duceppe came out on top.

To reach Quebecers beyond the French debate, we had decided, for the first time ever, to invest heavily in the air war in Quebec. Federal cuts to culture and the Conservative changes to the Young Offenders Act emerged as big issues in Quebec, so we produced a very negative anti-Harper ad with a dark, ominous message about what he was doing to Canada.

But now the ground shifted. "As soon as the financial crisis hit, we were just looking to survive," recalls Brian Topp. "It was such a jarring thing to happen mid-campaign. And it was an X factor—it pulled you off your election game plan that you had mapped out and created a lot of question marks for a period of time. In the end, though, it did feed into a larger narrative of management and steadiness around the economy."

That narrative helped Harper, despite a misstep he made near the end of the campaign. A week before voting day, Harper mentioned a silver lining to the plunging stock market. As many retirees were seeing a significant percentage of their savings wiped out, Harper told the press the crisis was an excellent buying opportunity for those seeking bargains. He later fleshed out his argument in an interview with CBC's Peter Mansbridge. "We always know that when stock markets go up, people end up buying a lot of things that are overpriced, and when stock markets go down people end up passing on a lot of things that are underpriced. I think there are probably some gains to be made in the stock market."

Jack took Harper to task for his unwise comments, but the story was quickly overshadowed by a Dion misstep. While taping a sit-down interview with the local CTV affiliate in Halifax, Dion, with the cameras rolling, needed a do-over when he couldn't understand a question about the economy. CTV decided to air the embarrassing footage, and the Conservative campaign pounced. "What yesterday showed was that the Leader of the Opposition, when asked a straightforward question about what he would do for the economy, he has no answer but a carbon tax," Harper told reporters.

Dion didn't do himself any favours with his hapless performance on CBC TV the next morning. Host Heather Hiscox kicked off the interview by airing the footage, which she called "painful to watch."

"Maybe it's because I have a hearing problem. Maybe it's because it's my second language, but I did not understand the question," Dion explained in his heavily accented English.

"It certainly has been getting a lot of viewing on YouTube," Hiscox responded, "and you can read Canadians' reactions online when they see it, and one caught my attention particularly. 'He's so flustered by not understanding the question that I feel sorry for him. On the other hand, it proves he doesn't have what it takes to be prime minister.'" That pretty much summed it up.

We were also hurt by our own limitations in the closing days of the campaign. We'd gone in with the first three weeks of the four-week campaign scripted, but we'd left our endgame plan fluid so that we could nail it down mid-campaign. "The key mistake of the 2008 campaign was that we did not come up with a strong close. We had a good start, a good middle, but we didn't freshen it up again. That was fatal," recalls Topp.

As Topp remembers it, he came to a private decision ten days before election day: he wasn't going to be campaign manager next time around. "I was sitting in the corner office, and I needed something new to say. I couldn't come up with something new to say. Somebody else had to do this. It was time for new people with new ideas."

Without a new idea for our endgame, we decided on a repeat of our launch. Our message was solidified, not amplified. Our "United with Layton" slogan urged all Canadians who didn't support Harper, approximately 65 per cent of the electorate, to back the NDP. We wanted to own the market share of this target audience. Jack addressed the issue directly in an ad entitled "Chalk Talk" with an unapologetic appeal.

"Most Canadians don't want to see Mr. Harper in power. In fact, lots of Canadians are saying 'anybody but Harper.' So the big question is, who's really up for the job? Stéphane Dion and the Liberals have run such a confused campaign they'll be spending the next two years wondering what went wrong and fighting amongst themselves. The real alternative to Mr. Harper is me, Jack Layton. For strong leadership on the side of everyday families like yours, vote New Democrat."

By this point in the campaign, the media were writing off Dion's chances and speculating about how many seats he would lose. Talk of his anticipated resignation and a drawn-out leadership contest to follow circulated widely among the punditry. Jack's appeal was a reflection of this dynamic: he wasn't asking Liberals to abandon their party so much as asking them to buy insurance that someone would be there to take on Harper.

Our message fit the reputation Jack had rightfully earned in the last Parliament, but it didn't have the punch needed for an endgame message heard by voters over the Thanksgiving weekend before heading to the polls. Without question, that cost us seats.

I'd known about a week before voting day that we were heading for a bitter disappointment. Technically, we were running our best campaign ever with an even stronger leader. We were humming along while the Liberals were flailing with a weak leader. But our internal polling showed the vote was not breaking our way. If it wasn't there in the last four or five days, it was likely not coming. This realization, compounded by exhaustion, made the final week hard. "What is it going to take?" I asked myself.

ONE OF OUR CAMPAIGN'S PRIORITIES was to show that we had a solid foundation to expand our caucus in Quebec. At a bare minimum, that meant we needed a victory for Mulcair in Outremont, but we also wanted to lay down more beachheads, including one in Gatineau. Early in the counting process on election night, it looked as though we might have failed at both. The television networks were showing that Mulcair was trailing.

Raymond Guardia, who was serving as the master of ceremonies for the NDP on election night at Guvernment nightclub in Toronto, phoned Mulcair's long-time assistant, Steve Moran, to find out what was going on in Outremont. "Steve, what the hell is going on up there?" he asked.

Moran had poll-by-poll breakdowns the networks didn't have yet, and he told Guardia the early returns were from the west end of the riding, where Mulcair's support was weakest. "Don't worry, don't worry, those are the bad polls. We're in fine shape," he said.

"You better be fucking right," replied Guardia.

He was. Mulcair won his seat, the first time a New Democrat had been elected in Quebec during a general election in which we increased our popular vote in the province to 12 per cent. But Mulcair was still the lone NDP MP from Quebec. Françoise Boivin, who had stood next to Jack for the campaign kickoff on the banks of the Ottawa River, came a strong second in Gatineau behind the Bloc but still fell three thousand votes short. And we hadn't been able to translate Mulcair's toehold in Montreal to other seats on the island, despite Jack's five visits to the city during the campaign to bolster our star candidate in Westmount–Ville-Marie, Anne Lagacé Dowson.

We were stuck in the Bloc's frame. Our ominous, hard-hitting ad against Harper had ended up sending votes to Duceppe, not us. We had made the ballot question about stopping Harper, and for that voters had turned to the Bloc, not us. This was an important lesson we took into the next campaign, as we watched the Bloc showing signs of weakness in 2008, dropping four points from 2006 to 38 per cent of the vote in Quebec.

Our disappointment about Quebec matched how we felt about the overall results. We'd spent the most ever and run a technically excellent campaign, but we garnered 75,000 fewer votes than in 2006, and picked up just 8 new seats. We hadn't cracked 20 per cent nationally, picking up just 0.7 per cent of the popular vote to get to 18.2 per cent. The Liberals under Dion had lost 18 seats—and 4 per cent of the popular vote—but they were still more than 1 million votes ahead of us, even after getting 850,000 fewer votes than in 2006. The Conservatives had increased their popular vote by just 1.38 per cent, to 37.7 per cent, but that was enough to win them 16 more seats and return them to power with a stronger 143-seat minority government.

After three campaigns and some impressive gains, the NDP was almost back to its all-time high in popular support, with thirty-seven seats, the second-biggest caucus in the party's history. How should we interpret the results in assessing where the party should go from here?

There were two options.

The first was to accept the party's historic place. Gerald Caplan, who had served as the NDP's campaign manager in 1984, advocated this route in a campaign post-mortem in an election blog at globeandmail.com. "Just as Canadians seem instinctively to have set a ceiling beyond which they won't trust Stephen Harper, so too for 75 years there's been a rigid ceiling on NDP support," Caplan wrote. "It's an ironclad truth that doesn't become less valid just because many New Democrats won't face it. The question is what the party does with this truth. At the moment, that question is not even being asked. Denial doesn't encourage honest discussion. Look—if you can't be government, you either try to influence or you fold your tents. You don't pretend 'real' power is within grasping distance."

The second option, and the one we would take, was to recognize that if the party was ever to break through, it would need to reject this defeatist attitude. This wasn't about denying our history: it was about defying it.

CHAPTER 9:
BUILDING FOR THE BREAKTHROUGH

Jack was a planner. Back in 2004, before his first election campaign as party leader, he had tapped his mentor and long-time friend Terry Grier to head up a low-profile group to consider scenarios in anticipation of a minority government. The minority government materialized, but the NDP didn't hold the balance of power, so the scenarios remained theoretical.

Jack reactivated the committee during both the 2006 and 2008 election campaigns under the leadership of Brian Topp. Each time, Grier, former Saskatchewan premier Allan Blakeney and Ed Broadbent talked through all options, including those for forming a governing coalition in a minority Parliament. After the 2006 vote, the sketch of what a parliamentary arrangement might look like collected dust for a while. The Liberals and the Bloc took turns at keeping the Harper government afloat for little or nothing in return. In the 2008 campaign, the work of the group took on new urgency after Jack spoke openly in the press of his resolve to work with the other parties for the good of the country.

On September 22, in the midst of the election campaign, one of the hosts of CTV's *Canada AM* had asked Jack if he would "entertain even the notion of entering into a coalition with the Liberals in order to get the Conservatives out of power."

Jack made it clear he would partner with another party for the greater public good. "Well, you know what? I'll work with any political party. I think people have seen that if they look back to my days on a municipal council. You roll up your sleeves and you try to solve a problem. I think right now the problem we have is Stephen Harper and his Conservatives. They're taking the country down the wrong path," he said.

The Tories had jumped on Jack's comments, saying a vote for the NDP would mean the return of a Liberal government. Dion made an emphatic statement that painted him into a corner: he would never consider a coalition with the NDP. Dion's denials aside, the NDP scenarios committee got down to the business of mapping out options for Jack. His preferred option was an NDP government, but if the voters returned a minority Parliament, he wanted options for how the NDP could play an effective role.

On the morning of election day, Topp and deputy campaign director Sue Milling had met with Jack to review the scenarios developed by the group. They showed him a copy of the letter to Dion the group had drafted on Jack's behalf. Short of an NDP government, the preferred option was a two-party governing coalition, including a joint Cabinet, if the seats captured by the NDP and the Liberals together added up to a majority. The letter, crafted with the understanding it would be made public, spelled out the details.

Jack made some changes to the letter, signed the final version and tucked it away in an envelope. Then we waited for the election results. It turned out Blakeney, the astute statesman from Saskatchewan, had been right. He had predicted the Tories would capture about 140 seats, making an NDP/Liberal governing coalition all but impossible without the support of the Bloc. The Tory win of 143 seats torpedoed the possibility of a two-party coalition government. Together, the NDP and the Liberal seats totalled 114, well short of what was needed.

Jack gave it a few days to let the results sink in. Then, on October 18, he called Dion to see if the Liberal leader wanted to explore options. Dion said it wasn't the right time. Perhaps those discussions could take place later, he told Jack. After the call, Jack debriefed Topp. They agreed there was no window to pursue the options, so the letter to Dion remained in the envelope.

Two days later, Dion announced he was resigning as party leader but would stay on until his successor was chosen. The following day,

October 21, Topp appeared on a panel with Conservative senator Hugh Segal and Liberal senator David Smith, the Liberal campaign chair. Afterwards, Topp, who later chronicled this time in Canadian politics in his book *How We Almost Gave the Tories the Boot*, had a chance to chat with Smith. Once he got back to the office, Topp prepared a written account of this conversation for Jack.

"I told him I was a little sorry that Mr. Dion was staying on as Liberal leader since that made it difficult for people in Parliament who might have been thinking of kicking the Tories out. He clearly knew exactly what I was talking about. He replied that whether or not Dion remained during the interregnum, the Liberals will be fully engaged in the next leadership race and could not contemplate anything ambitious in the house... There was a faint suggestion that something might be possible after the [leadership] convention," Topp wrote to Jack.

"Your report makes sense when we consider their perspective and the project that lies ahead of them," Jack replied.

Then, on November 27, Harper and his finance minister, Jim Flaherty, provoked the opposition.

On Saturday, November 29, just forty-seven days since Canadians had gone to the polls and denied Stephen Harper his elusive majority, the Grand Hall at the Canadian Museum of Civilization, on the banks of the Ottawa River in Gatineau just across from Parliament Hill, was buzzing with politicians, government officials, media flacks and political aides in tuxedos and gowns. The annual Parliamentary Press Gallery Dinner usually generated plenty of gossip by the time the evening of drinking, roasting and toasting was over. This year was different: the event was high octane right from the start.

The cocktail hour had barely begun, but the place was electric, the rumour mill in overdrive about Harper's shaky grip on power. Could the NDP and the Liberals actually pull off forming a coalition government? Would the Conservatives have the nerve to prorogue Parliament to avoid a bullet to the head?

"Looks like we'll be working together, comrade," Liberal MP Scott

Brison joked to me when I arrived. This didn't seem so far-fetched after the preceding forty-eight hours.

The previous Thursday, Flaherty had released the government's Economic and Fiscal Update. The NDP and the other opposition parties had gotten a sneak peek in a lock-up held on our home turf. Room 308 of the West Block on Parliament Hill, where the NDP held its weekly caucus meetings, was a grand room with vaulted ceilings and large windows. It was showing signs of age, but we had spruced it up with pictures of our past leaders, from J.S. Woodsworth to Tommy Douglas to Alexa McDonough.

I went into the lock-up with other staff to help draft the NDP's press release and the talking points that would guide our response. We knew Conservatives were approaching the new Parliament as though they had an outright majority. Harper's office had already leaked to the press that their update would include a commitment to eliminate public financing for political parties; that was a provocative move designed to bankrupt the Liberals, who had failed to recalibrate their fundraising efforts after corporate donations were restricted and then abolished. We also knew the government wanted to suspend the right to strike in the public sector and to eliminate pay equity for women in the federal civil service.

But we weren't prepared for the government to remain completely silent on how to deal with the global financial crisis. The giant U.S. investment-banking firm Lehman Brothers had filed for bankruptcy protection earlier that fall, and the Canadian economy had plunged into a recession in October.

Yet, there was no game plan in the update to spur Canada's slumping economy or help those who were out of work. There was no stimulus package, nothing on employment insurance. Instead, Flaherty projected small surpluses through 2012–13 and promised a few measures to rein in spending and make credit available to some businesses. Mulcair, in his capacity as finance critic, was sitting next to me at our table. We looked at each other. "What's your take?" he asked.

"There's nothing in this thing at all about the recession," I said.

"I know. We can't support this," Tom said.

For the Fiscal and Economic Update to pass, the Conservative government needed one of the opposition parties to back it in a confidence vote in the House of Commons, scheduled for the following Monday. Otherwise, the government would fall. Each of us had enough seats to hold the balance of power. All three parties emerged from the lock-up with the same message: there was no way in hell we were going to support it.

Harper's team had figured the Liberals would let the fiscal statement pass. After all, Dion had already announced he would step down as party leader once a successor had been chosen. But it was so off the mark that even Dion couldn't swallow it.

"I intend to meet him tonight to start the process. He's saying no because he knows our option can work and Duceppe will support it. Good job, we are prepared," Jack wrote to Anne McGrath and Topp late Thursday afternoon. Jack was reacting to Dion's definitive statement to the press that there was no way the Liberals would support the fiscal statement.

Jack was convinced there was a brief window of opportunity for the NDP to get some of our agenda implemented through a coalition, even though his senior team had reservations. But we didn't have the time we wanted to think it through. "I am not going to follow him down another rabbit hole," I told Kathleen Monk, the deputy director of strategic communications, after our meeting with Jack about his plan. "With Jack, we were always overreaching. This is crazy. This can't work. And Jack kept pushing and pushing," recalls McGrath. At first, we didn't think we could pull this off. Eventually, Dion gave in. The letter to Dion became the starting point for Jack's team of negotiators. Led by Topp, the team comprised members of the "scenario committee," including McGrath, Broadbent and Blakeney, who flew in from Saskatoon. The goal was to lock up the coalition and have a new majority as quickly as possible. That way, we could show the Governor General that, unlike Harper, the NDP and the Liberals had the confidence of the House and therefore could govern.

The Liberal leadership race was already underway. This gave us some leverage with Dion's designates at the negotiating table in the mid-afternoon on Friday, November 28, where Topp and BC NDP Member of Parliament Dawn Black faced House Leader Ralph Goodale and Ottawa consultant Herb Metcalfe. Dion's plan, it turned out, was to strike a deal by Monday and use the accord to "unresign," as Topp put it. Therefore, the Dion team had an incentive to move quickly.

But while we were focussed on negotiating policies that would help families, Dion had to contend with leadership hopefuls who saw these coalition discussions as an obstacle to their own ascendancy. That's probably why Michael Ignatieff spent so much time talking to Harper's director of communications, Kory Teneycke, at the Parliamentary Press Gallery Dinner on Saturday night. Teneycke and Jack both sat at the CTV table, where Jack regaled his seatmates with a story about how in high school he had put together a coalition with some unlikely allies to become prime minister in a mock Parliament.

Ignatieff made a point of seeking out Teneycke later that evening, and the two spoke at length in the middle of the hall, attracting more than a few glances. Key strategists on Ignatieff's leadership campaign had already told Topp they were confident Ignatieff would win the Liberal crown the following May and go on to win a general election in the fall of 2009. As Teneycke later revealed, Ignatieff told him at the dinner how uncomfortable he was with the coalition.

"He was doing his best impression of Hamlet, trying to very clearly demonstrate his anxiety and conflict around whether or not this was the right move," Teneycke recalled. "From my read, this was more about concern that Dion would hold on as leader than it was about any greater interests of the country. I was a useful prop for him that night."

Throughout the evening, Teneycke was sending intelligence back to staffers in the Prime Minister's Office, who, like us, were working around the clock. At this stage in the episode, the Conservatives were on the ropes and the PMO had begun to backtrack to blunt the coalition's momentum. The day before, on Friday, the government had announced it would drop the elimination of political party financing and remove the ban on strikes by public service workers.

The government had also cancelled both a confidence vote on the government's Fiscal and Economic Update and a Liberal opposition day to avoid a separate confidence motion, both scheduled for Monday. That pushed off a confidence vote in the House until December 8. Conservatives were buying time, hoping the coalition partners would start to make mistakes. And we did.

The first one came the very next day. On Sunday, Harper's office released a recording of the NDP's caucus conference call from a day before. Details about participating in the caucus teleconference had been sent in error to Conservative MP John Duncan instead of NDP MP Linda Duncan. The Conservatives secretly sat in on the private conversation, recorded it and then released it.

Kathleen Monk and I were grabbing a quick lunch at the Centretown Tavern just around the corner from the NDP's caucus offices. The television mounted on the wall was tuned to one of the all-news channels, and we saw the words on the screen at the same time: "Leaked NDP conference call."

We leapt up from the table and rushed back to the office, where we spent the rest of the day pushing back against Tory spin that suggested Jack's comments during the teleconference had been something they weren't: an indication that he had been conspiring with the Bloc for months to bring down the Harper government.

The second misstep came on Monday, when we handed Harper the opportunity to change the channel away from his failure to hold the confidence of the House and onto the supporting role of the Bloc in the NDP-Liberal coalition. Dion's office, eager to show it was in control as it battled internal Liberal politics, took the lead in coordinating a press conference to announce the coalition deal and the policies it would pursue. The planning meeting was convened by Dion's chief of staff, Johanne Senécal, in the Opposition leader's office. We sent Anne McGrath and Karl Bélanger.

At first, the idea that Duceppe would be present at the signing ceremony on December 1, even though he was not part of the coalition, hadn't struck any of us as something to be concerned about. After all,

Duceppe had kept the Conservative minority government afloat by voting with Harper on matters of confidence on numerous occasions over the past two years, and in 2004 Harper had signed a joint letter with Duceppe and Jack to the Governor General at the time, Adrienne Clarkson, inviting her to turn to the three opposition parties if the Liberal minority under Paul Martin failed to enjoy confidence in the House.

But the image of Duceppe shaking hands with Jack and Dion sank the coalition in English Canada. "The Conservatives could not have scripted it better," recalls Teneycke. Two days later, on Wednesday, December 3, Dion's inept prime-time address in response to the prime minister placed more doubt in his ability to lead the coalition.

Dion's office had informed us early that afternoon that an agreement had been reached with the television networks to broadcast statements by Harper and Dion during prime time that evening. Anne McGrath contacted CTV News president Robert Hurst and tried to muscle Jack's way in. By late afternoon we had been rebuffed by the main networks but had secured time after Dion's address on the all-news networks. Jack would deliver prepared remarks from the podium in the foyer of the House of Commons, where the networks could easily take the feed.

At 7:01 PM EST, Jack watched the prime minister's address in his Centre Block office with McGrath and Bélanger. I was downstairs in the foyer of the House of Commons with the gathered media after having put the final touches on Jack's remarks for that night.

"Instead of an immediate budget, they are proposing a coalition... This is a pivotal moment in our history," Harper said in his address. "Tonight I pledge to you, Canada's government will use every legal means at our disposal to protect our democracy, to protect our economy and to protect Canada," he concluded. Then nothing.

Word quickly spread throughout the foyer that Dion's team had delivered their tape late to the networks. They had to fill the time with something, and the reporters covering the evening's events began to lay into Dion. On CTV with Lloyd Robertson, bureau chief Robert Fife said Dion's inability to deliver a tape on time "borders on incompetence."

Fife continued: "Maybe Mr. Layton should have come on instead of Mr. Dion, because we know Jack would have definitely been able to get that tape to us on time."

Robertson replied with a chuckle, "Indeed, he knows how to play that game."

Each minute that passed seemed like an eternity. At about 7:20, Monk turned to me in the foyer and suggested we should put Jack up now, before the main networks signed off: screw Dion. I told her no. "We have an agreement with Dion's people, and we're sticking to it." Dion's address began airing at 7:28 PM EST, but not before CTV had signed off without airing his address. The CBC had decided to stay on. Dion's videotaped address was out of focus and amateur, and the Liberal leader delivered an incoherent message.

Then it was Jack's turn on the all-news channels. "This is a remarkable time in history," he began.

> The opposition parties acted together with the common goal to give hope to Canadians to help them come through these difficult times. For the first time, the majority of the Members of Parliament chosen by the people set aside their differences for the good of Canada and for the good of every Canadian. On Monday, the two leaders of the proposed coalition sent Her Excellency the Governor General a letter making it crystal clear that the majority of Members of Parliament no longer have confidence in this Conservative government. Nothing we have heard tonight changes this fact. Tonight Mr. Harper had an opportunity to chart a new course to accept some of the ideas that we have been putting before him. But he did not. And tonight we are announcing that if it pleases Her Excellency we will arrange that every New Democrat Member of Parliament will indicate individually and together formally their lack of confidence in this government. A new kind of government with a new kind of politics is ready to serve: one that will put the economy and working families first.

The NDP caucus had gathered in the party's West Block room to watch the televised addresses. It was part of a farewell event for the party's long-time director of organization, Heather Fraser, and its national director, Éric Hébert-Daly. There was a collective groan when Dion's video clip aired, because everyone knew what it meant.

Jack delivered a solid performance, but the story of the night wasn't him—it was Dion.

"It's all over, dude," a senior member of Ignatieff's leadership campaign wrote to Topp a few minutes after Dion's speech had aired.

"How so?" Topp replied.

"The chief spokesman can't speak."

The next day, Harper asked Governor General Michaëlle Jean to prorogue Parliament. She acquiesced, and Parliament was shut down until the end of January. Six days later, on December 10, Ignatieff was chosen as interim Liberal leader by his caucus. As the new interim leader, Ignatieff made it clear he was open to voting non-confidence on the Conservatives at the first opportunity. That would now be January 27, 2009, when Harper would table his next budget.

Jack spent the Christmas holiday period and the weeks before Flaherty tabled his early budget trying to get through to Ignatieff and have him honour his signature to the Governor General; during the coalition negotiations, Ignatieff, along with every other member of the Liberal caucus, had signed a letter to the Governor General indicating the caucus had no confidence in the Conservative government and was united behind the coalition. But as Olivia recounted later, "The conversation went nowhere. It completely went in one ear and out the other."

"We handed him the opportunity," says Olivia today. "We took enormous amounts of risk, and he said no. It was quite depressing, actually. Jack kept hoping and he wouldn't give up. He thought maybe [Ignatieff] would change his mind."

Instead, Ignatieff returned to Parliament in January and decided to prop up the Conservative government. The Liberals, he announced, would let the budget pass in exchange for regular updates to Parliament on the impact of economic stimulus projects.

Ignatieff spun it as putting the Harper government on probation. The Tories turned things around, using the reports as opportunities to trumpet the work of the government. Jack saw Ignatieff's decision to support Harper differently. "We have a new coalition on Parliament Hill. It's a coalition between Mr. Harper and Mr. Ignatieff," he told reporters on January 28.

"Jack took it a bit hard, but he moved on. He put in everything he had there trying to persuade the Liberals to join with the NDP," recalls Olivia.

Our play for replacing the government failed. But we had laid down important markers on which to build. Jack's approach to politics was always about getting results. He had tried to get rid of Harper and take a direct role in governing the country.

In Quebec, significantly, this was a defining moment in Jack's leadership. The Bloc's backing of the coalition had elevated the NDP to a party that could attain power in Ottawa. The Bloc, coming up on its twentieth anniversary, could never do that. In the short term, Harper's successful demonization of the Bloc cost us support in Western Canada, but it set the table for us in Quebec: it told voters there that they could send MPs to Ottawa not just to oppose Harper but to replace him.

IF WE NEEDED MORE PROOF that the Conservatives were running a permanent campaign, the devastating anti-Dion ad that had begun airing on Super Bowl Sunday in February 2007 had provided plenty. The Tories hadn't come up with the concept of the sustained political campaign, but they were becoming its Canadian pioneers.

The original badge of honour belonged to Patrick Caddell, who, as a young pollster, said in a lengthy memo to president-elect Jimmy Carter in December 1976 that "governing with public approval requires a continuing political campaign." In 1980, journalist Sidney Blumenthal, who later became a senior advisor to President Bill Clinton, chronicled how campaigning had become a form of governing in his book *The Permanent Campaign*. The book's subtitle summed it up well: *The Inside Story of the Revolution in American Politics—How Consultants and Media Wizards Package and Sell Candidates for Public Office Before, During and After their Election.*

Jack's team disagreed fundamentally with the Conservative Party's ideas and policy prescriptions for the country, but we had grudging respect for the way Harper and his operatives executed their permanent campaign. We wanted to match them. In its Canadian application, the Conservatives used every tool at their disposal to define themselves and their opponents, from fundraising appeals to statements in the House before Question Period to the bills they tabled in Parliament. While they were breaking the Liberal hegemony by redefining the Liberal Party, they were also identifying the icons they would use to define Canada: the North, the monarchy, stable economic stewardship, and law and order.

For generations, by their design, the Liberal Party brand and the Canada brand had been indistinguishable: the maple leaf flag, the Charter of Rights and Freedoms, bilingualism, multiculturalism and national unity. Harper set out to change that by replacing those things with symbols he defined as Conservative.

Successive minority Parliaments had provided the perfect opportunity for Harper to set up his permanent campaign. If the NDP was going to take him on and compete at his level, we too would have to build support in between elections—and do a better job of defining ourselves and our opponents. If you love campaigning, you live the permanent campaign. And we did.

By the time the dust had settled after the coalition crisis, Jack had made key personnel decisions. Following the 2008 campaign, he appointed Anne McGrath as his chief of staff. Anne and I had first met in the late 1980s and knew each from our student movement days. Over the previous year, we had developed a close working relationship.

Brian Topp had informed Jack before the 2008 campaign ended that he would not serve in his same capacity in the next campaign. He remained a key advisor, though, and he recommended to Jack that the next campaign be run from inside the operation. Jack had been party leader for six years now, and our internal capacity was developed enough to evolve into a full-time political machine.

Jack appointed me national director of the party and campaign manager for the next election. I made sure before accepting that I had a mandate from Jack to do the things I needed to do to modernize the party. The ideals of the "project" were well ingrained in both McGrath and me. We'd be working in tandem towards a common goal, and now the three of us would begin a new tradition of dinner together, usually every Tuesday before the weekly caucus meeting on Wednesday mornings. Jack called us his "CEOs," and he was the chairman of the board. Jack announced my appointment officially in March 2009, after the senior campaign team had completed an exhaustive post-mortem of where we stood.

Through Jack's first three election campaigns, we had reassembled the traditional vote base that the NDP had lost throughout the 1990s; we could now count on a base of between 16 and 19 per cent of the population. We had the second-largest caucus in our party's history with beachheads in all regions of the country, notably in Alberta and Quebec, and in rural, urban and ethnic communities. Unlike in 1988, when NDP support had been highly regional—in Ontario, B.C. and Saskatchewan—our vote and our caucus were now national. We had built up Jack's profile and popularity, and we had transformed the party brand and identity to one that was leader-focussed.

We had also taken our place in the big leagues with our 2008 campaign, matching the Conservatives and the Liberals on financing and in tactical areas such as the leader's tour. Most importantly, we now had a core campaign team that had worked together through three election campaigns in five years, creating bonds based on trust. In regular electoral cycles, that would have taken twelve years.

The campaign team assessed every aspect of what we would need to do to get to the next level, end the incremental gains and make a breakthrough. Basically, we needed a better message, delivered by a stronger campaign machine, to a bigger audience.

We tackled the stumbling blocks, one by one. We knew we had to start with the machinery: the party operation and the campaign must become one and the same. A new mantra in the party office kept us focussed: if what you're doing doesn't contribute to us winning more seats in the next campaign, you shouldn't be doing it. But we were encumbered by an outdated structure that didn't allow us to do our jobs.

When the party was founded in 1961, it was set up as a confederation, with a weak centre and strong provincial sections. Provincial membership was linked to federal membership, meaning if you joined the Ontario NDP or the Manitoba NDP, you automatically became a member of the federal NDP. You didn't get to pick one level or the other. Recruiting new members and renewing memberships was the responsibility of the provincial parties, which meant provincial NDP offices managed party lists. Under contractual obligation, provincial bodies forwarded these names and addresses to Ottawa when the federal party needed to communicate with the membership.

By 2009, there were growing tensions between the federal party and its provincial cousins over how often Ottawa could communicate with members, particularly how many times in a given year we could solicit money.

Under Jack's leadership, the federal party had begun to look at fundraising in a modern way. We watched how other jurisdictions were doing it, including in the U.S., and knew we had to overhaul our approach. Drew Anderson, who came on board in 2005 as the party's director of development, understood that fundraising was not a burden but rather an extension of our communications strategy, one more way to carry our message further and engage our supporters—particularly our most ardent activists.

When I rejoined the party office as national director, we ramped up both the sophistication and the aggressiveness of our fundraising effort. In addition to crafting strategic pitches that aligned with the party's overall positioning, we adopted the simple mantra that people don't give money unless they're asked, and the more you ask, the more they give. We wanted the resources to go toe to toe with the other parties.

Our challenge became immediately apparent. In all areas critical to our success—membership, recruitment, fundraising and organizing—the federal NDP essentially outsourced responsibility to busy provincial sections with their own interests and campaigns to run. And most of the provincial parties had a different vision of fundraising. They also had a stake in limiting the amount of access the federal party had to the members. Under the rules of engagement, we had to get permission to send out fundraising appeals. Usually, the answer was no. This was an unworkable structure for running a permanent campaign.

Under the rules, the federal party also contracted the field operations to the provincial sections. Each year, we paid the provincial offices to hire organizers to find federal candidates, organize federal riding associations and do the administrative work for Elections Canada. We had no oversight over field staff, though, so if the provincial officials who managed our field workers didn't like the federal party's directives, they could just rewrite them. Decisions were often made for the benefit of the provincial section, meaning federal work took a back seat.

Over the years, this organizational structure had resulted in a federal party that was weak and dependent on the better-resourced provincial sections. However, the frequency of recent federal campaigns under successive minority governments opened up the opportunity for swift and deep changes to this structure, and we took it.

Under Jack's direction, one of my first tasks was to assess, and if necessary get rid of these contracts with the provincial sections. That would allow the party to execute our aggressive fundraising plan and to overhaul the federal party's organizing department under the leadership of Nathan Rotman, the talented organizer who had cut his teeth in Olivia's office in Toronto.

We were guided by two objectives as we entered into discussions with the provincial sections of the NDP: to build a better field organization dedicated to the federal effort that would report directly to Ottawa and to get unfettered access to the membership. This access was vital to us. The provincial parties were far more timid when it came to fundraising. Once I became national director, I fielded at least one complaint a month from a provincial party about how we were fundraising too much in "their" province.

By the end of the year, we had come to agreements with each province to achieve both objectives.

We'd extricated ourselves from an unworkable structure and secured peace inside the party. Now it was time to bolster our campaign capacity at the riding level. That meant we needed to help NDP district associations raise money. We knew there was a connection between a candidate's ability to spend the legal local maximum and their ability to win. In fact, virtually every winning campaign in 2008 had spent the legal maximum. In those that spent close to the legal maximum, the candidates nearly won.

The local maximum is set based on the number of voters in a riding; the central limit is based on the number of candidates a party runs on its slate. In 2008, for the first time ever, the NDP had spent the legal maximum on our central campaign. Our next step was to increase the number of local campaigns that did the same. To get there, we increased our fundraising staff and ramped up the training we provided to fundraisers.

Campaign headquarters can simply transfer money to campaigns, but that's very expensive. It also breeds laziness at the local level. We didn't want such a culture to get established, so we conducted research to find out why local district associations weren't fundraising. Fear of rejection played a role, it turned out, but so did an arrangement that saw provincial offices claw back a portion of all money raised by their local provincial riding associations. Such an arrangement did not exist at the federal level. We asked ourselves: If clawing back local fundraising deterred the activity, what if we paid riding associations to raise money?

We came up with the "Local Victories Fundraising Challenge": for every dollar raised by a local district association during a set period, the federal party would match it by fifty cents. The response was overwhelming. One hundred and thirty riding associations took part, raising hundreds of thousands of dollars for their local campaigns. It was a novel concept that not only gave the federal office a sneak peek into the finances of the ridings but, more importantly, rewarded local initiative.

The next area to fix when it came to the machinery of the party was candidate search. Once a federal election was called, the central campaign spent about $500,000 each day to get out messages. Last time around, we'd spent five full days dealing with the fallout from unsuitable candidates, squandering about $2.5 million. This wasn't fair to party activists who had worked hard to raise that money. We'd also blown a lot of capital and hadn't looked ready for prime time.

Jack moved quickly after the 2008 campaign to fix the process. At the first federal council meeting after the election, the governing body of the party approved a new candidate approval process. In the past, vetting had taken place after the local riding had chosen a candidate. That meant it was tricky—and often too late—to instruct a local association to unselect their candidate and start over. Under the new system, potential candidates had to go through a rigorous vetting system in advance. Now, nobody was eligible to run for the party nomination without my signature on their application form.

In the run-up to the next campaign, we rejected more than two dozen applications. This saved us potential embarrassment and money, and it empowered people at the local level to raise the bar on candidate search and recruitment. Local leaders rejected some people outright, knowing they would never get through the federal screening process.

This internal work was an important, largely invisible, part of setting up the infrastructure for the next campaign. The other piece was the public work we did on branding. In a permanent campaign, you seize every opportunity to showcase and communicate your aims and goals. The party's convention in Halifax in August 2009 was organized through this lens.

Conventions had evolved dramatically under Jack's leadership. Before he became leader, party conventions were well known as painful, process-driven affairs mired in "points of order" and long rants from the plenary floor. Not enough people inside the party seemed to be thinking about the story they wanted to tell people beyond the walls of the convention. Being fixated on process also wasn't fun for participants.

We studied the conventions of other political parties to learn as much as we could about what might make sense for us. U.K. Labour brought people from social movements to their conventions and provided training and skills development to their own activists. Both the Democrats and the Republicans in the U.S. were skilled at theming conventions. We took everything we could and translated it into the Canadian context.

Unlike other parties, the NDP sets its convention delegate fees very low—$199 compared with up to $1,000—and provides travel subsidies for disadvantaged groups to ensure all our party members can afford to participate. This is expensive, though, so if we fail to articulate our message and train at the grassroots level, then we have missed an opportunity and blown some serious money.

Building on the work we had done at our Quebec City convention in 2006, we transformed the 2009 convention in August into a made-for-TV showcase that promoted our message to the media and the voters at home. We put our political stars onstage, just like the Americans. When we weren't promoting our message to the outside world, we were running training seminars for delegates. In total, we offered twenty-three hours of training on local fundraising and campaigning. The modern convention is part political rally, part training boot camp.

We were also in Halifax just months after the Nova Scotia NDP's historic election breakthrough. The stories of the provincial party and the federal party ran on similar tracks. Both made uphill climbs after being told for years they would never win opposition, let alone government. Premiers Darrell Dexter of Nova Scotia and Gary Doer of Manitoba delivered keynote addresses at the convention. Their campaign managers also led talks to explain how their teams had won. Marshall Ganz, architect of Barack Obama's grassroots organizing model for the 2008 presidential campaign, spoke to delegates, as did Betsy Myers, the Obama campaign's chief operations officer.

We had spent the previous three years fully intertwining Jack and the federal party. Now, we wanted to move the public over from liking our leader to voting for his local candidates. We developed "Team Layton" as our main brand and unveiled it at the Halifax convention. We boiled the entire convention, in both internal training sessions and public messaging, down to one word: winning.

It had been nearly a year since Harper had provoked the coalition crisis, and we were getting our house in order.

CHAPTER 10:
THE NEXT TIER

I nearly fell off my chair laughing when I saw Michael Ignatieff, the man who had spent the last eight months propping up Stephen Harper, on my television screen chirping, "Mr. Harper, your time is up."

It was September 1, 2009, and I was sitting in my office at party headquarters. Ignatieff was in Sudbury, where his caucus had gathered for a strategy session before the fall parliamentary session was to begin. He was arrogant enough to think that in a minority Parliament where all three opposition parties held the balance of power, he alone would be the one to trigger the next election campaign.

Ignatieff made his announcement without the courtesy of an advance call to the two other opposition parties, assuming they would follow suit. But in a minority Parliament, you have to think carefully about all your opponents, trying to figure out what each is thinking and how each might react. Ignatieff and his team seemed incapable of thinking about what Jack might do. The last election had been just eleven months earlier. Since then, Ignatieff had failed to make the case to the Canadian people for another election. In fact, he had spent much of his time helping the Conservatives implement their agenda.

We had decided to have some fun with Ignatieff back in February, when the Liberals were propping up the Harper Conservatives on a confidence vote for the fiftieth time. In return, they got nothing. We ordered a cake and put a "50" candle on it with the two party logos and had a few NDP MPs do a photo op in the foyer before Question Period.

Judy Wasylycia-Leis, Malcolm Allen, Irene Mathyssen and John Rafferty cut the cake and offered pieces to Liberal MPs.

Since 2004, the first of the string of minority Parliaments, Jack had acted to keep a government in power only in return for something New Democrat MPs had been elected to achieve. In the fall of 2009, he again embraced the approach that had worked for him since the 2005 NDP budget. Just as he had with Paul Martin, Jack made it clear to Stephen Harper that he was willing to consider keeping the government alive, but his support wouldn't come for free.

Ignatieff returned from Sudbury to news that the Conservatives planned to bring in employment insurance relief for long-tenured employees who had been out of work for a significant amount of time. Ignatieff had said the Liberals planned to table a non-confidence motion at the first opportunity. Jack knew the country was still in a recession, though, and unemployed workers were hurting. He said the NDP would look at the EI proposal.

On his instructions, I made calls to contacts in the PMO to alert them that Jack was serious about supporting a major initiative on employment insurance. Neither side wanted to enter into negotiations, especially behind closed doors, but there was nothing stopping us from using all the tools at our disposal to reinforce the idea that New Democrats would exercise their balance of power responsibly for Canadians if the proposal was worthy.

When the Conservatives revealed they would invest an additional $1 billion for the unemployed, it was obvious the initiative would help a lot of people. It was a gamble for Jack to vote for the package. But we needed to send a signal to voters, including progressive voters in our universe, that the point wasn't who we voted with but rather what we voted for. Improving access to employment insurance was a hallmark issue for the NDP, and Harper was putting down a good chunk of change.

"How are you weathering the storm?" a senior Conservative strategist emailed me after Jack announced his decision to support the EI proposal.

"We are in the field now to assess our position. Anecdotal evidence suggests we chose right," I responded.

By the time the dust had settled a few weeks later, Ignatieff's approval rating had plummeted ten points, from 29 per cent in August to 19 per cent in October. Jack's approval numbers had held steady, at 34 per cent.

The way Jack and Ignatieff conducted themselves in a minority Parliament was a study in contrasts. This was a particularly important moment that would help set the stage for the next election campaign on the question of leadership.

But so, too, would another issue that crept up on us that winter—cancer.

WHEN I GOT OFF THE phone with Anne McGrath on the evening of January 13, 2010, I turned to my wife and began to tear up. "It's Jack, he has prostate cancer." We had been married for more than a decade, and she'd never seen me so upset. During the call, McGrath had walked me through Jack's diagnosis, emphasizing the excellent survival rates for prostate cancer. Still, I felt as though I had been run over by a bulldozer.

McGrath was preparing me for our dinner with Jack a few nights later. He had told her about his diagnosis on Boxing Day, right after he got the results. Since his father had had prostate cancer, Jack was judicious about his annual screening test. Now, he was about to start treatment, so he wanted the three of us to talk through the next steps.

We met at the Buzz Restaurant on Bank Street on January 15. Jack had just come back from a four-day western tour that took him to Campbell River, Courtenay, Kamloops, Edmonton, Saskatoon and Regina, and he was confident and upbeat. His father had beaten prostate cancer, he reminded us, and he was going to do everything to beat it too. Jack viewed his diagnosis as a condition rather than a disease. He also talked about the inspiration he drew from Olivia. She had been diagnosed with thyroid cancer in 2004 and was successfully treated.

We agreed that Jack would hold a press event in his riding with Olivia and make the announcement himself. A written statement wouldn't do. Successful leaders connect with people from their own daily lives. Cancer touched virtually every Canadian family, and Jack

184

was adamant about going public. "I want to do this. I have to do this," he said.

This would be one of the most important announcements of Jack's political life, and we wanted it to be pitch perfect. The senior team had already decided to start presenting Jack as more three-dimensional, encouraging him to talk more about the fact that he was a regular guy. About two-thirds of the way through the first draft of the speech prepared by our writing team was a startling statistic about the number of men who were diagnosed with prostate cancer every year in Canada. "Don't bury the lead," I said to myself. "That's the opening sentence." I quickly made the change and made sure the statement talked about his supportive friends and family, including his dad's battle, and how determined he was to beat it. Jack didn't change a word.

On February 5, on his way to the Estonian Hall on Broadview Avenue in Toronto to make the announcement, Jack called Harper to give him a heads-up. The two men disagreed ferociously on matters of policy but liked and respected each other personally. Jack signed off by giving Harper some dietary advice. "That red meat is going to kill you," he told the prime minister.

Jack then walked into the room packed with reporters with Olivia by his side. He looked good, and he sounded the way he felt: confident and optimistic.

"This year, more than twenty-five thousand Canadian men are going to be diagnosed with treatable prostate cancer. And I've recently learned that I'm one of them. It's the same kind of prostate cancer that my dad was diagnosed with seventeen years ago. He, like the overwhelming majority of Canadian men with prostate cancer, fought it and won. His treatments were successful, and I intend to bring to this battle the same sense of determination and optimism that he did. I'll have his genes on my side as well. Like my dad, I'm a fighter, and I'm going to beat this.

"I have an amazing team. I've got great friends, and I have an incredibly supportive family. As some of you know, my wife, Olivia, knows a thing or two about taking on cancer and winning, having been diagnosed with thyroid cancer just a few years ago. She won her battle, and

I'm going to win mine as well. Recently the party marked the seventh anniversary of my becoming leader, and without question we have accomplished a lot. But there's a lot more to do. We recognize that there is still work ahead of us to build that caring and green Canada that we believe in and know is possible. And I can't wait to roll up my sleeves on Monday morning and get started."

Jack did just that. The NDP caucus went about its business as the effective opposition, while the Liberals continued to flounder. After his misstep the previous September of trying to trigger an election for which no groundwork or outreach had been done, Ignatieff was now in no mood to talk about one. "We've had three or four elections in the last few years, and I got told clearly by Canadians last autumn, 'Don't do that again,'" Ignatieff explained to reporters in March 2010, confirming that the Liberals would let all confidence votes related to the latest federal budget clear the House of Commons.

Jack had his own issue to stick-handle. The Conservatives had decided to put the gun registry back on the agenda through a proxy: backbench Conservative MP Candice Hoeppner tabled a private member's bill to scrap it. (Hoeppner returned to using her birth name after this period, and she is now known as Candice Bergen.) The move took aim straight at the NDP. Our caucus was an even mix of urban MPs who favoured the gun registry and rural MPs whose voters tended to oppose the registry. The kicker for us was that, on principle, Jack permitted free votes on private member's bills. This opened up another front—attacks from the Liberals. Michael Ignatieff, who had already announced that he would direct his caucus to vote to keep the registry, tried to make this about principled leadership.

Jack knew the numbers: 12 NDP MPs had told their constituents they didn't support the registry. If all of them voted to kill the registry alongside the 144 Tory MPs, the bill would pass. Jack knew the NDP couldn't be responsible for killing the registry, though. This would be political suicide in some cities, especially in Quebec, where the gun registry was very popular.

The caucus would need to hammer out a game plan for the upcoming vote at its retreat in Regina in September. Before that, Jack and the senior team worked on the gun registry positioning for him. We came up with a proposal to fix the registry, and Jack announced it on August 30. The compromise, in legislation to be introduced in the House, would address the frustrations of northern, rural and aboriginal Canadians, Jack said.

The next day, Ignatieff responded at the Liberal caucus retreat in Nova Scotia. "You know the problem with the NDP? Do you know what it stands for? No Darn Principles." After the Liberal attack, I tweeted: "For the record, if the Liberals want to run the next campaign on a contest of principles, we're kinda ok with that." Olivia added her own two cents on Twitter: #LPC united and principled? What about on abortion rights, Afghan war and the 120 votes in support of #CPC in #HoC?"

The spin war was one thing, but this was going to be the trickiest policy issue Jack would face as leader. He had to secure enough votes to defeat Hoeppner's bill. Jack wrote to senior staff on September 7, a week before the caucus retreat was scheduled to start. He didn't want "too much emphasis on our rural objectives (most of caucus won't relate). I have another suggestion focussing on going to Saskatchewan [for the caucus retreat] because we're not going to be shut out of our Birthplace! We're going there because we have several winnable seats there where we intend to defeat Conservatives."

He also wanted to use the messaging we had developed for him: "A leader you can trust." "Emphasizing the leader will be important for several reasons," he wrote. "Helping drive the gun vote where we need it to go. Making sure there's no doubt about who's in charge; test-driving messaging that our team has developed; showing the world that the caucus has confidence in the Leader (given the attack—that unity and message will be key)."

Working with Jack, we landed on a strategy to change the terms of the debate in Regina. The previous Liberal government had bungled the file spectacularly, we agreed. They had barrelled ahead without paying attention to rural sensitivities and had allowed a $2 million initiative to balloon into a $1 billion project. Others could talk about the past or focus on policy, but Jack was going to talk about bridging the divide between rural and urban. He would make his comments in public, as well as in private.

"We'd rather bring people together than pull them apart," Jack declared in a public address to the federal and provincial caucuses on September 13 at the Saskatchewan legislature.

Later that day, at a nearby hotel where the federal caucus was meeting behind closed doors, Jack acknowledged there were legitimate complaints about the gun registry and concerns from rural communities that needed to be addressed. He wasn't an advocate of the status quo, either, he said, urging caucus members to keep an open mind.

"We've had many discussions about the gun registry in this caucus over the seven and a half years that I've been leader. Some of them have been very emotional. I want our discussions here to be more measured," Jack said.

"We need to move into a new phase of discussion that is mindful of the politics of this issue, its impact on our party, our caucus, and the next election, and is more open than you perhaps thought possible. The way we deal with this issue is a test, and we must pass.

"There is a difference between a free vote and free rein," he continued, saying the party needed "to find a solution and move out of the dangerous rhetoric of either saving or abandoning the registry... We have worked hard to build a caucus that respects each other, that tackles differences honestly and always with an eye to solutions rather than a winner-takes-all approach. That requires flexibility—from me, but also from you... Some MPs may be feeling resentful that I've put pressure on them to make the move to oppose the Conservatives and work with me to find a solution. Have I put effort and resources into persuading some of you? Yes, I have. It's my responsibility. Have I put effort into persuading our colleagues who are staunch supporters of the registry to accept the changes that will make it possible for our rural MPs to shift position? Yes, I have."

When the caucus retreat ended the following day, Jack left the room to face the media. We were on the second floor of the hotel, and it was a short elevator ride to the ground floor, where the press conference was being held. We knew the gun registry was all reporters would want to talk about. Jack turned to Anderson, who had been appointed as the party's director of communications earlier that spring, and asked, "Okay, what are we saying?"

"It's not about the issue, it's about national unity," Anderson told Jack just before the elevator doors opened.

Jack proceeded to the media room, walked to the microphone and declared, "I am confident that the government will not win the gun registry vote."

Ten days later, Jack proved his deftness on the file. Six NDP MPs voted with the Conservatives, not twelve. Jack had succeeded in ensuring the registry survived without forcing rural MPs to vote a certain way. He had engaged in quiet diplomacy, including enlisting Ed Broadbent to make calls, and got the math just right. The bill to scrap the registry was voted down 153 to 151.

"Having a rural MP be told how to vote by an urban leader on an issue that was in rural Canada a values issue was something Jack understood and refused to do," recalls former Saskatchewan NDP MP Dick Proctor, a party stalwart and confidant of Jack's on rural affairs. "It was better to have the rural MP come to their own conclusion on the registry. That's something their constituents would understand. Being told what to do wouldn't fly."

We had passed a major test, but we still had some mopping up to do. The Conservatives had launched a substantial radio and advertising blitz in rural ridings held by New Democrats that fall, indicating the NDP could expect a full-out assault against them in the next election, focussed on the trust issue, if they flipped on the gun registry. We had been building messaging around Jack and trust, and we weren't going to cede that territory to the Conservatives.

We tapped our English-language ad agency in Toronto, Open, to produce TV ads featuring Jack delivering a simple message. Harper's government had campaigned on lowering taxes in the 2008 campaign, then negotiated harmonized sales tax deals with Ontario and B.C. that saw the price of consumer goods rise in the middle of a recession.

"Another cold Canadian winter's coming. Times are tight and your home heating costs are skyrocketing. So why doesn't Stephen Harper get it? He's giving tax breaks to the big polluters, and doing nothing to help you. It's time for Canadian leadership to make your life more affordable," Jack said in the ad.

The ads, which began airing on October 24, were heavily weighted to run in rural areas. They delivered a blunt message to the Conservatives: if they wanted to have a fight on trust, we were up for it. We liked our odds if the question was: Who do you trust on guns versus who do you trust to give your family a break?

WITH THE REGISTRY VOTE AND the politics around it behind us, it was time to return to getting ready for the next election campaign, which would likely be the spring of 2011. Jack continued his treatment for prostate cancer, and his doctors felt good about his progress. He also felt good. Next on our list was identifying the next tier of New Democrat voter. We had two tracks: English Canada and Quebec.

Over the previous three campaigns, we'd been successful at reconstructing our traditional voter base. Between the 2000 and 2008 campaigns, we'd gone from thirteen to thirty-seven seats and from 1 million to 2.5 million votes, making impressive gains.

We were pleased with our recovery, but we weren't satisfied. We had squeezed out thirty-seven seats from about 18 per cent of the voting public, including just one seat in Quebec with 12 per cent of the vote there.

Now we wanted to identify the voters who could get the party to 25 per cent of the popular vote and beyond. We knew there were millions of Canadians who were open to voting for us but weren't for one reason or another. We wanted to know who these people were, where they lived, what their political attitudes were, what they had in common with our voter base and what it would take to move them.

We posed the challenge to Viewpoints Research, our polling firm. In the past, they had done large untargeted baseline polling. Those horse-race numbers gave us our universe; they indicated who was supporting us (our base) and who was thinking of supporting us (swing voters). But a baseline poll of a thousand people really didn't teach us much. Respondents were only spoken to once briefly. We needed to learn much more. The numbers were also statistically insignificant to drill down in specific regions or within demographic profiles. With this sample size, for example, there were only fifty respondents from the Prairies who were considering voting NDP but hadn't yet done so. This number was just too low to guide a multi-million-dollar election campaign. It simply wasn't good enough.

We asked Viewpoints to develop a model that used the most modern methods to do research differently. Their innovative model was a hybrid, the best of both worlds: a massive interactive voice-recorded poll of tens of thousands of people to get more accurate numbers *and* a longer attitudinal poll solely of those in the "next tier."

The interactive voice-recording poll Viewpoints designed was an automated, easy and quick five-question poll. People would respond by pressing numbers on their phone pad. This new survey allowed us to reach a lot more people—twelve thousand—in a shorter amount of time. The larger sample size also allowed us to drill down into ridings to get a more accurate picture of support. In the past, we had had to make the decisions about whether a riding was in play or not based on data from only a handful of people. Now, we could make determinations on a sample of several hundred responses.

The next step in the process was to micro-target, zero in on the people who could get us that 25 per cent of the vote, and then tailor our campaign message to them while also maintaining the support from our base. If you indicated the NDP was your first choice in the initial survey, you were out right away for the long attitudinal poll. If you indicated that the NDP was your second choice or that you were leaning towards the NDP or had a favourable impression of Jack, you were in. Of the twelve thousand people we questioned initially, we decided on 5 per cent to target further. This time around, we conducted an attitudinal poll, asking this smaller group about policies that mattered to them and their thoughts about the party leaders.

The profile of this cohort was fascinating. They were older than our base by about ten years, on average, and economically more secure. More of them were paid salaries, rather than wages, and they were higher up the ladder at work. They were concerned about their young kids and their aging parents, but unlike many in our base, their financial concerns were longer term. They weren't worried about putting food on the table that night.

Our base was over-represented by women voters, but there was no gender bias in this next tier of voters. They were also predominantly Liberal voters. We delved deeper in focus groups, held in Halifax, Toronto, Oshawa and Nanaimo. Participants told us without prompting that above all else they wanted a leader they could trust. We hadn't heard that as clearly and as often as we were hearing it this time. Across the board, they were unhappy with what they were seeing in Ottawa. Parliament seemed to focus on itself, not on them. Nothing was getting done, people said, though they did like Jack's emphasis on trying to make it work. This sentiment was strongest in industrial Oshawa, where the local economy was linked to the health of the auto industry. People there saw a direct connection between the level of their suffering and the lack of action in Ottawa.

The focus groups liked virtually every argument we put to them about Harper. They agreed with the sentiments that Ottawa had changed him for the worse, that he was out of touch and that he was more interested in helping big business than struggling families. Figuring out what to do with Ignatieff was trickier. We learned that Liberal voters did not like him. Yet people in traditionally held Liberal ridings still saw no good reason *not* to vote for their Liberal MP.

In our focus groups, we approached Ignatieff a few different ways. First, we tested his position on torture. In the early days of his becoming Liberal leader, we had hammered him on that to build a firewall around our base, and it had proved a very effective fundraising pitch. We wanted to know what the next tier thought of it.

The moderator played news clips of Ignatieff endorsing torture, then asked focus group participants to write down their reactions. Their responses were puzzling, because they were neutral. We asked them again and still nothing.

Yet when the moderator read out loud what Ignatieff had said, the groups reacted negatively. Ignatieff was so unlikeable and condescending with his high-minded language that they had just been tuning him out. We would need to find a way to tap into that sentiment in order to move those votes. Torture wouldn't be the issue, though.

Our main attack against Dion in the 2008 campaign had been that he voted with Harper so many times. Ignatieff had developed his own pattern of ducking out just before votes in the House of Commons so that there would be no record tying him to support of Harper. But this strategy gave him a new problem: statistics indicated that Ignatieff was not showing up in Parliament. On March 7, 2011, the *Globe and Mail* crowned Ignatieff the MP with the worst attendance record in the House of Commons. We took this information and tested it in focus groups. The response wasn't compelling, but strong enough to pursue further. The campaign team had a hunch the issue had potential to stick, so we directed Open to come up with an ad we could test.

During our debriefings on the results from the focus groups, we realized the dominant theme was that Parliament wasn't working. It was as though Ottawa was broken. If Obama made Washington the problem, maybe we could make Ottawa the problem, we concluded.

As a perennial third- or fourth-place party, we faced the same challenge during each election: Who was our main opponent? The Conservatives? The Liberals? The Bloc Québécois? In this campaign, what if we could bundle all of our opponents together and brand them as the status quo: they were the reason nothing in Ottawa was working. Whatever region you lived in, or whatever problem you had, Ottawa was the problem, and voting NDP was the answer. Ottawa was broken, and we were going to fix it.

We developed this message for voters in English Canada, but it folded nicely into the message we were crafting for Quebec. We knew Quebec had the ability to act collectively and move in one direction electorally. In 1984, Mulroney's Progressive Conservatives had gone from one to fifty-eight seats. In 1993, the upstart Bloc had gone into the campaign with seven MPs and emerged with fifty-four.

Our focus was on Bloc supporters in Quebec since the research showed we were overwhelmingly their second choice. We knew from focus group tests that Duceppe was popular, but also that a level of fatigue with the Bloc had set in as the party founded on the goal of separating from Canada celebrated its twentieth anniversary in Canadian Parliament.

This couldn't be personal, however—if we criticized the Bloc or Duceppe, we'd come across as a party that didn't understand the sophisticated terrain in Quebec. Quebecers liked that the Bloc represented their interests in Ottawa, so we needed to find a compelling reason for these voters to leave the Bloc without attacking either the party or its leader. We asked ourselves: If Harper is so unpopular in Quebec, how attractive is the Bloc's claim that it could stop a Harper majority? It had used that claim in the final stages of the 2008 campaign, and we were sure the party would use it again. What if we were to make the case that this election should be about stopping Harper from forming a government at all? That would be our brand differentiation: we could replace Stephen Harper, and the Bloc could not.

We turned to Carl Grenier, with whom we had worked in the 2008 campaign, to transform this approach into concepts for our Quebec ads. We were looking for a soft pitch: "If you vote the same way, you'll get the same results." Our Quebec team had been meeting with Grenier on a monthly basis for about a year, and he presented us with a number of concepts. One of them showed a hamster running around and around in its wheel, getting nowhere. Guardia, Anderson and Bélanger's eyes got wide. The approach seemed to capture the problem, so we took it into focus groups we set up in Montreal and Gatineau.

The focus groups initially confirmed what we knew: they liked the NDP and our leader, but their support for Duceppe seemed rock solid. We asked them about the idea of doing the same thing and getting the same results. They shrugged. Then we showed them Grenier's hamster ad. In focus groups, you usually get people who say, "good ad" or "bad ad." This time we got silence, though people had been nodding their heads at the tagline: "It has to change. NDP." There was something there, but this was certainly no eureka moment.

Thinking through our English-language ads took a lot longer. The advertising pros at Open were already working on the Ignatieff attendance ad, but we needed an overall concept for the campaign. We knew leadership worked for us, so Open initially suggested Jack as the pitchman to describe a series of problems; for example, "Stephen Harper is hurting health care." What wasn't evident, though, was that the NDP was the solution.

Then a light bulb went on. The crew at the ad agency had gotten the perception that we saw Jack as the primary pitchman for the things we were selling—better health care, better pensions, a cleaner environment. But Jack wasn't the pitchman, we told them, he was the product. People were yearning for a leader they could trust, someone who could actually get things done. Jack was what we needed to sell, not better health care.

The people at Open came back a few weeks later with an idea that captured what we were looking for. Ottawa was a cartoony place, they explained, so let's show people just how absurd things had become. An example was a Tim Hortons, in New Westminster, B.C., that had been turned into an emergency ward at the overcrowded Royal Columbian Hospital. Tim Hortons as an emergency ward? Giving tax breaks to companies that ship Canadian jobs overseas? The leader of an opposition party rarely showing up for work? Senators charged with fraud yet still sitting in the Senate? It was so bad it was comical. The idea was to juxtapose these absurdities with Jack and his steady leadership.

The theme of the cartoon ads, developed for the front end of our campaign, allowed us to bounce from issue to issue and from Harper to Ignatieff without looking as though we were switching gears or strategies. The world that we created stayed the same. Every ad, with the Peace Tower as the backdrop, reinforced the same idea: Ottawa was broken. Jack always came onscreen at the end as the leader who would fix it.

In the new year, we shot the election ads, a series we called "Not So Great Moments." We also developed a pre-election advertising concept, shot the ads and allocated $500,000 to air them beginning on

February 28, 2011. The pre-election ads were built around the concept of "Canadian Leadership," an issue that had emerged organically from our focus groups. In the wake of the gun registry vote, though, one of our rural MPs questioned whether it was wise to emphasize the theme of trusted leadership. "Are you nuts? We can't run on trust," the MP said after I presented our plan to the caucus.

The Conservatives must have picked up the same sentiment about a yearning for leadership in their own research. On January 17, they launched an anti-Liberal ad called "Ignatieff. He didn't come back for you," evoking a similar sentiment to their earlier "Just visiting" ad. Both highlighted the Liberal leader's long tenure outside the country. A week later, the Conservatives launched the tagline they would later use during the campaign. "Here for Canada" set up a direct contrast between the Conservatives and us, with our "Canadian Leadership" messaging. We were happy to have a fight over who was standing up for Canada.

Ignatieff was probably less excited about that fight. By February, his approval rating had sunk to 13.6 per cent.

With March right around the corner, everything seemed to be falling into place.

Then, I got a call. "It's Jack. It's his hip," a subdued McGrath told me. My heart sank.

"How bad is it?" I asked.

"They think he has a fracture. He'll likely need surgery," said McGrath.

With a potential election just weeks away, what were we going to do?

CHAPTER 11:
PULLING THE TRIGGER

Jack's doctors couldn't say for sure how long the recovery period would be after his surgery on March 4. A few days before the procedure in Toronto, Anne McGrath phoned me with an update. I'd brought campaign tour coordinator Ira Dubinsky into my office to join us on the call. Conservative Finance Minister Jim Flaherty would be tabling the federal budget before the end of the month, and that meant we could be heading out on the campaign trail soon.

"Will Jack be able to walk up the stairs to get on the plane?" I asked.

"We don't know yet," McGrath answered.

"Do we need to plan for a lift to get him into the plane?" asked Ira.

"Don't know," McGrath said. "But with each week that passes, he will get better. So if the election doesn't start for a few more weeks, he may not even be on the campaign trail with crutches. The one thing you need to understand, though, is that if he goes too hard, he could hurt it again and then he's back to square one."

"Shit. We need a backup plan," I said. After spending two years mapping out a campaign game plan fronted by our best asset—Jack—we now had to work out the logistics of him being on crutches or worse. We also knew that we would be the ones to decide the timing of an election. The Liberals and the Bloc had both been signalling to the media that they would be voting against Flaherty's budget, regardless of what was in it.

WE FIGURED THE LIBERALS WERE leaving the timing of the election to us because they had misinterpreted the results of three by-elections held just a few months earlier.

Pundits often elevate by-elections into something they are not, taking local results and reframing them as a national trend. By-elections are fundamentally different from a general election, however. They present an opportunity for people to base their votes on something other than who should lead the country. Sometimes, by-elections can be instruments to send a message. Sometimes, the results reflect simply the strength of a local candidate.

Three very different seats had been up for grabs in November 2010. The rural Manitoba seat of Dauphin–Swan River–Marquette became vacant when the Conservative MP Inky Mark stepped down. The Vaughan riding, north of Toronto, was being contested after Liberal MP Maurizio Bevilacqua resigned to run for mayor. Winnipeg North, an NDP stronghold, was vacant after long-time NDP MP Judy Wasylycia-Leis decided to run for mayor of Winnipeg.

The Tories had easily held the seat in rural Manitoba, though the NDP vote went up ten points. Our second-place finish was well ahead of a distant Liberal Party candidate. In Vaughan, the Tories picked up the long-held Liberal seat by running former Toronto chief of police Julian Fantino. The NDP vote completely collapsed.

Of the 40,000 votes cast in the riding that night, our candidate garnered just 673, or 1.7 per cent of the vote. The outcome was disappointing. Vaughan had never been a winning riding for us, but in the last three federal elections, under Jack's leadership, we had captured close to 10 per cent of the vote there.

But that wasn't the worst news we had to break to Jack that night in November.

The NDP and its predecessor, the CCF, had held the Winnipeg North riding for sixty of the last eighty-five years. In Kevin Chief we had a strong candidate with an inspirational personal story, but Chief lost by eight hundred votes to a popular local MLA. Kevin Lamoureux, only one of two Liberals in the Manitoba legislature, had spent the previous two decades as a constituency man. (Chief, a young aboriginal community leader, would go on to become a cabinet minister in Manitoba premier Greg Selinger's NDP government.)

The loss in Winnipeg North was devastating. But after a comprehensive debrief about the race, including a poll-by-poll breakdown on voter turnout and voting patterns, we concluded local forces had driven the results. This was about a long-time MLA who had motivated his provincial constituents to vote for him and about our own inability to motivate white working-class voters and traditional ethnic supporters in the riding.

In other words, this was no Liberal resurgence in Western Canada. It was certainly not the sudden emergence of "Iggymania" or a rejection of Jack. But that's how the Liberals appeared to see things. Our loss in Winnipeg North was proof that we were vulnerable to the Liberals even in our "safe" seats in the West, they concluded. If they could just drive two-way race polarization between themselves and the Conservatives in the next election, they figured our vote would move to them, allowing the Liberals to pick up seats. This view not only helped Ignatieff's team shape their strategy for the next campaign; it meant the Liberals wanted to go to the polls quickly.

During the run-up to the budget in early 2011, Jack stepped into the space vacated by the Liberals and the Bloc. He returned to the frame that had worked well for us in the past: the NDP wanted to make Parliament work to get things done for Canadian families. That meant he was going to tell Harper what we wanted in the budget, wait to see what was in it, and then decide whether the NDP would support it.

All eyes were now on Jack. We seized the opportunity to telegraph our values and priorities to the public. Allowing voters to compare our values to Harper's priorities, we figured, would give us a running start on the story we wanted to tell if there was a spring campaign. But we had to ensure the media understood that Jack's decision would be based on the merits of the budget alone, not on whether we were ready for an election campaign. This message would also strengthen Jack's hand in his budget discussions with the prime minister.

In January, I wrote a memo about our campaign readiness and leaked it to the media. Addressed to Jack but intended for reporters, the memo detailed how many candidates we had nominated, and it confirmed the booking of our tour plane and our $21-million budget to fight the campaign. Our team was "prepared to wage an aggressive federal election campaign at any time," stated the internal memo, reported in the press.

This set things up nicely for Jack's meeting with Harper on February 18. The two had spoken on the phone on December 17 about Jack's proposal to strengthen the Canada Pension Plan. The call had ended with a plan for the two men to meet in the new year to discuss that and "any other budget asks we may have," Anne McGrath wrote to senior staff in a brief about the conversation.

The two leaders and their chiefs of staff, McGrath and Nigel Wright, met at 4 PM in the Prime Minister's Office at Langevin Block. Jack, experiencing pain in his hip, was having a hard time moving around and getting in and out of cars, so we had arranged to use a minivan to drive him to the meeting just a few blocks from his Ottawa apartment. Helpful PMO staff had arranged for Jack's assistant, Eiman Zarrug, to drive the van through the gates at the side of the building to minimize walking.

The four sat on the leather couch and armchairs, rather than at a meeting table, to make sure Jack was as comfortable as possible. Things began cordially. Harper inquired about Jack's hip and mentioned that he "avoids all activities that may lead to injury. Saw how difficult it was for [Peter] McKay to lead the party on crutches when they negotiated the merger of the parties," McGrath later told senior staff in an email to debrief us about the meeting.

Jack laid out for Harper what the NDP wanted to see in the budget: the removal of the GST from home heating bills, a restoration of the ecoENERGY Retrofit program, an increase to the Guaranteed Income Supplement for seniors, changes to the Canada Pension Plan and a plan to increase access to family doctors. Our asks were clear and affordable, and they reinforced our values. "He was very clear, no notes, hit every point, well matched with the PM," McGrath wrote. "PM believes that our home heating proposal would be about $2.3 billion per year. One half of that in direct costs and the other half in compensation to the provinces. Reason for provincial compensation is that removing it affects the base. Jack challenged him on the provincial compensation and gave examples of seniors turning off their heat."

Harper also estimated that our senior provisions would cost $3 billion. On the Canada Pension Plan, Harper "indicated an openness to CPP improvements but that he won't do that now since there is strong pushback to what amounts to a payroll tax increase. Says he's not slamming the door, though it is undoable in the current climate," McGrath wrote.

Jack "pressed the point about the value of improving retirement security through the public plan. Highlighted low admin costs, belief there would be public support. Harper said he's not arguing against CPP expansion but made it clear he's not going to put that in this budget."

There was also some discussion about demographics and "funny stories about dads," McGrath wrote. "Harper's dad would map out routes and times to get to a game and they'd arrive almost an hour and a half early. Then he'd analyze the trip and muse that if they'd missed a connection they'd be late. Layton's dad would cut it close to the wire and had unusual techniques (such as getting Jack to open his door to get traffic to stop so they could move into another lane) to get through Montreal traffic."

At the end of the meeting, McGrath wrote, Harper "said that he is not seeking an election. Said, 'you will make your decision.' With respect to our proposals, he said they will make some effort. Jack said that we will look at the budget as a whole. Will also look for any surprises that wedge us, items we can't support. Both Wright and Harper noted that what was presented was consistent with what we've been saying publicly."

Over the next few weeks, Jack repeated our main message over and over again in the public: if these items are in the budget, we'll vote for it. If they're not, the NDP caucus will vote against it, triggering an election. It was now up to Harper to decide whether Parliament was going to live for another day.

Now, though, with Jack's hip fracture, we had a huge obstacle to overcome.

Jack had begun feeling pain early in the new year after getting some good news about his prostate cancer from his doctors before the Christmas holidays. On December 16, he received an update from one of his physicians telling him that his PSA had declined further to near non-detectable levels. "Thanks, Doc!" Jack wrote back. "Glad the blood-work shows a good result, again. I'm feeling very well indeed. I have gained weight. I'm going to have to watch the calories a bit! My tailor is going to be busy if I keep this up," Jack wrote, explaining that he was working out five or six times a week.

But the pain he experienced in January prevented him from flying to Ottawa from Toronto to deliver a speech at the party's federal council meeting. "We didn't realize it was the hip," Olivia recalls. "We knew something was wrong, but it took a while to find the fracture and we thought it may heal itself. But it just got worse."

Two weeks after his meeting with Harper about the upcoming budget, Jack underwent hip surgery without complications. He was clear on one thing during this period. "My health will not be a consideration. We are going to assess what's in the budget and decide whether it's worth supporting on its merits. Period," he told me.

Nonetheless, we faced a skeptical press. Columnist L. Ian MacDonald captured the sentiment: "Being Irish, Flaherty knows blarney when he sees it... Flaherty knows perfectly well the NDP doesn't want an election in which it stands to lose up to a dozen seats, and in which its leader would be put through a punishing grind while still in recovery from prostate cancer."

Budget day, on March 22, fell just eighteen days after Jack's hip surgery, and he still needed a crutch to get around. Jack wasn't nervous about a possible election, even though he was working through a lot of pain. "Jack doesn't work that way. Jack makes decisions based on principle. If the budget is bad, he'll vote against the budget. He'll run a campaign if he needs to. He's not scared of anything; he's willing to take that risk," said Olivia of Jack's state of mind at the time.

That same sentiment was what had got Jack to Parliament Hill on March 9, five days after his surgery, to cast his vote for a generic drug bill that would make it easier to distribute patented medicines, including those used to treat AIDS, to the world's poorest countries. The private member's bill, sponsored by Ottawa Centre MP Paul Dewar and pushed by the NDP since 2009, had passed the House of Commons, despite opposition from a few Liberals and many Conservatives.

"He insisted that we go and vote on the drug bill," remembers Olivia. "We struggled to get Jack in the van. We drove for hours so that he could hobble in for the vote. We won the vote, and the goddamned senators—the unelected Senate—didn't deal with it before the election—so it's killed."

The sight of Jack hobbling around on Parliament Hill with a crutch fuelled speculation. On the night before the budget was to be released, Evan Solomon, the host of CBC's *Power & Politics*, emailed Jack. "There is of course lots of talk and speculation these days and that is par for the course for politics. I get it. And we will talk politics and budgets tomorrow and I look forward to it. But: there is also lots of loose talk about you, your health and stepping down.

"Jack: I don't deal in rumours and health issues and personal family issues for me trump all else. So off the record: you doing ok? Is it way out of line to have folks deal in this type of speculation? I don't want to go over any lines here at a fraught period but I do appreciate how sensitive all this is. And I don't want to traffic in hurtful gossip either," Solomon wrote.

The next morning, before setting off for the budget lock-up, Jack replied to Solomon. "Thanks for asking, Evan. Hip improving ahead of schedule. I got married with a cane so I can do my job with one too. No truth to the speculation. Health will play no role in our decision on the budget," he wrote. (In 1988, Jack broke his leg in a bicycle accident just before his wedding to Olivia.)

At 2 PM, Jack, finance critic Tom Mulcair and deputy critic Chris Charlton headed into the lock-up for opposition parties in the Promenade Building on Sparks Street, two blocks from Parliament Hill. This way, the opposition parties had a few hours to see what was in the budget before Flaherty released it to the public at 4 PM.

The Department of Finance had set up separate rooms for each of the opposition parties, so Jack, Mulcair and Charlton had the luxury of privacy to talk things through with senior caucus staff. Departmental officials were available to answer questions, and they guided our team to the sections of the budget that would contain the provisions Jack requested.

There was no mention of relief for the high costs of home heating. There was no money to revive the popular ecoENERGY Retrofit initiative into a permanent program. The budget included a statement about how the government would study the future of the public pension plan, but the line felt empty, and it certainly didn't commit to improving the Canada Pension Plan. The government also said in the budget that it would increase the Guaranteed Income Supplement for half of all seniors who were living in poverty, but such a move fell short of what Jack was seeking.

Mulcair and Charlton huddled, and there was no ambiguity for either of them: there wasn't enough in the budget for us to support it, and they told Jack so.

Jack, under tremendous pressure, listened to them intently. He also peppered NDP staff with questions on the technical points in the budget. He made his decision in a few minutes. He spoke seriously, but he was also relieved that the decision had been as clear as it was. "Okay, here we go," Jack said as he walked out of the lock-up. He now had to tell Canadians about his decision, knowing it meant we were heading to the polls.

McGrath, who was in the lock-up with Jack, had to get him back to Parliament Hill without word leaking out. They called for an elevator in the Promenade Building, and when the doors opened, there were a few Liberal staffers already inside. "So?" one of them asked. "Let's wait for the next elevator," McGrath said to Jack.

The media were awaiting Jack's verdict in the foyer of the House of Commons. A press conference was scheduled to start after Flaherty's budget speech inside the chambers. The foyer was packed with reporters, who encircled the wooden podium that had been set up for Jack. His prepared remarks, written quickly during the lock-up and printed on plain white paper, had been left for him by senior staff and were turned upside down.

The assembled media tried to read Jack's body language as he approached the podium using his crutch, but he had his poker face on. They knew the budget didn't meet our party's demands, but many in the press gallery were convinced that Jack would find a way to avoid an election to give himself more time to recuperate and the NDP a chance to climb in the polls. Jack set them straight.

The prime minister "had an opportunity to address the needs of hard-working, middle-class Canadians and families, and he missed that opportunity. He just doesn't get it," Jack told reporters. "New Democrats will not support the budget as presented."

One of the reporters had a last question for him. "How is your health? Will you be well enough to go on a five- or six-week election campaign? I mean, it's a gruelling business, as you know."

"Better by the day," Jack replied.

Two days later, Jack arrived at Ottawa Hospital at 7:30 AM to have the stitches from his hip surgery removed. Two days after that, on March 26, the election campaign began.

In early March, Kathleen Monk and I had made the rounds of the news bureaus in Ottawa to walk them through our game plan and try to convince them to cover our election tour. This was always a challenge: to break through the horse-race coverage of the blue team versus the red team that squeezed the NDP out of the game. Unless reporters travelled with our tour, breaking this pattern would be even harder.

On March 9, we'd met with the CBC's parliamentary bureau at the broadcaster's Ottawa headquarters on Sparks Street to lay out why the CBC needed to pay attention to the NDP campaign. Monk walked through the logistics of the tour, highlighting the fact that I had cut our rates for accompanying media as an incentive for cash-strapped media outlets to join us.

As I laid out our strategy, I was direct about what our research showed. I took the group through a region-by-region analysis of where we were targeting new seats and which demographic groups we would be aggressively pursuing. I walked the group through Jack's strong leadership numbers and how we expected to use those to our advantage, including in Quebec, where we were the second choice of Bloc voters, who were growing weary of their party.

At the end of our presentation, veteran CBC reporter Terry Milewski folded his arms, leaned back in his chair, looked straight at me and said, "Well, that's all very well and good, Brad, but it sounds like a lot of bull-shit. Every time an election rolls around, the parties come in with their numbers and try and convince us that something magical is going to happen."

Milewski was challenging me to provide further evidence for the scenario I had just laid out. The CBC would eventually sign on to cover the whole tour, but not all media outlets thought it was worth their time or money, including Postmedia News and the *Globe and Mail.* In fact, fewer outlets agreed at the outset to cover the entire 2011 tour compared with the 2008 campaign. Because certain outlets wouldn't be with us for each of the five weeks of the campaign, we would see the number of reporters on the NDP tour increase with our rising fortunes. At the beginning of week four, for example, we were down to twelve reporters on the tour with us, but the number would jump to twenty-one for the last week of the campaign.

Our campaign script for this election was carved up into three periods. In the first period of the game, we would answer the question, "What is this campaign about?" We would make the case for why Stephen Harper had to go. We needed to be bold and interesting so that we wouldn't be written out of the early campaign stories. During weeks two to four, we would provide the meat to reinforce our message: daily announcements, the platform launch and the televised leaders' debates. In this second period, we would contrast ourselves with the Liberals and the Bloc, and outline why they weren't the solution. The third period would be our endgame—our closing arguments in the last days of the campaign. In the final sprint, we would seek to motivate our voters and show momentum with energetic rallies and whistle stops. Here, Jack would be the focus.

Drew Anderson and I had worked for months on Jack's opening statement. As lead writer, Drew spent a lot of time talking things through with Jack. "Drew, I want more personal stories in my speeches, I want to connect. I need them in there, because I draw off them to get into the zone about what we're doing," Jack told him.

Since Jack had grown up in a middle-class family, Drew made sure to include other people's stories that would give Jack an energy boost as he delivered his opening volley. We knew he could nail the speech. Our biggest concern was whether he would be able to stand comfortably for the duration.

Jack worked through the pain and delivered his speech beautifully at our campaign kickoff on Saturday, March 26. With supporters behind him in a ballroom at the Château Laurier, he stood at a podium adorned with the words "Canadian Leadership/ *Travaillons Ensemble.*" For those in English Canada, the message emphasized our ballot question: leadership. It was also a subtle reminder that Ignatieff had been out of the country for most of the last thirty years, a fact ingrained in people's minds after the Conservative "Just Visiting" and "He didn't come back for you" ads. In Quebec, our tag was intended as an antidote to the Bloc, a party that wasn't interested in working in any constructive way in the House of Commons. We were inviting progressives and anti-Conservative voters in Quebec to join with those outside the province to defeat Harper.

Jack took aim at Harper in his speech, emphasizing that the Conservative leader had become what he had once professed to despise. This segued nicely into our main message, which lumped our opponents together: "Ottawa is broken and it's time to fix it," said Jack, with his daughter, Sarah, and granddaughter, twenty-one-month-old Beatrice, in attendance. "He promised he'd finally clean up Liberal-style scandals. Instead, he's just created new scandals of his own. After five years, Stephen Harper has failed to fix what's wrong in Ottawa. In fact, he's made it worse."

The campaign tour was designed to hammer home this point for the next three days—and to show that it was New Democrats who could defeat Conservative candidates in many regions of the country. For many political pundits, the idea of Tory-NDP races, especially in the West, was a foreign concept, despite the data we had to back us.

To inoculate ourselves against the expected Liberal frame (the election was a choice between Ignatieff and Harper), we started our tour in Edmonton, where NDP candidate Linda Duncan had won the Edmonton–Strathcona riding in 2008. Duncan held the only non-Conservative seat in Alberta, and the NDP had come in second in the majority of the other seats in the province. Jack was in Edmonton on day one of the 2011 campaign to emphasize this point. The NDP tour then travelled to Surrey, Regina, Brantford and Kitchener, visiting Conservative ridings we were targeting. In many, we had come a strong second in 2008.

Whenever we travelled by plane, the tour staff made sure to get Jack onto the tarmac before anyone else. That gave him extra time to climb stairs free from the watchful eyes of reporters or their cameras. We didn't want stories about his health to get in the way of our narrative.

But Jack's limited mobility in the opening week of the campaign hampered our ability to pull off the kinds of events we had developed for him. Our plan had been to put Jack in situations where he thrived: town halls and energetic rallies surrounded by supporters. Harper and Ignatieff, both more wooden and less personable, weren't comfortable in these settings, so we wanted to set up this contrast to showcase Jack's leadership strengths. We were confident Harper would stick to a tour plan that played to his different strengths but figured if Ignatieff tried to emulate Jack, we would be drawing him out of his comfort zone and into ours, setting up a nice comparison for the voters. Unfortunately, Jack's hip didn't allow us to do this at the outset.

During the opening days of the campaign, we employed what is known as the "rolling barrage" tactic, named after the strategy the Canadian Armed Forces employed at Vimy Ridge during World War I. Since the leader's tour had been developed well in advance of the writ drop, we were able to reinforce the message of Jack's stump speech with local radio ads and leaflet drops to households on the day he arrived in each new city. Our message was always the same: New Democrats were the ones who beat Conservatives here. Even if they weren't paying much attention to the campaign, chances are people would hear or read that if they were part of the 65 per cent of the non-Conservative vote, they should vote NDP to defeat the Conservative incumbent. We pressed play on our message, rewound and pressed play again.

Ignatieff had pressed play on his own message before the campaign began with his "red door" and "blue door" analogy, a reference to the colours of the Liberal and Conservative parties. "You go through the blue door and you get jets, you get jails, you get corporate tax cuts and you get miserable knockoffs of the real article. But you go through the red door and you get compassion, you get fiscal responsibility and you get a government relentlessly focussed on the real priorities of Canadian families," Ignatieff told reporters. "There are only two choices."

The opening days of federal campaigns were always a challenge for us. The other parties ignored us to marginalize us, and the press usually followed suit after filing one pro-forma story about the kickoff of our campaign. We had to work like hell to get written into the cut and thrust of the daily cycle. This time around, Jack had just had hip surgery. Even though his energy level was on par with that of Harper and Ignatieff, we were already fighting a perception of a slow start.

It didn't help when Harper told reporters on day five, "We could also have a debate between Mr. Ignatieff and myself, since after all, the real choice in this election is between a Conservative government or an Ignatieff-led government that all of these other opposition parties will support."

Ryan Dolby, our candidate in Elgin–Middlesex–London, dropped a bomb on us on the same day, March 30. The day had started off well. In the morning, Jack had held a great event in Oshawa to announce a key plank of the NDP's job creation plan: cut the small business tax rate and return the corporate tax rate to 2008 levels. "As prime minister, I wouldn't use your hard-earned tax dollars to reward companies that ship jobs to the States or overseas," Jack said, speaking from the premises of Kitchen Studio, a custom cabinetmaker. "I'll target investment to create jobs right here at home. I'll reward the job creators."

The *Globe and Mail* covered the story online, pointing out that the "New Democrats have run well in this working-class community... so it is easy to understand why the party is targeting this riding." But the same reporter was baffled by our destination later that day. "What is more difficult to comprehend is the visit that Mr. Layton will make to Bramalea–Gore–Malton, west of Toronto, on Wednesday afternoon, where the Conservatives were in a tight race with Liberal incumbent Gurbax Singh Malhi in the last election and the New Democrats ran a distant third." In fact, we were running a star candidate in the riding, local community activist and lawyer Jagmeet Singh. Singh would come within 539 votes of defeating Conservative Bal Gosal in the 2011 election and get nearly 4,000 more votes than the Liberal candidate. (He went on to win the first NDP seat in the Peel region in the provincial election later that year.)

The plan was for Jack to visit the MDA Robotics plant in Singh's riding in Brampton before a scheduled rally for the candidate later in the afternoon. I was on the phone when Nathan Rotman came into my office and laid down a handwritten note that read "Ryan Dolby is about to quit, throw support to Libs."

I cut short my call. "Does Jack know about this?" I asked Rotman.

"We just got the heads-up now," he replied.

"Shit. Jack's about to start at MDA."

I called Anne McGrath right away. She and Jack were travelling in an RCMP car, so she put me on speakerphone. They had just arrived at MDA, so we didn't have a lot of time to go over the messaging. The press would know about the defection soon.

Jack never panicked in these situations, but it was a blow. According to McGrath, his face said it all when he got the news: disappointed and a bit discouraged. "There was a sense that things were beyond our control, and there was a possibility that... we would be stuck back into that old [Liberal] frame," recalls McGrath. "It was bad. It was really bad."

The fact that Ryan Dolby was a member of the CAW, and Jack was about to enter a facility full of CAW members, made the timing even worse. CAW past president Buzz Hargrove had backed the Liberals in English Canada in previous campaigns, part of his flawed strategy to block the Conservatives, and Hargrove's successor, Ken Lewenza, would also be on hand at MDA that day.

We'd learn later that the whole thing was a set-up. Dolby had been talking to the Liberals for weeks, and they had hatched the plan before the campaign even started. Now, though, we had to develop a fast plan of attack. We decided to run towards the issue, not away from it. "Let's get into Dolby's riding as soon as possible. Show them we're not going anywhere," I told tour director Ira Dubinsky. "Find the biggest hotel ballroom you can for a rally. Let's get right in their faces. Red door, blue door, my ass."

After Jack's scrum at the MDA facility, I called to pitch our strategy to him and McGrath: "We want you to go to London and have a rally."

Jack loved the idea. "Let's do it," he said.

By that evening, we had another NDP candidate in place, local riding president Fred Sinclair. Four days later, we organized a large "London 4 Layton" rally in the riding. "We weren't afraid to fight," recalls Nathan Rotman.

Our strategy was risky. We didn't know whether there were more turncoats out there. The day Dolby quit had been brutal. "Jack Layton has been saying that his party, and not the Liberals, has what it takes to beat the Conservatives. But just five days into the campaign, at least one of his own candidates did not buy the message," the *Globe* reported. But the newspaper was back in London on Monday for the rally. "Layton Gambles in Rally in Defector's Riding—and Wins," the headline said. On election night, Fred Sinclair would come in second behind the Conservatives in the riding, getting 12,436 votes, or 25 per cent of the vote. The Liberal candidate backed by Dolby came in a distant third, with just 6,800 ballots cast for him.

WE WERE DISAPPOINTED AT THE end of the first week of the campaign. The media had reported that our crowds were a little thin, we had lost a candidate, and the leader's tour didn't have the energy of past campaigns. We had to go slow at the beginning, to give Jack time to get stronger, but things were flat.

On Sunday morning, after seven days of campaigning, I called Brian Topp for a pep talk. "Should we be worried we're not doing as well in the polls?" I asked.

"Worried?" Topp replied. "Usually, we are a lot lower at this stage in the campaign."

We had a game plan that was well researched, and we were sticking to it. I took heart from a line I remembered from *Audacity to Win,* the book by David Plouffe that chronicled Barack Obama's surprising victory over Hillary Clinton for the Democratic nomination and then the presidency. Plouffe, Obama's campaign manager, quotes Mark McKinnon, George W. Bush's chief campaign ad man: "I'd rather have one flawed strategy than seven different strategies."

It wasn't time to panic, but it was time to up our game and insert colour events to boost our campaign script and reinforce Jack's strengths. I called the tour and communications team into the boardroom at campaign headquarters. "With Jack on the mend, we've got to juice up our tour hits. I want Jack serving coffee at Tim Hortons. I want him pouring beer at pubs. I want to see Jack doing this kind of stuff incorporated into the rest of the tour," I told the team.

That evening, on Sunday, April 3, 1 million Quebecers tuned in to the popular Quebec television talk show *Tout le monde en parle* (everyone's talking about it) on Radio-Canada to see a relaxed and very likeable Jack. The influential show, hosted and co-produced by Guy Lepage, had approached us before the campaign to invite Jack to come on the show. They'd offered us a few dates, and we took the earliest one available. Jack had taped the segment on the previous Thursday while he was in Montreal to announce that Cree leader Romeo Saganash was running for us in the northern Quebec riding of Abitibi–Baie-James–Nunavik–Eeyou. Jack had been wooing Saganash for a few years, and he was a star candidate for us.

Quebecers liked what they saw on their television screens: the NDP leader was becoming *le bon* Jack. Over the next two evenings, on April 4 and 5, pollster Angus Reid was in the field. The results, published on April 7, confirmed what we already knew from our own internal research.

We were running a strong second behind the Bloc in Quebec, leaping ahead of the other federalist parties.

Jack was exercising every day on the campaign trail; we even had a physiotherapy table set up in his hotel rooms. His sister, Nancy Layton, a retired physical education teacher, was travelling with the tour and served as his trainer. Jack had traded his crutch for a cane, but we needed more from him. It was time for me to give him a little kick in the pants.

"He was definitely lacklustre, and the media were really on his case about the health stuff," recalls Anne McGrath, who put me on speakerphone to talk to Jack during a campaign break at a Winnipeg TV station. "It's a $20-million campaign," I reminded him. "Everyone is putting their heart and soul into this. Everyone is counting on you. It's time to get off the bench. This is what we've been working for. The project won't get fulfilled unless you turn it on." It was good for Jack to hear. Physically, McGrath recalls, you could see him getting energized. He sat up straighter, and his eyes got wider.

Jack picked up the pace during week two, and he made some strategic announcements about the HST and home heating costs, shipbuilding and the Navy, veterans and crime in key ridings in British Columbia, Manitoba and northern Ontario. These issues were intentionally against type. But I woke on the morning of Sunday, April 10, to another depressing poll, just as we were set to release our platform. We were a few points down from the previous Sunday, now standing at 13 per cent in the Nanos tracking poll.

Jack had directed me to ensure our platform was released before the debates, slotted for April 12 and 13. For parties like ours with a diverse constituency, the platform can be a nightmare. It could sabotage your campaign, and it seldom helped. We needed this one to actually help us.

Our idea for the 2011 campaign was to write a platform that was modest and focussed. We wanted to head off the expected knock against us as the party that wanted to do too much, too fast. So instead of announcing large multi-billion-dollar new programs, we would concentrate on smaller, more immediate things. We captured our approach in the title: "Practical First Steps."

Brian Topp had agreed to stick-handle the platform, and he worked with Peter Puxley, director of the newly created policy branch in Jack's office on Parliament Hill, to ensure the document worked its way through the appropriate channels in caucus. The idea was to narrowcast our commitment to reach our target voters and not give our opponents much to shoot at. We'd watched the Conservatives pull off this approach in earlier campaigns, and we thought it could work for us.

Copying the Conservatives didn't mean aligning with them. In fact, we set out to highlight items in our platform that would reinforce our differences. Since Harper's campaign would have the ability to set the agenda in the daily media cycles, we had to anticipate what his campaign issues would be and make sure we had something meaningful to say about the issue. If the Conservatives were talking about jobs, we needed to talk about jobs. If they were talking about seniors, so did we. That way, media and the voters could hold up the two competing visions and compare them.

"What's our response to a Conservative corporate tax cut?" I'd put to our talented policy team in a bear-pit session during platform development.

"A corporate tax increase?" answered one.

"No," I responded. "Our response to a corporate tax cut is a small business tax cut."

"What's our response to the Conservatives' purchase of multi-billion-dollar F-35 fighter jets for the air force?" I asked them.

"Cancelling the contract and opening it up to tender?" someone suggested.

"Wrong. Our response is to invest in replacing our aging naval fleet," I said. "Their military priority is planes; ours is ships," I said.

We had to be more than the party that would undo what the Conservatives were going to propose. Reversing bad Conservative policy was important, but the bigger questions about our platform had to be: "Who do we speak for? Who do we represent? Who will we help compared with the people they would help?"

The Conservatives wanted to help the profitable multinational corporations; we wanted to help the mom-and-pop shops. The Conservatives believed job creation came about through giving tax cuts to big companies with no proviso against shipping jobs overseas; we wanted to create jobs by helping those who were hiring in their communities and weren't outsourcing. They stood for the big guys. We stood for the little guys.

I directed our policy branch to use the numbers from the Department of Finance as a starting point for our fiscal framework. We wanted to debate priorities, not our fiscal assumptions. We also used the Conservatives' timeline for balancing the budgets.

It helped that both the Liberals and the Conservatives released their platforms earlier than we did. The Conservatives had signalled that they would be running on the budget that they had tabled in the dying days of Parliament. We looked for commonalities between the Liberal and Conservative platforms to see how we could further distinguish our offer to voters. Then it hit us: both parties had back-end loaded many of their commitments into the third or fourth year of their mandate. People needing pension relief would have to wait, while corporate tax cuts would kick in right away. We seized on this, firming up a marketing strategy for the platform launch to highlight five priorities that Jack would act on in the first hundred days. It meshed well with our plan to use the platform launch to reinforce our strength in the campaign: Jack was someone you could trust to get things done.

We wanted to make sure the visuals coming out of the platform launch would be Jack delivering a rousing speech before cheering supporters, held after the briefing to the media in a ballroom next door at the Hilton Hotel on Richmond Street in Toronto. It would be left to me, Drew Anderson and Peter Puxley to lead the technical briefing and field the inevitable questions from reporters about the NDP's low standing in the latest public opinion poll. Before the town hall–style event, we'd played a short animated video. We'd produced it at the end of the first week.

The tone of the video was more defensive than Jack's optimistic delivery of the platform at the town hall, but the underlying message for both was informed by the "Seven Habits of the Working Class" set out by American author Henry Olsen. Olsen had interviewed Patrick Muttart, a strategist on Harper's team at the time, as part of a study into the characteristics of working-class voters. Olsen, drawing on Muttart's insights, identified these as: hope for the future, fear of the present, pride in their lives, anger at being disrespected, belief in public order, patriotism and fear of rapid change.

Drew Anderson had posted this list next to his computer to remind him what was on Harper's mind, and we used it to craft Jack's key lines at the platform launch. Surrounded by supporters, Jack delivered a speech about the values that informed our platform and insisted that voters had a choice. "People will try and tell you that you have no choice but to vote for more of the same. But you *do* have a choice," he said. At the end of his remarks, Jack signed the platform document. The picture said it all: "You can trust me. I'm putting my good name to these commitments."

We knew Jack did well on character, and that was the field on which we'd compete. We weren't running away from the commitments in our platform—far from it. But people weren't going to decide their votes based on a line-by-line analysis of each party's platform. They were going to vote for someone they trusted.

We got straight-up coverage of our platform launch, and our internal polling ticked up a day later. It would never dip again. The external polls started showing the same trend: Jack rose above Ignatieff in the Nanos Leadership Index and stayed there. The first debate was in forty-eight hours. Was it just possible that we could turn this election around?

CHAPTER 12:
DEFYING HISTORY

It was thirty minutes before the French-language debate was set to start at Ottawa's National Arts Centre on April 13, 2011. Jack, feeling buoyant after his performance the night before in the English-language debate, was trying to stay loose in his room backstage. He had taken his last painkiller that morning, prescribed to help with his recovery from hip surgery, and he had a question for his physicians.

Under the subject line "A glass of wine tonight?" Jack emailed: "So far so good, my friends. After this evening's debate, I'm wondering if I can celebrate. If not, no problem, I'll survive. Thanks for everything."

This was typical Jack. He had always eaten healthily, and after his diagnosis with prostate cancer, Olivia had put him on a strict vegan diet. He sometimes checked in with his doctors about diet, too.

After the debate that evening, Olivia, Brian Topp, Anne McGrath, Raymond Guardia, Karl Bélanger and I watched Jack savour a glass of red wine at Zoe's Lounge at the Château Laurier. His doctor had given him the go-ahead, and there was definitely a lot to celebrate.

Early on in our relationship, Jack had showed me footage of the debate performance he'd participated in during his unsuccessful run for Toronto mayor in 1991. He was not a great performer, and he knew it: he looked wooden and sounded unsubstantive. During his three campaigns as NDP leader, he'd improved his debate performance each time after a shaky start in 2004. In 2008, although his performance was strong, it hadn't fundamentally changed the race.

This time around, we needed to shake things up. I tapped Topp to be the lead on debate prep, and he decided on an approach that had worked for his previous boss, Roy Romanow. Topp tossed out our traditional playbook, in which we had Jack studying the policy briefs on every subject we thought could come up during the debates, then memorizing lines in both languages to capture complicated policies in short sound bites. Topp ditched this for a simpler approach: Jack and his senior team would talk out the overall goals and objectives for the debates, then get them wired into Jack's DNA. Jack already knew the issues and policies; he needed to live and breathe our strategy to get them out there effectively.

This new approach didn't mean we failed to determine how best to use the debate format to Jack's advantage. As in past years, we role-played so he could practise responding to expected arguments from Harper, Ignatieff and Duceppe in both languages. But the conference room at the Marriott Hotel in Ottawa where we did our debate prep was bare. We had one flip chart and a marker. There were no binders full of materials, no army of policy wonks. The room held just Jack's inner circle and those impersonating the other debaters: Bélanger was Duceppe, Guardia was Harper and Anderson was Ignatieff.

We wanted Jack to land his punches in the first sixty minutes. Many Canadians would tune out after that and reporters would already be crafting their stories. "We need more zingers. Go write some one-liners," Topp instructed Bélanger and Anderson.

During our last session, Brian Topp asked each of us in the room for a final comment. "Any last words of wisdom before we adjourn here?" Topp asked.

I went last. "This is it, Jack," I said. "Tonight's the last time you'll get to speak directly to millions of Canadians. You know the format, and you know what you need to say. The message is in your DNA. Go out there like this is the last debate you'll ever do," I said.

Jack's eyes teared up, and he raised himself on the balls of his feet behind the practice podium. "I don't think this will be my last one. Maybe I'll do one more," he said.

We'd all gone into the National Arts Centre for the first debate feeling anxious, but there was no need. Jack had grown much more comfortable in his skin over the years, and he was in control from the start. He undercut Harper with targeted messages and memorable lines. "You've become everything you used to fight against," Jack charged. "I don't know why you need to build more prisons, when the crooks seem so happy in the Senate." In reference to tackling youth crime, he reached out to the Twitter generation when he told Harper, "That's been a hashtag fail."

Jack also knocked Ignatieff down. "If you want to be prime minister, you better learn how to be a Member of Parliament first," he told the Liberal leader. "You know, most Canadians, if they don't show up for work, they don't get a promotion." Even though we'd laid the groundwork with a "Not So Great Moments" ad about Ignatieff's attendance problem, Ignatieff's team seemed taken aback by this line of attack during the English-language debate, and he fell hard.

Handling Duceppe in the French debate was going to be a bit trickier. Our focus groups in Quebec had told us they didn't respond well to the NDP criticizing Duceppe. But again Jack was up to the challenge. Duceppe's pitch was that people had to vote Bloc to hold Harper to a minority. "I know I won't be prime minister, and you won't be either," Duceppe told Jack.

Since we knew that would be coming, we'd developed an effective rebuttal. Hold it, the line went, Harper's in power now. Instead of just slowing him down, shouldn't we be working to replace him? The Bloc had "some good ideas sometimes, but you're like a hockey team made up of defencemen," Jack said. The NDP, by contrast, can "score goals... The NDP can do it because we have the possibility of forming a government."

So it was quite a toast at Zoe's that evening after the debates were over: Ignatieff had been knocked down, and Duceppe looked like he was in trouble.

WHEN ED BROADBENT LOGGED ONTO his computer on the morning of April 21 from his holiday home in England, where he spent part of the year, he knew the news he read could change the course of the campaign.

For the first time ever, the NDP was leading in Quebec, catapulting ahead of the Bloc in a new poll published in the Montreal newspaper *La Presse*.

The sun hadn't even risen yet in Canada, but Broadbent wanted to send Jack a congratulatory email to start his day. "Fantastic! Just got the CROP poll in Quebec. I almost had a tear in my eye. My warmest congratulations for making real by strong leadership and determination what some of us believed in and worked for a long time ago. Congratulations again! And a big hug to boot. Now bring home the bacon," wrote Broadbent, who also spoke to Jack regularly during the campaign. He'd decided not to run himself after the 2004 election because his wife, Lucille, was ill with cancer. She died in November 2006.

Jack was in Thunder Bay that morning preparing for a scrum with reporters. He was so busy he hadn't had a chance to check his personal email account, nor had he heard the news of the poll. Campaigns are like that: a bubble is purposely built around the leader. Bélanger and McGrath debated whether to brief Jack about the CROP poll before the press event, and they decided to give him the good news. The new poll showed the NDP in Quebec surging to 36 per cent, five points ahead of the Bloc. Even among francophone voters, the NDP was now within four points of the Bloc, at 34 per cent to the Bloc's 38 per cent.

Jack was ecstatic. The long slog in Quebec had sometimes seemed futile, but things were clicking this time. On April 14, the day after the French-language debate, Jack was at La Cage aux Sports at the Bell Centre to watch game one of the playoffs of the Montreal Canadiens against the Boston Bruins. The fans were in a partying mood, and Jack was on fire. The pictures that came out of the event were gold. Not only that: Jack got an unexpected chance to do some sportscasting.

Jack and the tour team had arrived at the bar just before the national anthems. When Bélanger noticed that CKAC, a popular French-language radio station, was there doing live hits, he asked if they would like to interview Jack. They immediately said yes. Jack was just settling in to the interview in the opening minute of the game when, at two minutes and forty-four seconds into the first period, Brian Gionta scored for the Canadiens. The place erupted, and Jack was live on the radio describing what the whole province was feeling as Montreal took the lead.

HOST: Good evening, Jack Layton.

JACK: Good evening.

HOST: Happy to have you with us tonight at La Cage aux Sports at the Bell Centre.

JACK: [Loud cheers.] Here we go! They scored! The Habs just scored their first goal, just like I predicted. Tonight, the Habs will win.

HOST: This is a sign. Right when we went on air... they scored a goal.

JACK: Wonderful.

HOST: Wonderful. Jack Layton's first words led the Montreal Canadiens to score a goal, ladies and gentlemen. Isn't that fantastic?

JACK: Right at the beginning, they took control of the game, and they did a very good... and look at that, look at the replay. That's something else.

But bringing home the bacon was still no sure thing. Like Broadbent, Jack knew that a campaign on the ascendancy, while a lot more fun than a campaign stuck in last place, had many potential pitfalls and land-mines to avoid. We repeated our clear, consistent message to Quebecers, reinforced in our television ads that had played in high rotation since March 31. They were part of our biggest ad buy ever in the province. Set to playful carnival music, the first fifteen-second ad starred the hamster spinning in its wheel. The line *"La politique fait du surplace à Ottawa"* (Politics is going nowhere in Ottawa) appeared, followed by *"Il est temps que ça change"* (It's time for that to change). The tagline at the end read *"NPD Travaillons Ensemble."* Once the ad had run for five days, we rotated in barking dogs in place of the hamster.

What viewers didn't know about the first wave of Quebec ads was that the hamster brought in to star in the ad had died on the set. His replacement was so lethargic that Grenier's production team had to run a loop of him spinning in his wheel for the ad that actually aired.

We couldn't have created a more apt metaphor about the state of affairs than the Bloc itself did. Its campaign slogan, *"Parlons Québec"* (Let's talk about Quebec), reinforced our message. "Thank you, Jesus," we thought to ourselves. "Talk, talk, talk about Quebec, that's all they can do. What about getting results for Quebec?"

They had left the playing field wide open, and we moved in. The Bloc's entire campaign was lazy and ineffective. Their platform highlighted a handful of themes. Sovereignty was not one of them, which also helped us: we were poised to do better in a campaign that wasn't framed as a debate between federalism and sovereignty. With the Bloc's raison d'être off the table, we were on equal footing to fight it out with them on issues such as jobs, health care, the environment and trust.

On April 18, Duceppe had called on Quebecers not to be taken in by Jack's smiling face. "Me, too, I find him a nice guy. I train with him in the gym," Duceppe said. "But we are not now deciding to vote for someone who is training with me, but who is defending Quebec's interests." He'd repeated his new line of attack a few days later, using a scripted hockey metaphor to repeat his point. "Jack Layton plays against Quebec, but he plays with a smile," Duceppe told reporters.

What Duceppe couldn't have anticipated was that we were ready for such an accusation. Grenier, our ad guy in Quebec, had developed a concept for us before the campaign that addressed the issue of Jack's personality. The thirty-second ad opened with regular Quebecers talking about Jack.

"Isn't he too nice to be a politician?" asked one. "Hasn't he got himself too close to real people?" asked another. Then Jack appeared onscreen chuckling: "I cannot promise not to be nice, but we need to improve our health care system, build a green economy, bring our troops home, support the arts, support culture, protect the French language. Let's work together for families. There is a lot of work to do."

Jack wasn't sure of the script when Grenier first presented it. Grenier was so committed to it, though, that he convinced Jack, Guardia and Anderson to get the ad in the can at least, saying, "Let's just shoot it, it doesn't cost any more." When Grenier lobbied to put the ad on the air, Jack said no because he felt there was no context. "Come on," he said. "Nobody has said that about me. I'm not being accused of it." So we'd made a deal with Grenier: if one of our opponents criticized Jack for being too nice, then we'd revisit it.

As soon as Duceppe played the nice card, Anderson's ears perked up. He called Grenier immediately. "How soon could we get the ad on the air?" he asked. Jack and I agreed it was time to pull the trigger on the ad, titled "Vox Pop," and it was broadcasting within hours.

On April 23, Easter Sunday, we showed up in Duceppe's backyard for an NDP rally. Before the event started, Guardia checked out the line to get into the Olympia Theatre in the heart of Duceppe's riding. The line stretched a few hundred metres from rue Sainte-Catherine to boulevard René-Levesque. When Guardia looked around the corner, he could see that the line just kept going and going from there.

The night before, in Toronto, Jack had convinced his two children and their families to join the campaign for a day. The whole gang hopped on the campaign plane in the morning: Jack's daughter, Sarah, and her husband, Hugh, and their daughter, Beatrice, and Jack's son, Mike, and his partner, Brett.

When the aircraft landed in Montreal, Jack and his family climbed onto the bus for campaign staffers. Jack typically travelled with Anne McGrath in a car provided by the RCMP, but today was different. As the bus wound its way from the airport to the event, a campaign staffer pointed out all the NDP signs as they neared the Olympia Theatre. It was Gilles Duceppe's riding, so "it was very much a 'Whoa, wait a second. Why are there so many NDP signs?'" recalls Mike Layton.

Then the bus pulled up to the venue, and everybody saw the lineup around the block. "Is this for us?" Mike recalls people asking. "That's when we realized this was real."

Jack's speech, delivered to a cheering crowd, was the Quebec version of our "Don't let them tell you it can't be done" message. After the rally, Jack stole four hours to be with his family. "We went rogue," jokes Mike. Jack secured an eight-seat van from the campaign's security detail, and the family drove around town in the unmarked vehicle.

Their first stop was Schwartz's, Jack's favourite smoked meat shop, though his father had preferred Bens. After Mike picked up sandwiches for the group, they drove up Mont Royal to visit Robert Layton's grave. "We got lost trying to find my grandfather's tombstone," recalls Mike.

From there, the family drove by the house Jack had lived in as a young boy, before the family moved to Hudson. The home is a classic two-storey brick house on Westminster Avenue in Montreal West. The tour continued with a stop at Layton Audio on rue Sainte-Catherine in downtown Montreal, the latest incarnation of the piano store founded by Jack's great-grandfather in 1887. The family drove by the Montreal Association for the Blind, also founded by him, and ended their tour with a stop at Gilbert Layton Park, named after Jack's grandfather. "It was just a fantastic family moment," recalls Mike Layton of the day.

The day had gone very differently for Duceppe: this was the moment his campaign panicked. After the release of the CROP poll that showed the NDP in first place in Quebec, Duceppe and his team took the weekend to re-tool. They would decide to abandon their "Only the Bloc can stop Harper" claim and replace it with a direct plea to traditional Bloc voters to come back home. It was too late.

The Bloc's internals might not have looked exactly like our numbers, but they couldn't have been pretty. The voter identification polling we conducted on April 23 in targeted ridings in Montreal showed levels of support that were so high that the company contracted to do the automated calls offered to run larger samples on its own dime to verify them.

Among 2,204 respondents in the Rosemont–La Petite-Patrie riding, 1,582, or 67 per cent, said they were voting for Jack Layton and the NDP. In Duceppe's Laurier–Sainte-Marie riding, the number was 63 per cent. On the easternmost tip of Montreal in the Pointe-de-l'Île riding, our support hit a staggering 73 per cent.

On the day we held our big rally in Montreal, Duceppe's Twitter account had issued a note saying, "This election is a battle between... Canada and Quebec." The post was later removed. But in a pep talk to volunteers that day, Duceppe had narrowed his pitch to make sure hard-core separatists turned out to vote: "We want Quebec to become a country. We must fight for that in Ottawa."

Two days later, Duceppe dragged out eighty-year-old Jacques Parizeau, Quebec's former premier and leader of the Parti Québécois. "Canada's federal system is full of traps. It's time to get out of it," Parizeau told a small room filled mostly with staffers. "I'm sending out a message to the supporters of the Parti Québécois, to unite and mobilize with all of your energy to support the Bloc in this last week."

Parizeau was seeing what Ed Broadbent was hearing over in England. Broadbent often talked to his daughter during the campaign; she was a nursing assistant in Gatineau and lived in nearby Buckingham, Quebec. As he recalls, "At the end of the first week, she said, 'Dad, they're starting to talk about the NDP at work.' Ten days, later she said, 'Dad, they're putting up signs in Buckingham for the NDP.' I said, 'You're kidding.' She said, 'No, true story.' Two days before the election, she said, 'Dad, I think we're going to win.'"

From his vantage point in Montreal, former prime minister Brian Mulroney was watching a similar arc. On April 28, former Ontario NDP leader Stephen Lewis and Mulroney were chatting in Mulroney's Montreal law office. Lewis, who in 1984 had been appointed by Mulroney to serve as Canadian ambassador to the United Nations, was in town from Toronto for a luncheon at the Mount Royal Club that Mulroney was hosting for the Stephen Lewis Foundation. Before heading off to the fundraiser, the two talked politics.

"I think Jack is going to become Leader of the Official Opposition. He's going to win more seats than I did in Quebec in my first outing," Mulroney, who had won fifty-eight seats in 1984, told a startled Lewis. Like Broadbent's daughter, Mulroney had been picking up vibes over the course of the campaign to lead him to this prediction. "I'm often stopped on the street; people talk to me," Mulroney explained later. "If you were a politician, if you had run for office yourself, particularly if you had run in Quebec, you know you have a bit of a sense. I didn't think there was much doubt that this was going to happen."

Mulroney may have felt confident, but our view was that a lot can happen in the last week of a campaign. Coming out of Easter weekend, we were leading in Quebec and held second place behind the Tories nationally after leapfrogging ahead of the Liberals. Momentum was on our side. It was time to roll out a strong endgame advertising blitz to reinforce our campaign's motivating message and blunt any reverse momentum or strategic voting. We couldn't screw this up. Going into any campaign, you enter the writ period with an idea of what your endgame message will be. It's best to have a few options for a solid close, but you need to be nimble enough to tailor your endgame message to the quirks of the campaign. The message has to flow from your core offer, solidify your vote and motivate your supporters.

In Quebec, our plan to reach our target voters in the province had played out beautifully during the first two periods of the campaign. We were nearing a level of support, especially among francophone voters, that could result in a flood of seats going our way.

Our original idea for our endgame ad blitz in Quebec was the right one, so we stuck to it. Our campaign in the province had struck the right chord, and we were going to ride this one out. The ad, shot and directed by Grenier before the campaign's launch, started off with a young woman, representing a Bloc voter, explaining that in the past she hadn't voted for the war or environmental degradation or against her language and culture. This time, she was voting for change. In the second part of the thirty-second ad, Jack and Tom Mulcair talked about how they'd stand up for the environment, bring our troops home from Afghanistan and protect Quebec culture and language. The ad didn't reference the Bloc and was careful not to attack the party directly. It conveyed the message that the woman hadn't done anything wrong by backing the Bloc to this point. However, the ad made it clear that if voters didn't do something different, they were going to get more of the same: we'd be stuck with Stephen Harper. The ad, which aired more than any of our Quebec ads, ended with the tagline that was working so well for us: *"Travaillons ensemble."*

We had settled on our endgame message for the rest of Canada during the second week of the campaign. We'd known going in that our closing argument would have to be motivational to get our base to stay with us. We'd gathered footage for the final ad during our platform launch, the energetic town-hall event Jack had hosted. We'd brought in extra cameras to make sure we had shots of Jack from multiple angles, including the moment he signed the platform to signal his commitment to it.

Our best asset, Jack, was front and centre in our final ad. He started by delivering the line "People will try and tell you that you have no choice but to vote for more of the same. But you do have a choice." This assertion was meant to debunk the red door/blue door Liberal frame.

After Jack listed his easy-to-remember, family-friendly priorities in a voice-over, accompanied by strong visuals of him on the campaign trail meeting regular people, he delivered closing lines that packed an emotional punch.

"Together we can do this." (We were careful not to define what "this" was, to let the audience project.) "You know where I stand." (We wanted to hammer home the point that trust was the ballot box question.) "You know I am a fighter." (Jack had fought prostate cancer and was recovering from hip surgery. We wanted to remind voters that he would continue to fight like hell for them.) "And I won't stop until the job is done," Jack told the crowd at the town hall to great applause, closing out the ad. (The media reported that Ignatieff had already been in talks with the University of Toronto, arranging a soft landing if his foray into electoral politics didn't pan out. The "Just Visiting" tag had also stuck. Our message underlined permanence and determination. Ignatieff was a flight risk; Jack was in it for the long haul.)

By the time our ad aired in the last week of the campaign, Jack's lines, written to solidify and motivate our base, were casting a much wider net. We reinforced them with a refreshed stump speech Jack delivered in targeted growth areas, including Dartmouth, Saint John, Saskatoon and Courtenay.

Our opponents took notice, hitting back with endgame attack ads. The Tory spot, called "Blind Ambition," was similar in substance and tone to an earlier attack ad against Ignatieff. "They say ambition can be blind. Just ask the NDP's Jack Layton," the ad said, showing black-and-white images of Jack and Duceppe set among dark shadows. "Jack

Layton and his coalition with the Bloc Québécois: he did it before, he'll do it again. And Canada will pay the price." Harper had been warning voters about an Ignatieff-led coalition with the NDP, supported by the Bloc. Now, Harper changed his stump speech to warn the country of an NDP-led coalition government.

It appeared the Liberals had never anticipated finding themselves in this predicament in the last week of the campaign: entrenched in third place and fading fast, with a surging NDP emerging as the main contender against the Conservatives. Their ad felt rushed. Entitled "Not so fast, Jack," it tried to scare voters by talking about the "unprincipled" NDP and its "incredibly inexperienced candidates." "After twenty-six years as a career politician, shouldn't Jack Layton know better? The NDP: evasion on gun control and chaos on the economy, higher taxes, no real team. Not so fast, Jack," the narrator warned, as a stoplight turned red to the sound of screeching brakes.

Once our endgame ad and the counter-attacks had time to sink in with voters, public opinion polls revealed what our internal numbers showed: the NDP still had upward momentum, the Liberals were still dropping and the Tory vote was slipping. We were closing in on Harper as the non-Conservative vote broke in our favour.

Ipsos-Reid polls always had the NDP lower than did other polling firms, but even they showed us at 33 per cent in a poll published on Friday, April 29. We were up nine points from the previous week and trailing the Conservatives by five points, now at 38 per cent. The Liberals had dropped to 18 per cent, down three points from the previous week.

WITH JUST THREE MORE CAMPAIGN days left, we had the momentum. But we had also seen our support drift away from us in the last seventy-two hours of a campaign, so we had to get the close of the endgame right.

Just after 2 PM on April 29, I was reviewing the stump speech Jack would deliver the next day in Burnaby, B.C. This would be our last weekend rally, and I was finessing the endgame message. Over the final few days, we wanted to close the deal with as many undecided voters as possible and lock in our supporters.

We were on a bit of a high from the day before, when more than eighteen hundred people had come out to see Jack in Saskatoon. It was our largest rally of the campaign to date, and the mood on the tour was electric. After being brushed off for a chunk of the campaign, the tour was now packed with representatives from various media outlets. Reuters and Bloomberg had joined the tour, and Al Jazeera was lining up election-night coverage. "The staffers on the NDP bus are obsessed with Journey's 'Don't Stop Believing.' Appropriate I guess," CBC's Rosemary Barton tweeted that night.

But things were about to change. As I worked on Jack's rally speech, I received an email at 1:54 PM from a reliable source, asking me to call her. "You want to call me on my cell," she wrote. When she didn't immediately hear from me, she emailed me back nine minutes later. "Seriously" is all it said. I took a few more minutes to finish up the speech and then I called her.

"Look, you didn't hear this from me," she said, "but the *Toronto Sun* has a hatchet job coming out in tomorrow's paper on Layton. Something about a massage parlour back when he was on city council. You need to be prepared."

I quizzed my source to assess the credibility of the claim and deduced this was for real. After I hung up, I turned to Jess Turk-Browne, the deputy campaign director I shared an office with during the campaign. "Close the door," I said to Jess. "Have you ever heard of an incident in Toronto about Jack and a massage parlour?"

"No, never," she replied.

The key to being able to defend your boss is to know everything in their past, no matter how bogus or embarrassing an allegation might be. It isn't just about being prepared; it's about trust. We thought we knew about all of the possible attacks that could be levelled against Jack from his thirty years in public life. We didn't know about this one.

I called Kory Teneycke, Harper's former director of communications, who was now a vice-president at Québecor Média, heading up the upstart Sun TV News. Québecor also owned a series of newspapers, including the Sun chain.

"Kory, it's Brad Lavigne. Look, I hear that you guys are running with some bullshit about Jack and a massage parlour from 1996. Do you know anything about it?" He was quiet. I broke the silence. "If you assholes run anything that even suggests any wrongdoing, I am going to spend my life's work amassing the resources to rain holy hell on your fucking heads. If there is one ounce of this that isn't absolutely 100 per cent fucking true, I am going to sue you fucking people for every goddamned dime that Péladeau [Québecor's chief executive officer at the time] has. Are we fucking clear?"

"Let me check into this and get back you," Teneycke said. He called back shortly after. "It looks like the story checks out. We have our sources, it's being run through legal and we are running with it. It's going in our papers tomorrow, and it will be on Sun TV tonight at eight. The *Toronto Sun* is looking for reaction. Here is the number of the guy at the *Toronto Sun*. Call him," said Teneycke, who later acknowledged to me that he knew nothing about the story until my call.

I turned to Turk-Browne. "Well, that didn't work." I called Anne McGrath and told her that I needed to talk to Jack immediately and that he needed to be alone. It was a pretty light day on the campaign trail because of the royal wedding. The media was all Will and Kate, all the time. After a mid-morning rally in Kamloops, the tour would be flying to the Vancouver Island North riding for an evening town hall in Courtenay at 6 PM local time.

When I reached McGrath, she and Jack were in the RCMP car and had just arrived at the airport for the flight to Courtenay. As the plane was being loaded, Anne sent a staffer to find a quiet spot in the hangar. The staffer found an office, and Jack sat in there on the couch. I filled him in on the situation as best we knew it.

"What do I need to know here, Jack?" I said.

"This is bullshit. Nothing ever happened," he assured me. He hung up the phone and turned to McGrath. "I need to call Olivia. Can I have the room?" By this time, the media were sitting on the tarmac waiting for Jack and Anne. They were getting antsy.

A few minutes later, Jack and McGrath called me back. We scheduled a conference call for when their plane landed. In the meantime, I would engage our legal counsel and develop our media lines. I called Brian Topp and walked him through the situation. "Any advice?" I asked.

"Call Olivia. Get her to make a statement. She's the best validator you're going to have on this," he said.

He was right. Olivia was eager to help in the push back. She remembered the incident and couldn't believe Sun Media, vocal critics in the past of both her and Jack during their time on city council, was trying to resurrect the story now. At the time of the incident, Jack and Olivia had told their long-time friend and Olivia's advisor at city hall, Bob Gallagher, about it. The incident was known around Toronto political circles, but it never made the newspapers. Jack was never charged with anything, and because Jack hadn't done anything wrong, he and Olivia didn't think anything more of it.

I quizzed her for all the facts and details so that we could craft a statement. We needed to get this right. Good crisis communications requires acting quickly and getting your side of the story out.

When the plane landed in Courtenay around 3:30 PM local time, the tour shuttled reporters to the Crown Isle Resort, where they would have a place to file and a few hours of downtime. It was a beautiful spring day as the bus pulled in. As McGrath recalls, the lilacs were in bloom, the fire hydrants were painted gold and a deer was running across the golf course.

McGrath darted off to a corner of the parking lot. There were golf carts whizzing by her, but this was the most private spot she could find to join a conference call with Topp, Turk-Browne and me to develop strategy. Most of the journalists were already goofing off. Some were at the driving range, where Nancy, Jack's sister, was teaching people how to perfect their golf swing. Others had headed to the bar with tour staff.

We were running against the clock. We had our media lines ready to go by now, and Olivia's statement was undergoing a final edit. It was time to brief Monk and Bélanger about what they were about to face as the campaign's spokespeople. Olivia's statement would be released before Sun TV went to air with the story at 8 PM EST, 5 PM in B.C.

In the meantime, we forwarded Monk, Bélanger and McGrath the final lines: "This is a smear campaign of the worst sort. This is another reason why we need change in this country. On the eve of an election, someone decided to go over the top now in attacking Mr. Layton. This is simply the latest attempt at character assassination. Mr. Layton has participated in 8 election campaigns in the past 16 years—no one has ever tried to make this an issue. This was a registered massage therapy clinic around the corner from Mr. Layton and Ms. Chow's house. Ms. Chow was aware of the appointment."

We wanted Olivia's statement to form the basis of our response and be part of every story filed that night. We didn't want reporters to scrum Jack in case he started deviating from the lines or got too far into the weeds with the details. That could be done by others later. The minute the public saw Olivia saying she knew about the incident, they would see it shouldn't be a problem for them. This was about a man getting a massage at a registered massage establishment licenced with the City of Toronto. This was a smear. That was the message.

When Sun TV and QMI, the wire service for Québecor's papers, teased on Twitter that they had a bombshell of a story that could change the election campaign, reporters travelling with the NDP started to suspect something was up. QMI reporter Kristy Kirkup, on tour with us, got a call from her newsroom to fill her in on her company's scoop. One thing was working in our favour: most journalists held Sun TV in such low regard that they were skeptical of the story before even knowing any details.

Three minutes before air time, we released Olivia's statement to the press.

"Sixteen years ago, my husband went for a massage at a massage clinic that is registered with the City of Toronto. He exercises regularly; he was and remains in great shape; and he needed a massage.

"I knew about this appointment, as I always do.

"No one was more surprised than my husband when the police informed him of allegations of potential wrongdoing at this establishment. He told me about the incident after it happened.

"Any insinuation of wrongdoing on the part of my husband is completely and utterly false, which is why after 16 years and 8 election campaigns that my husband has campaigned in, this has never been an issue.

"In the last hours of this election, this is nothing more than a smear campaign in an attempt to question my husband's character. This is another reason why politics in this country need to change, and on Monday, Canadians will have their chance to do just that."

We released the letter party lawyer Brian Iler had sent to Sun Media. It read in part,

> The facts are that Mr. Layton had obtained a massage from a massage therapist, but had no knowledge whatsoever that that therapist's location may have been used for illicit purposes. He does recall being advised by the police at the time that he did nothing wrong, but that the location was questionable, and to be stayed away from... Any statement or inference that Mr. Layton's actions or behaviour was other than the facts stated above would be without any factual basis, would clearly be made with malice, and ought not to be published. In fact, it would be irresponsible in the extreme for any such story to be printed. Damages, as you will appreciate, would be very significant.

The Sun story had been out for thirty minutes when reporters covering the NDP tour cornered Monk for a comment at an impromptu scrum. We hadn't anticipated this. The group was about to board the bus to the high school for Jack's rally, set to begin an hour after the story broke.

The mood on the tour had gone from jovial and light to brutal inside an hour. Monk bore the brunt of it, surrounded by a hoard of reporters with cameras who peppered her with questions. There were around a dozen of them, but it felt more like a hundred, she recalls.

"Why is there no statement from Mr. Layton himself, as he is the one that is subject to the allegations?" asked the *Toronto Star*'s Joanna Smith.

"I have gotten you comment from Ms. Olivia Chow," Monk said.

"We're requesting comment from the leader, who is here on the election campaign," interrupted Smith.

"Okay. We're good? Should we get on the bus?" Monk interrupted.

Monk was cut off again by another reporter who repeated innuendos and unsubstantiated allegations by Sun Media. Trying to get the reporters to move along, Monk told them the "event happened over sixteen years ago, and eight election campaigns have happened since that time. I suggest that we get ready, because we have a rally to go to."

Quebec reporters on the tour asked for a statement in French, so Bélanger jumped in. He'd been hovering throughout the scrum. He made a short statement, then decided to get out of there. In his haste, he walked right into a bank of fake trees in the lobby and had to push himself through. Luckily, his escape wasn't caught on tape.

After Monk had briefed headquarters about the unplanned scrum, we decided to have Jack make a brief statement on camera on his way into the high school, where seven hundred people were waiting for him. He wouldn't take any questions.

Jack stepped in front of the cameras and stuck to the lines. "It's unfortunate to see these smear campaigns starting in these last few days of the campaign. Absolutely nothing wrong was done, there's no wrongdoing here, but yet the smears start. This is why a lot of people get turned off politics and don't even want to get involved, and I think it's very unfortunate," he said before walking away from the pack of reporters. The media tried to follow him, but Jack kept on moving. One cameraman tripped and fell amid the chaos.

Inside the school gym Jack turned it on, delivering one of his best performances of the campaign. After the town hall, the team on the ground made sure he exited through a side door into an awaiting RCMP car.

Back at headquarters, we drafted separate lines to distribute to the local campaigns and sent them out at 9:31 PM, after I had signed off on them.

"Tonight, the self-professed conservative Sun News Network launched yet another smear campaign against Jack Layton. A statement by Olivia Chow repudiating the claims dating back from 1996 can be found here.

"This is the same kind of dirty attack politics that have become all too common in Ottawa in the last 5 years. It's part of why Ottawa's broken—and we have to fix it. Don't let your campaign get distracted. Our opponents see that our message is resonating and they want to knock us off it. Don't let them. If you needed proof that we are making conservatives very nervous, this last-minute smear is it. Keep up the great work!"

I gathered with a few senior folks in my office that evening to watch things unfold. Within a few minutes of the Sun broadcast, it appeared the story wasn't as bad as I'd feared. The best news was the reaction on Twitter. Within minutes of the story breaking, the twitterverse had turned on Sun TV, with journalists and commentators attacking the news outlet:

"Canadian politics hits new sordid low. Am sick at heart" (Frank Graves, EKOS). "It's a sad episode for Canadian politics" (Gerry Nicholls, former president of National Citizens Coalition). "I do enjoy that the cop in the Layton story boasts of the force's professionalism in not leaking it" (Adam Radwanski, the *Globe and Mail*). "Somebody at Sun should have had the news judgment, [if] nothing else, to realize. But then if they were about news or judgment they wouldn't be Sun, would they?" (Andrew Coyne, *Maclean's*). "Wow. You've got to be shitting me? 15 year-old story, no charges" (Stephen Wicary, the *Globe and Mail*). "Gosh, I hope this isn't some other lowlife trying to undermine #SunTvs credibility" (Tabatha Southey, the *Globe and Mail*). "Attack on Layton seems desperate & small. It may help him more than hurt, given apparent national mood." (Keith Baldrey, Global B.C.).

None of this changed the frame of the story in the *Toronto Sun*. Sun readers in Toronto woke up on Saturday morning to a giant picture of Jack's face on the front page of the paper with the words "BAWDY POLITICS" in large font. The subhead read: "Layton found naked in massage parlor: Former Cop; Wife denies he did wrong."

Our getting out in front of the story meant the coverage in the other media outlets was a little more nuanced. We'd stayed calm. We'd assembled our facts, developed a game plan and then executed it. But we'd also been very lucky to get the tip from my source earlier in the afternoon. That had given us a few hours to develop a response.

The worst thing you can do in such situations is hide and let your opponents have the field to themselves. We got our best validator out front, calmly and consistently delivering our message. Olivia's statement had also blunted the sting.

Of course, we didn't want any stories on the last weekend of the campaign to be about a massage sixteen years ago. And we still had to get through Jack's scrum that day in Vancouver. He was bombarded with questions, but he did a good job of sticking to the script and avoided getting weighed down by any insinuations.

The story also had our opponents a bit on the defensive by then. Both the Liberals and the Conservatives were forced to answer questions about whether they were behind the smear campaign. The Liberals in particular were vulnerable to the charge. They were in desperate shape, and news quickly surfaced that the party had shopped around the story to the media in the past.

The *National Post*'s Jonathan Kay turned to Twitter on Saturday to reveal what he knew in a series of tweets. "For those who care, someone tried to shop me the Layton-massage story 2 yrs ago (without docs). It was a Liberal fixer," wrote Kay. "To repeat: I have no idea who leaked the Layton/massage story this time around. But, if I had to *guess*, I'd say the most desperate party." "Michael Ignatieff was *not* Lib leader when Layton story was shopped to me by Libs. They shopped it to me on Oct 12, 2008."

The following day, Kay revealed even more damaging information in a news story. "I was shown a copy of a Liberal Party lawyer's Access to Information request seeking details of the massage bust—and I have retained that ATI request in my files," Kay told the *Montreal Gazette*. "Kay wouldn't say who the lawyer is, saying he promised the person his or her name wouldn't come out."

Liberal strategist and blogger Warren Kinsella also weighed in, confirming the story had already made the rounds among politicos in Toronto, where Jack and Olivia had plenty of enemies. "A Sun reporter called me about this story [Friday] afternoon. Before he could even describe what it was about—he said it involved 'a major political figure and the police'—I told him I already knew what it was about. In Toronto, and amongst many political people, this story has been pretty well-known for years. Someone came to me about it two years ago. I looked at what they had, thought about it for about sixty seconds, and then urged this person to forget all about it. I certainly planned to," Kinsella wrote on his blog.

The Liberal campaign now had their own problem to manage just before election day: denying they had had a hand in trying to tear down the guy who had just passed them in the polls.

Before all hell broke loose on Friday afternoon, I had already decided to fly out to B.C. on Saturday morning to attend the rally. It had been a whirlwind twenty-four hours, but I wanted to get a feel of the campaign up close. I was happy to be on the ground with McGrath and Jack in Vancouver. The *Toronto Star,* a Liberal-friendly newspaper, had endorsed us that morning. Angus Reid's last poll of the campaign, published that day in *La Presse* and the *Star,* showed us at 33 per cent, just four points below the Tories; the Liberals had dropped below 20 per cent. The poll also showed that Harper was now statistically tied with Jack as the "preferred Prime Minister" (31 to 29 per cent). Ignatieff was at 11 per cent.

Before the rally started at a film studio in Burnaby, Jack was at the nearby Hilton Hotel doing pre-taped interviews with media outlets. During a break, he wanted the three of us to have a moment alone. Jack insisted on a group hug. Some people saw Jack as a bit schlocky, but that was who he was: optimistic, loving and affectionate. "I just want to tell you two how much you mean to me and how much I appreciate everything you've done. So thank you," he said to Anne and me.

Not long after, Jack headed to the rally and took to the stage. "The winds of change are blowing across this great country of ours. You can feel it," Jack said to a packed hall. "And my friends, the winds of change are even blowing in Quebec." That line garnered the loudest applause of the day.

OUR SENIOR CAMPAIGN TEAM SET up shop at the InterContinental Hotel in downtown Toronto on election day. The hotel adjoined the Metro Toronto Convention Centre, where Jack would likely speak for the first time as something other than the leader of Canada's third or fourth party.

Despite the last-minute attempt to blunt our momentum, our internal tracking polling had showed we were still on the ascendancy on Saturday night, our last day in the field. Nanos's nightly overnight tracking poll had picked up the same trend on Saturday night: for the first time in the campaign, the NDP was tied with the Conservatives in his sample of decided voters that evening: 33.8 per cent each.

The other campaigns knew what we knew. On election day, the Liberals pulled volunteers and staffers from ridings across Toronto and poured their resources into trying to save Ignatieff's seat of Etobicoke–Lakeshore. The Bloc did the same in Montreal, focussing all their efforts in Duceppe's riding.

Drew Anderson was the lead on Jack's election-day speech, and we had prepared several versions: Conservatives win a majority with us as the Official Opposition; Conservatives win a minority with us holding the balance of power; we win a minority. I had told Anderson and a senior speechwriter in the campaign, Jim Rutkowski, to use the word "spring" in all the speeches to emphasize the theme of renewal. We settled on "Spring is here, my friends, and a new chapter begins."

Once the different versions of the speech had been put to bed, there was nothing left to do but wait. Election day is quiet for the leader and his inner circle; the job is done, and now it's up to the organizing crews around the country to pull the vote. The Herculean task was carried out under the leadership of our director of organization, Nathan Rotman.

Results always arrive in waves, starting in Atlantic Canada, where polls close before the rest of the country. As they started to roll in, I got a sinking feeling. There were a lot of Liberal holds, and we only had two pickups. I had to remind myself: we had always anticipated that Atlantic Canada would be the last Liberal holdout.

There was a quiet, nervous energy in our makeshift war room when the Quebec results started trickling in. It began with Gaspésie–Îles-de-la-Madeleine, the very French riding at the mouth of the St. Lawrence in the Atlantic Time Zone. We were leading. That was a very good sign. Then, when the polls closed in the Eastern Time Zone, the floodgates opened, and we passed the tipping point: no matter how the votes split in other provinces, we would have more seats than the Bloc and the Liberals at the end of the night, leapfrogging over both in a historic breakthrough.

In Ontario, the trend was showing a Liberal collapse in the country's most populous province. It looked as though Harper's last-minute message over the weekend, instilling fear about the NDP forming government, worked in enough places. We held our own, though, and won a record twenty-two seats, besting the Liberals both in the popular vote and in seats. They won just eleven seats across Ontario.

And for the first time, the Liberal fortress of Toronto crumbled. Most of the outskirts went blue, and the urban core and the east side of town went orange. It was now cool to be a New Democrat in Toronto, in sharp contrast to 2003 when Jack had become leader.

We remained upstairs in our hotel suites at the InterContinental, waiting quietly for the results from Western Canada to see whether Harper would get his majority. We were ecstatic about where we stood, but none of us showed the excitement we were feeling. The energy in the room downstairs, where we had booked our election-night party, was very different. The place lit up when the Toronto results were announced, showing eight NDP seats.

The ballroom was like a rock concert filling up before a big show. We had had to book the adjacent ballroom to accommodate the record crowds, many sporting fake moustaches in honour of Jack. While people waited, we played video clips from the campaign trail. They chanted Jack's inspirational lines in unison: "Together we can do this. You know where I stand. You know I am a fighter. And I won't stop until the job is done."

Just after 10 PM local time, I sent a note to Anderson. "Speech is good," I wrote, signalling him to load the "Conservative Majority, NDP Official Opposition" speech into the teleprompter.

When all the dust had settled, the NDP had won 103 seats and come in second in another 121 ridings. We'd taken an amazing 59 seats in Quebec, besting Mulroney's 1984 showing by 1. We would get our deposit back in all but two ridings, by far the highest percentage of any of the parties.

There were still some heartbreakers. The splits didn't go our way in Halifax West. In Sault Ste. Marie, our thoughtful MP Tony Martin was narrowly defeated by a Conservative. In Winnipeg North, Rebecca

Blaikie, the party's amazing Quebec organizer for all those years, lost by about a hundred votes to one of only four Liberals who managed to win a seat west of Ontario. Blaikie had returned to her hometown a few years earlier to work as a community organizer. Had she run in Quebec, she would have been on her way to the House of Commons.

In Saskatchewan, our popular vote had risen to 32 per cent (compared with the Liberal Party's 8.5 per cent, and 56 per cent for the Tories), but lopsided boundaries with huge swaths of rural land tossed in with urban communities meant we failed to win a single seat. Nettie Wiebe was within 540 votes of knocking off a Tory backbencher in Saskatoon–Rosetown–Biggar, but that was the closest we'd come. In Alberta, although we'd solidified ourselves as the alternative to the Tories, the gap was too big to overcome, even in Edmonton, where Linda Duncan was again the sole NDP MP elected. In British Columbia, we had targeted Vancouver Island North and Nanaimo–Alberni, but we had come just a little short in both ridings, losing to Conservative candidates.

In the end, with 166 seats, Harper got his majority, just as the networks had called it. Now it was time for each party leader, in turn, to address their supporters and other Canadians on live TV. Those with fewer seats went first, so Jack, Anne, Brian and I took more time than usual to make our way down to the hall.

Even so, we showed up a bit too early; the big losers of the night, Duceppe and Ignatieff, hadn't wrapped up their speeches yet. Brian Topp noticed that Jack, ecstatic but exhausted after a gruelling campaign that had begun just twenty-two days after his hip surgery, was in pain. Jack was standing in the long corridor, facing another fifteen minutes of waiting on his feet. We got him a chair.

"I can't sit if everyone else has to stand," the newly elected Leader of the Official Opposition said. What to do? wondered Topp. We needed Jack ready to deliver the speech of his life. "Well, I'm going to sit down," said Topp, seating himself on the floor.

"Okay, now we're equal," Jack said, laughing as he took his seat.

CHAPTER 13:

113 DAYS

It had been a whirlwind spring for Jack, and immediately after the election on May 2, he switched gears and turned his mind to building the office of the Leader of the Opposition. He was supported by an eleven-member transition team: MPs Tom Mulcair, Libby Davies, Malcolm Allen, Jean Crowder and David Christopherson; advisors Brian Topp, Matt Hebb and Bob Dewar; and staffers Ray Guardia, appointed Jack's special Quebec advisor; chief of staff Anne McGrath; and me, newly appointed as Jack's principal secretary.

Our new centre of gravity was the Opposition leader's office, so that's where I'd be working along with Anne and Karl Bélanger, who would continue as senior press secretary, and George Soule, Jack's executive assistant. Jess Turk-Browne and Nathan Rotman left party headquarters to join us. They would oversee the hiring and training of Hill staffers, by far the biggest staff complement in the NDP's history. My mandate was to maintain the political momentum we had gained during the last campaign. The plan was for me to spend two years in Jack's office on Parliament Hill, then return to the party office to prepare for the next campaign, set for 2015.

With senior staff and the transition team in place, we next had to put together a strong Shadow Cabinet. New Democrat MPs would be sitting directly across from the government side for the first time in our history. Jack agreed that we should match up Harper's Cabinet picks with people who would make for a strong contrast and shine as NDP counterpoints to Tory cabinet ministers during Question Period.

The Shadow Cabinet took many days to build, since we had to balance region, gender and experience. It wasn't easy, especially with so many new MPs, the majority of whom we did not know much about. Jack also insisted that everyone—all 103 New Democrat MPs—be given a job to do. He had been close to his late father and had learned lessons about caucus management from him. Not long after the May vote, Jack reached out to his dad's old boss, Brian Mulroney, who had appointed Robert Layton to his Cabinet in 1984 and later as his long-time national PC caucus chair. "He and I worked very closely on areas of caucus relations," Mulroney said of Jack's father, "and he had spoken to Jack about the way I'd handled caucus."

Jack called Mulroney and the two spoke for about an hour and a half. "I have gone from A to B here, and B is the Official Opposition with a large delegation of Quebecers who have never been in Parliament before," Mulroney remembers Jack saying. "They don't know a great deal about the rest of Canada and vice versa, and so caucus management is going to be the highest priority for me, as it is for any leader in the British parliamentary system who understands the true nature of political success." Mulroney continued, "Without the caucus, you can't get across the street. Without caucus loyalty, you can't get anywhere, and so Jack said to me, 'Look, everybody knows about your success with caucus, starting with my own father. I'd like to talk to you about it.' All I could tell him is how it had worked for me, and he took it all in."

The press gallery wrote their predictable stories, musing about whether the NDP team, especially our young Quebec caucus, was ready for prime time, but we knew we had the bench strength to go toe to toe with Harper's team. We aimed to set up pairings that would not only highlight our talent but also contrast the fundamental differences between the two parties.

Jack appointed former Canadian Auto Workers union negotiator Peggy Nash from the Toronto riding of Parkdale–High Park as finance critic to go up against former Mike Harris cabinet minister Jim Flaherty from the GTA riding of Whitby–Oshawa. He put environmental lawyer Megan Leslie from Halifax up against climate change deniers Peter Kent and Joe Oliver, ministers of the environment and natural resources respectively. Jack assigned the young Alexandre Boulerice from the

Montreal riding of Rosemont–La Petite-Patrie as critic for the Treasury Board, up against another alumnus of the Harris government, Tony Clement.

In total, 42 per cent of the Shadow Cabinet were from Quebec and 40 per cent were women. Our team was young, fresh proof of what it looked like when two political parties with real differences squared off against each other.

The party's general convention in Vancouver, set to run from June 17 to 19, 2011, meant Jack couldn't stop to take a break after the election. We were marking the fiftieth anniversary of the party on the heels of our historical breakthrough, and we needed to put on a strong show, with Jack at the centre of it.

Jack was in good form at the convention in Vancouver, where he received an approval vote of 97.9 per cent in his leadership review. He was feeling fatigued when he flew back to Ottawa on the Sunday, but he took solace in the fact that the parliamentary session was almost done. He just had a few more sitting days in the House and one evening event that week at Stornoway, the official residence of the Leader of the Official Opposition. After that, he'd be able to head back home to Toronto for the summer to recharge. We were no longer in a minority Parliament, so we were all going to gear down over the next two months and come back recharged in the fall to take on Harper and start building for the next election.

Labour Minister Lisa Raitt had thrown a wrinkle into Jack's plan on Monday, June 20, when she tabled provocative legislation to order postal workers back to work; they had been locked out for a week after a few weeks of rotating job action. The NDP weren't going to be doormats, so we opted to filibuster the legislation. This meant the session would drag on past Thursday, but Jack thought it was important to draw attention to the government's attack on collective bargaining and buy time for the two sides to reach a settlement.

Jack felt unwell all week. He was supposed to make a quick detour to Montreal on Friday, June 24, to celebrate Saint-Jean-Baptiste Day, but even before it became apparent Jack would be stuck in Ottawa because of the filibuster, he'd told Bélanger he didn't think he would be able to walk the parade route. He was also showing some signs of discomfort on Wednesday evening, just before the filibuster was set to begin. Jack hosted a barbecue dinner that night for NDP caucus and staff and their families at Stornoway. He arrived a bit late because of his duties in the House and mingled before delivering a short speech. He was upbeat, but he seemed to be favouring one hip while relying heavily on his cane. I just figured he was exhausted.

By late Saturday, June 25, the fifty-eight-hour filibuster in the House of Commons was coming to an end. Jack had kicked off the debate on Thursday evening with an hour-long speech. He pressed forward despite the pain he was feeling and the "Union Jack" jeers from the government side. Over the next two days, he was in and out of the House to support the NDP MPs, including seventy newly elected rookies, who were rotated through Parliament for the around-the-clock debate. The filibuster had the effect of gelling the new team of inexperienced MPs, and Jack had insisted on being in the chamber for the final vote. As the vote neared, he turned to Mulcair, his new House Leader. "Tom, will you be able to give the wrap-up speech? I'm feeling a little discomfort," Jack said.

"Yeah, Jack," Mulcair replied.

"And can you scrum after it's all done?" asked Jack.

Mulcair stood up and gently patted Jack on the back. "Of course," said Mulcair. He was concerned, though, he recalls, because Jack's suit jacket was soaking with sweat.

In the days after the end of the parliamentary session, Jack was back in Toronto, doing a series of medical tests. He either cabbed to the hospital with Olivia or got a lift from his son or son-in-law. Either way, Olivia was usually with Jack. Other patients and personnel recognized Jack, but they didn't snap pictures of him. "People were respectful. I just think that people are not that intrusive in Canada. I think they respect someone's privacy," recalls Jack's son, Mike.

Jack pressed ahead with a few public events. On June 28, he and Olivia flew to Ottawa to host the annual summer garden party reception for Parliament Hill reporters at Stornoway. Instead of mingling, he sat at a table with his mother, Doris, and his mother-in-law, Ho Sze, who had both come to town for the event. Reporters inquired about how Jack was feeling, but they weren't aggressive about it, as they had been in March when he'd had hip surgery. "His hip is bothering him. He's not feeling well," Monk explained to anyone who asked. At the end of the evening, Jack and Olivia slept at Stornoway for the first—and only—time. He had been so busy in the weeks after the election that moving into the historic home just wasn't a priority for them.

Jack insisted on attending Toronto's Gay Pride Parade on July 3. Unlike in past years, he and Olivia sat in a rickshaw instead of riding their bikes or walking the route. Two days later, he attended a celebration in his honour hosted by members of the Chinese community in his riding.

On July 9, their wedding anniversary, Jack and Olivia hosted an engagement party at their home for Mike and his fiancée. "He was in good spirits," recalls Mike.

Mike and Sarah, Jack's daughter, had gone in on a video recorder and a good microphone as a gift for Jack and Olivia's anniversary. The idea was to continue a family tradition that Jack had started with his own parents. Jack would sit down with his old video recorder and ask his mother and father about their parents and grandparents, and about what life had been like for them growing up.

When Mike and Sarah purchased the gift, they didn't know how serious their father's illness was. "I don't think I ever realized that, and neither did my sister," Mike says when asked whether he believed his father could die.

The new video recorder was put to work right away. "Like he had done with his dad and mom, he sat down and we did these interviews, just me asking questions like, 'What was it like then?' We did it for a little bit, not as much as I would have liked, but we did do it for many hours, where it was just him and me shooting the shit... Sometimes other people would be there and they would chime in," Mike remembers. "So we got that time. Us doing the interviews wasn't an acknowledgement of an end coming near, [just that] we may as well try and document some of this, because people do die... He liked to tell stories."

Jack had a nice set-up in his bedroom on the third floor of the row house he shared with Olivia, the epicentre of their activism. The loft had an ensuite bathroom and a large balcony covered in flowers. He'd sit out on the balcony under the patio umbrella and hang out with visitors, read or listen to his iPod. He even received a haircut during a house call from his barber.

Jack was an optimist at his core, and this perspective had become even more pronounced after his diagnosis with prostate cancer in December 2009. "I often say getting a cancer diagnosis, in terms of your view of the world, it's a little like switching from watching black-and-white TV to watching colour," Jack explained in the NDP video shot in January 2011. "I'm old enough to remember what that was like. It's just such a difference. You look at every moment in your life as a gift, and that's a wonderful experience. Ironically, you'd think with a bad news diagnosis, if anything, you'd be looking at the greys, you'd be looking at the dark side. But at least for me, and I know for many people who are surviving cancer, it's the opposite."

Becoming a grandfather that year had been equally transformative for Jack. "There is nothing more exciting, thrilling and precious than holding a grandchild in your arms, and then how fast they grow and how fast it changes, and before you know it, they're getting heavy to hold in your arms," Jack explained in the video. "You're looking in their eyes, and they're looking at you. And when you're singing a song to them and when they're laughing and playing with you and you feel that hand going around that finger and squeezing—these are the intimacies you really can't put into words. I knew it was going to be great. I now know why grandparents all walk around smiling," said Jack, who noted his grand-daughter's birth on June 17 in his electronic calendar. "Born at 12:03 AM, Toronto Women's Hospital, such a happy day. Born 8 lbs, 1 oz." By the summer of 2011, Beatrice was a toddler, and Jack's daughter, Sarah, was expecting a second child.

Jack was preparing to receive the results of a major test later in July from the oncology department of the Princess Margaret Hospital. While he waited, he had some thoughtful meetings with Reverend

Brent Hawkes, pastor of the Metropolitan Community Church of Toronto, where Jack and Olivia were members. Jack was deeply spiritual, and the congregation suited them both: it was open, progressive and activist-oriented. During this period, Jack turned sixty-one.

Anne McGrath visited Jack at his home weekly, and she had already begun discussions with Jack and Topp about different options in the event that Jack needed to step aside for health reasons. When Jack received his major test results on Wednesday, July 20, he called McGrath. Olivia was by his side. It was evening, but McGrath was still at the office in Ottawa, she recalls. "The news isn't good. They found a new cancer. I'm going to fight it, but things aren't great," Jack, sounding apologetic, told McGrath. "I need you to present me with some scenarios," Jack said.

Earlier in July, Jack had asked Brian Topp, newly elected party president at the Vancouver convention, to review the NDP's constitution concerning the process for interim leadership. "Jack, you asked me about the rules on this matter," Topp wrote and then cited the relevant section of the constitution: "'Should the position of Leader become vacant at any point, the Council may, in consultation with the parliamentary Caucus, appoint a Leader for the interim period until a new Leader has been elected.' The trigger here is the office 'becoming vacant.'"

During their discussions, McGrath and Topp had decided that if Jack needed to step aside temporarily, they would recommend Nycole Turmel, who had been elected in the Quebec riding of Hull–Aylmer in May and who was caucus chair, to serve as interim leader.

Now McGrath—and Jack—knew the moment had arrived. "He was quite aware that he was going to step aside," McGrath remembers about their conversation on July 20.

"Walk me through your arguments," Jack told McGrath about the Turmel recommendation. The interim leader had to be someone bilingual, and it should be someone from Quebec but not someone who might go for the leadership at a later date, McGrath explained. Turmel was a new MP, but her long tenure as president of the Public Service Alliance of Canada meant she had significant experience running a national organization.

"He was in agreement with it. He was worried about it. He was worried about every possibility," recalls McGrath. Jack, Olivia and Anne agreed on the phone that Jack would make the announcement in Toronto on Monday, July 25.

Jack had received the results five days earlier than expected, and McGrath couldn't immediately reach Topp, who was on a canoe trip with his family. She enlisted Sue Milling, who contacted a park warden to find Topp. On Thursday, Topp called and got the news. McGrath also called the senior staff, one by one, into her office in Ottawa to inform us of the development.

"Things aren't good. Jack's not well. He's going to step down as leader. He's fighting a new battle, and he needs to take some time," McGrath told each of us. "Funny how you can be in shock when you can also expect something," says McGrath today.

Bélanger had just begun his holidays, so McGrath called him back to the office to speak with him in person, hinting there was an issue with Jack's health. When Karl arrived, Anne explained that Jack would be taking a leave of absence to focus on a treatment plan. "I let the news sink in, but I was not totally shocked," he recalled. He had spent a lot of time with Jack in June, and he knew about some new growing pain and discomfort.

While Karl was there, McGrath was able to get Jack on the phone. "That's when I was actually shocked for the first time, when I heard the voice for the first time. Anne had told me that he had lost a lot of weight and was pale, but she hadn't mentioned how raspy he sounded," Karl would later recount. "I quickly composed myself, and Jack started apologizing for interrupting my vacation. He apologized for what was happening."

"There is no need to apologize, sir. Anne informed me that this was why I make the big bucks," Bélanger joked.

Karl didn't call Jack "sir" very often. Jack didn't like it. "Call me Jack," he had told Karl after Karl called him "sir" when the two first met at the leadership convention. After that, "I would only use 'sir' when I wanted to signal he was taking himself too seriously, when I needed to lighten the atmosphere or when things were very, very serious. This situation qualified," Bélanger later explained.

At the end of their conversation, Jack's voice began to crack just as he started to apologize again for putting them through this. He couldn't complete his sentence. "It is our honour to serve you, sir," Karl said, "and we will see you Monday."

Kathleen Monk and Bélanger were put in charge of the press conference in Toronto, and their job was to organize it while making sure word didn't leak out in advance. They enlisted Rick Devereux from the party office and the production company Project X to produce the event. I was assigned, along with Topp, McGrath and Anderson, to help Jack and Olivia with the statement. It would fall to me to brief the staff on Parliament Hill in Ottawa, which we would do just before Jack's press conference.

McGrath flew to Toronto on Saturday morning. She had arranged with Nycole Turmel's assistant for Turmel to call her at 6:30 that evening, but Turmel did not yet know what the phone meeting with Jack's chief of staff was about. When McGrath arrived at Jack and Olivia's house in late afternoon, Jack was in the living room talking on the telephone with his mother, who split her time between Toronto and Florida. No matter what was going on in his life—even election campaigns—he spoke to his mother every day. That afternoon, Jack was talking to her about Turmel. He was concerned about asking his long-time friend to take on duties no rookie MP should ever be asked to assume—leading the Official Opposition while he fought cancer.

After he hung up, Jack and McGrath reviewed the scheduled call with Turmel. "Before the call, he wanted a full briefing. He was nervous about the call. He wanted me to go through the scenario again, how it would work," recalls McGrath.

Turmel called McGrath's cellphone at the designated time. McGrath spoke to her for a few minutes to prepare her a bit. "Jack isn't well, and he has something to ask you," she told Turmel, before passing the phone to Jack. "I felt really horrible for her," recalls McGrath. His voice was starting to get quite weak at that point, and he was emotional."

The call was brief. Usually, Jack and Turmel would speak to each other in French, but that evening, Jack spoke in English as he outlined his medical situation. "Will you step in as interim leader while I work on my health?" Jack asked her. Turmel immediately said yes.

Jack passed the phone back to McGrath, who thanked Turmel. "We will meet when I'm back in Ottawa, and we will be there to help you with all of it," she told the caucus chair. "I knew it was a shock," McGrath says today. "I knew she was feeling quite overwhelmed."

After the call, Jack's mother phoned to ask how it had gone. "Yes, Anne said it went well," Jack relayed. But he was emotional about what had just happened. Part of him felt as though he was burdening his friend with his illness. As his condition worsened, he felt he was letting other people down.

The next day, Jack emailed me a copy of the draft speech he and Olivia had prepared with Topp and McGrath. I was visiting family in B.C. with my kids for a long weekend on a prearranged vacation. I would now fly back to Ottawa early Monday for the press conference and return the next day to pick up my kids. Once I got a copy of the speech, I turned the picnic table at my brother's cottage into my workstation. The statement began like Jack's announcement about his prostate cancer had: it was direct and succinct about his diagnosis. The statement then transitioned to his recommendation for Turmel to serve as interim leader while he underwent treatment. He had also insisted on setting a return date, and the opening of Parliament on September 19 made the most sense.

For Jack, the statement was also deeply personal, and he wanted to weave a political call for building a green, caring Canada into his message of love, hope and optimism. I amended the love stuff, since it seemed a little un–prime ministerial to me, but Jack put it back in. This was who he was, and he was going to lay it all out in his own words.

By 8:30 PM in Toronto, the revisions to the speech were done, and Jack's statement was being translated.

Just after 8 AM on Monday, about six hours before the press conference, McGrath sent a note to me and the other members of the senior team. "Hi folks: Today will be a tough day for all of us and it's the start of one of our most difficult weeks. I have complete confidence that we'll all rise to the challenge. We will pull this off with sensitivity, professionalism, and clear heads. We've all been through a lot together and we will use all our resources to make sure that we are not set back," she wrote.

"Our goal is to replace this Conservative government with an NDP government and under Jack Layton's leadership we've come the closest ever. I feel confident that his contribution will continue and that part of his legacy will be the team that we've assembled. We've worked hard together under challenging situations and pulled off miracles. Let's keep that spirit in our minds and hearts this week. We will move on together, support each other and the interim Leader, and keep the Layton legacy going."

When Jack woke up on that hot Toronto day, his weakened, raspy voice matched how ill he felt. But he pressed ahead, labouring to put on the suit he would wear to make the most important announcement of his life. At 2 PM, he would go before the cameras to reveal he was stepping aside as leader of the NDP to fight a new cancer. He had insisted from the start on making the announcement himself. "I want to do it. This is something I need to do," he had told Kathleen Monk.

One of Monk's jobs that morning was to get Jack to the Hilton Hotel on Richmond Street, where he had launched the party's 2011 campaign platform just two months earlier, without any news cameras capturing images of him struggling to walk with his cane. He deserved that dignity. She arranged for Jack's assistant, Eiman Zarrug, to drop off him and Olivia at the loading dock at the back of the hotel before 11 AM so that he could arrive before the media advisory for the event went out to newsrooms.

Jack made it up the ramp and down the service hallway into the service elevator to head to his hotel room on the eleventh floor. He would rest and make some calls from there before going down to a second-floor room for the press conference. His progress "was long and tortuous and painful," recalls Monk. The hotel room was small, but she had booked it because it was the closest to the service elevator. Jack's children, Mike and

Sarah, were there, along with Brian Topp and Anne McGrath. The media team were downstairs setting up for the event.

Jack had to make a few key calls to leaders in the caucus, so McGrath had drawn up the list for him: deputy leaders Tom Mulcair and Libby Davies, deputy caucus chair Peter Julian and whip Chris Charlton. Jack was distracted after putting all of his energy and focus on the public announcement, and he needed a reminder before each call about whom he was calling and what he needed to cover. "Who's next?" he would ask McGrath as she dialled.

"Chris Charlton, MP for Hamilton Mountain."

"Remind me what she does again?"

"She's the new whip, Jack."

"Right," he said.

"It was a heartbreaking moment," recalls McGrath.

Mulcair was at his cottage in the Laurentians, where he didn't have a television, telephone or cell coverage. His assistant, Graham Carpenter, enlisted his father-in-law, who was in the region, to drive to Mulcair's cottage to give him the urgent message. Mulcair got through to Jack before the press conference started. Davies also missed his initial call but was able to reach Jack before the announcement. Mulcair jumped in his car with his wife, Catherine, to drive to his mother's place to watch the press conference.

As the press conference drew near, Jack headed back to the service elevator and down to the second floor. He rested in a holding room with Olivia and his children, along with McGrath, Milling and a few other staffers. A television was set up so that his family could watch his announcement from there, instead of having to watch it alongside reporters.

Just before the press event, McGrath alerted the chiefs of staff to the prime minister and interim Liberal leader Bob Rae about Jack's announcement. In Ottawa, fifteen minutes before the news conference was scheduled to begin, I brought together all caucus, MP and party staff as well as any MPs in town to brief them. Jack wanted everybody in the same room to watch the announcement, he had instructed me, to remind us that we were family and that we were going to get through this together. As the staff streamed in, they were relieved of their BlackBerries to make sure word didn't leak out.

The room went silent as Jack appeared on the giant television screen. His physical transformation in just a few weeks had been radical, and the silence was broken by gasps as people reacted to his dramatic weight loss, flushed face and shaky voice. Many of the staffers were looking at me for clues as to how bad his condition really was. I kept a brave face.

> Good afternoon. On February 5, 2010, I shared with Canadians that I, like twenty-five thousand other Canadian men every year, had been diagnosed with prostate cancer. I have received overwhelming support from my loving family, my friends, my caucus and party, and thousands of everyday Canadians. Their stories and support have touched me. And I have drawn strength and inspiration from them.
>
> In the closing days of the most recent session of the House of Commons, I suffered from some stiffness and pain. After the House rose, I undertook a series of tests at Princess Margaret Hospital in Toronto. My battle against prostate cancer is going very well. My PSA levels remain virtually undetectable. However, these tests, whose results I received last week, also indicate that I have a new, non-prostate cancer that will require further treatment. So, on the advice of my doctors, I am going to focus on treatment and recovery.
>
> I will therefore be taking a temporary leave of absence as Leader of the New Democratic Party of Canada. I'm going to fight this cancer now, so I can be back to fight for families when Parliament resumes.
>
> To that end, I have requested that the president of our party, Brian Topp, consult our parliamentary caucus and then convene a meeting of our party's federal council to appoint an interim leader. The interim leader will serve until I resume my duties. I intend to do so when Parliament meets on September 19.
>
> I am also making a recommendation on who the interim leader should be. I suggest that Hull–Aylmer MP Nycole Turmel be named interim leader during this period.
>
> Ms. Turmel enjoys unanimous support as the national chair of our parliamentary caucus. She is an experienced national leader in

both official languages. And she will do an excellent job as our national interim leader.

Let me conclude by saying this. If I have tried to bring anything to federal politics, it is the idea that hope and optimism should be at their heart. We CAN look after each other better than we do today. We CAN have a fiscally responsible government. We CAN have a strong economy, greater equality, a clean environment. We CAN be a force for peace in the world.

I am as hopeful and optimistic about all of this as I was the day I began my political work, many years ago. I am hopeful and optimistic about the personal battle that lies before me in the weeks to come. And I am very hopeful and optimistic that our party will continue to move forward.

We WILL replace the Conservative government a few short years from now. And we WILL work with Canadians to build the country of our hopes

Of our dreams

Of our optimism

Of our determination

Of our values...

Of our love.

Thank you.

In Ottawa, many of the staff were in tears. I opened the floor up for questions.

"What do you mean he's going to be back in September? He looks like he's dying," one person said.

"We can't think that right now. We have to keep working hard for our MPs. We have to make sure the interim leader has all the support she needs," I replied.

Watching from his mother's place in Quebec, Mulcair, too, was taken aback. "He'd had cancer for a while, and you'd always think that he's going to pull through. It wasn't denial. It was confidence. This guy is going to make it through this. But when I saw him on TV that day, I was very concerned," recalls Mulcair.

Mike Layton, watching his father on the television screen in the holding room, had a different reaction. "Why is he even bothering to do this?" he thought to himself. "I was convinced that it was a temporary situation. I didn't think his voice or colouring had changed that much, maybe because I was around him all the time. Typically, he was in pretty good shape. So none of that sunk in... Later on, I realized, 'Yeah, it was difficult when he was out there.' I think all of us... thought it was a temporary thing, or wanted to think that."

McGrath, feeling like a nervous parent at a dance recital, was relieved when the announcement was over. "I was so concerned for him getting through it. I was trying to put my strength, my force into him. I knew it was really important to him. He felt an obligation to do it, but I knew it was physically really hard for him and emotionally really hard," she recalls.

Jack stood up slowly after his announcement. With the help of his cane and with Olivia by his side, he walked back to the holding room behind the black curtain. McGrath hugged him; so did his children. Jack thanked everyone for helping him get through it. He was also very proud of himself. "My doctors weren't sure I'd be able to do it," he told the others. The group chatted until all the reporters had left the hotel, allowing Jack to avoid flashing cameras.

As Jack got into the car to head home with Olivia, Nigel Wright called McGrath. Harper's chief of staff had emailed her immediately after the press conference, saying the prime minister would like to speak with Jack, and the two had arranged this time. McGrath handed Jack her phone and the two men chatted briefly.

Not long after he got home, Jack posted a tweet, his last. "Your support and well wishes are so appreciated. Thank you. I will fight this—and beat it." Just after the dinner hour, McGrath sent an email to the senior staff.

"This was an incredibly tough day but we carried it off well. The Leader was very happy with the entire production and proud of his team. We have more to do but this was a big moment and I was confident all day that we could rise to the occasion. Everyone went above and beyond and put the greater goals ahead of our own personal feelings about the news we had to share with Canadians. The Leader did well and we all did well. It's a day to be sad but also to be proud and, as the Leader said, hopeful and optimistic. Thank you so much for being competent, patient, and always ready to do more."

Jack's mother, Doris, sent her son an email that night just after 10 PM. "Am sure you're tired after ordeal today—you deserve a good rest. Am going to bed now—hope to talk in the morning. Sleep well my sweet son—you are loved by so many more people than you can imagine."

JACK TRIED LIKE HELL TO push off death. A day after his press conference, he brought together his medical team and informed them he wanted to try whatever he could. "I'm going to challenge them," he told McGrath. He had always done the same thing with his political team in Ottawa. "He'd say, 'Assemble the team. Okay, we're at 20 per cent. How are we going to get to 25 per cent?'" McGrath remembers.

Ultimately, the aggressive new cancer cells took over, and Jack, a details guy and planner to the end, asked McGrath and Topp to work with him on crafting a final message to Canadians. Over the next few weeks, they spoke to Jack about what he wanted to say and worked on various drafts with him. It was important to Jack to keep the party's work going after his death, but he also wanted to strike an optimistic tone that would motivate people and give them hope.

On Saturday, August 20, Topp and McGrath went to Jack's house to do more work on the message with Jack and Olivia. By then, Jack found the stairs difficult to manage, so the family had transformed the living room into his bedroom with a hospital bed set up next to the front window. The four of them went through it word by word, using an iPad to take notes. Section by section, they read out loud what they had, and Jack interrupted. "Okay, walk me through our thinking," he'd say. Or, he'd stop to ask Olivia, "Is that okay with you, love? What about this?"

Periodically, Topp and Olivia would head up to the study on the second floor to input the edits on the desktop computer. McGrath would stay with Jack. He'd rest, and then the two would go through it again. After five hours, the letter was done. The plan was to release it after his death.

"To other Canadians who are on journeys to defeat cancer and to live their lives, I say this: please don't be discouraged that my own journey hasn't gone as well as I had hoped. You must not lose your own hope... You have every reason to be optimistic, determined, and focused on the future. My only other advice is to cherish every moment with those you love at every stage of your journey, as I have done this summer," Jack wrote.

To the members of the NDP, he wrote in part, "Let's continue to move forward. Let's demonstrate in everything we do in the four years before us that we are ready to serve our beloved Canada as its next government."

"Our caucus meetings were always the highlight of my week," Jack wrote to his caucus colleagues. "It has been my role to ask a great deal from you. And now I am going to do so again."

To his "fellow Quebecers," Jack wrote, "On May 2nd, you made an historic decision... You made the right decision then; it is still the right decision today; and it will be the right decision right through to the next election, when we will succeed, together."

"Many of you have placed your trust in our party," he wrote to young Canadians. "As my time in political life draws to a close I want to share with you my belief in your power to change this country and this world... I believe in you. Your energy, your vision, your passion for justice are exactly what this country needs today."

And "finally, to all Canadians," Jack wrote, "Canada is a great country, one of the hopes of the world. We can be a better one—a country of greater equality, justice, and opportunity... We can do all of these things because we finally have a party system at the national level where there are real choices; where your vote matters; where working for change can actually bring about change. My friends, love is better than anger. Hope is better than fear. Optimism is better than despair. So let us be loving, hopeful and optimistic. And we'll change the world."

"Jack was relieved," recalls McGrath. "He really wanted to make sure we were happy with it. He was always checking to make sure it was okay. Everything he did was as a team. He always said his two key words were 'team' and 'respect.'"

Early that evening, Topp and McGrath left the house, anticipating other visits over the next few weeks.

I had travelled to Toronto with McGrath a week earlier to visit Jack. We sat in the living room, next to his bed. He was in his usual chair with his bathrobe on. We all thought we had a few more weeks with Jack, so this wasn't goodbye but a check-in.

Jack had good days and bad days, and he wasn't feeling well the day of my visit. Our conversation was light as Olivia came in and out of the room. I mentioned the new polls, which showed us in a good position, to give him some assurance.

"Jack, I was on the phone this morning with Rob Fleming. We were recounting the story of how we encouraged you to run for leader," I joked, referring to that fateful night of drinking in Victoria with my old friend back in January 2001. He nodded and smiled. "I'll see you soon, Jack," I said as I left.

Throughout this period, Jack received dozens of emails from people expressing their love and concern. On August 8, he received a touching note from Laureen Harper. Under the subject line "A big juicy steak..." she wrote: "Good afternoon Jack and Olivia, I am sorry I didn't email you earlier to offer our best wishes (I know you talked to my husband). I was away hiking in the Yukon and lived days without any media. Just wanted to offer up a nice steak when you get back to Ottawa cooked by me. You are in our hearts and prayers (my heart, Stephen's prayers)."

Tom Mulcair also wrote to Jack that afternoon, sending one of his regular emails. *"Nous sommes avec toi"* (We're with you), read the subject line. *"Salut Jack, Juste un petit mot pour dire que Catherine et moi pensons fort à toi. Ton courage et ta détermination nous inspirent tous."* (Hi Jack, Simply wanted to tell you that Catherine and I are with you in spirit. Your courage and determination inspire us all.)

The day after Jack completed his letter to Canadians, Kathleen Monk spent the day at the house. She was there to begin the conversation with Olivia about Jack's funeral, something he and Olivia had talked about in the preceding weeks. He had even emailed some of his ideas to Olivia, which would later be incorporated into the service. It was the last email Jack ever sent.

When Monk left to catch her 9 PM flight back to Ottawa on August 21, she knew she wasn't going to see Jack again. "You could just tell," Monk remembers. She called McGrath when she landed to tell her. "We do not have three weeks."

Shortly after 11 PM, Jack's mother, Doris, called her son to say goodbye one last time. "Hi mom," Jack said softly. "You've had a great life, Jack. It's time to close your eyes and sleep now, son."

Just after midnight, Monk and McGrath received a quick note from Olivia, saying that this was it.

By then, family members and close friends had assembled at the house. Jack, the consummate planner, had made sure that his personal affairs were taken care of, party affairs were in order and his letter to Canadians was complete. He had checked off all of the boxes on his task list. He could let go.

Just before sunrise at 4:45 AM on Monday, August 22, 113 days after being elected leader of Her Majesty's Loyal Opposition, John Gilbert Layton—husband, grampa and sixth leader of the New Democratic Party of Canada—died.

CHAPTER 14:
THE LAYTON LEGACY

It was August 22, 2012, the one-year anniversary of Jack's death, and the team he had assembled was back together at Toronto's historic Necropolis Cemetery to attend a private ceremony for the interment of his ashes.

It was a perfect summer day, sunny but not too hot. McGrath, Topp, Anderson, Rotman, Gallagher and I joined Olivia; Jack's mother, Doris; and other family members and friends around a bronze bust of Jack. It had been sculpted by Olivia, who began her professional life as a sculptor after completing art school. Jack's headstone sat atop a piece of Laurentian pink granite from Quebec and was surrounded by a garden filled with his mother's favourite flowers. Some of Jack's ashes had already been sprinkled, and a Jack pine had been planted on the Toronto Islands, where he and Olivia wed. As well, some ashes had been planted with a memorial tree in the cemetery affiliated with Wyman United Church in Hudson, which he attended with his family as a child.

Regular Canadians had taken to the street by the thousands to mark Jack's passing in the days after his death, assembling at impromptu memorials across the country: the Vancouver Art Gallery, the Alberta legislature in Edmonton, at the foot of Mont Royal in Montreal, on Water Street in St. John's, as well as on Parliament Hill and at Nathan Phillips Square in Toronto. People left flowers and cans of Orange Crush, and picked up chalk and wrote messages about Jack on the sidewalk. Others lined up to pay their respects while Jack, remembered as a "happy warrior" by then U.S. ambassador David Jacobson, was lying in state.

"I will never forget the image of Jack campaigning as the happy warrior. His energy, his enthusiasm and passion for politics and for the Canadian people were undeniable. Something I will never forget. A standard for all of us," Jacobson said.

"The day he was dying, we didn't think there would be any special recognition for him," remembers Mike Layton. "So it was a big surprise when people showed up for him on Parliament Hill. It was this massive outpouring that nobody was expecting. Politicians just don't get that."

The extraordinary week had culminated in a televised state funeral for Jack at Roy Thomson Hall, where Jack and his family had attended the annual Christmas Eve service of the Metropolitan Community Church of Toronto. The family hadn't planned to walk from city hall, where Jack's casket had been lying in state, to Roy Thomson Hall, but just as the bells began ringing to start the procession, Olivia suggested they walk behind the coffin. It was a beautiful day, and Mike Layton remembers all the people who had lined Queen Street to pay their respects to his dad. "I felt pride. He got to do a lot and lived life totally to the fullest."

Rev. Brent Hawkes greeted the family at the hall, where he presided over the state funeral graciously offered to Olivia by Stephen Harper on the day of Jack's death. Since Confederation, the practice has been to offer a state funeral to people who have served as Governors General, prime ministers and federal cabinet ministers. Harper made a special exception in Jack's case, and I served as an honorary pallbearer alongside my former colleague Jamey Heath; Jack's mentor Charles Taylor; long-time friend and former Ontario NDP MPP Marilyn Churley; New Democrat premiers Darrell Dexter of Nova Scotia and Greg Selinger of Manitoba; former NDP premiers Roy Romanow and Gary Doer; former federal NDP leaders Ed Broadbent, Alexa McDonough and Audrey McLaughlin; Ken Neumann, national director for Canada, United Steelworkers; and former BC NDP leader Joy MacPhail.

The funeral, stately with a down-to-earth touch, was vintage Jack: uplifting with a good dose of music but also steeped in politics. "His remarkable letter made it absolutely clear. This was a testament written in the very throes of death that set out what Jack wanted for his caucus, for his party, for young people, for all Canadians," Stephen Lewis said in his eulogy. To his left, Lewis looked out at Prime Minister Harper; Harper's wife, Laureen; and a sea of Conservative cabinet ministers and other dignitaries, including former prime ministers Jean Chrétien and Paul Martin. To Lewis's right sat Jack's family and members of the NDP caucus.

"Inevitably, we fastened on those last memorable lines about hope, optimism and love. But the letter was, at its heart, a manifesto for social democracy. And if there was one word that might sum up Jack Layton's unabashed social democratic message, it would be generosity. He wanted, in the simplest and most visceral terms, a more generous Canada," said Lewis.

Olivia offered her own comforting words. "Let us not look behind us; let's look forward. Look at what we can accomplish together to make sure Jack's voice is not silenced. I think that's a good way to celebrate his life," she said in a video produced for the funeral, highlighting Jack's work over the years. Her message brought tears to the eyes of many of the people who had assembled by the thousands outside Roy Thomson Hall to watch the funeral.

The Necropolis, located in Toronto's Cabbagetown, had been a very special place for Jack. The family plot there included Jack's maternal grandparents, John (Jack) and Constance Steeves, and his father. Many prominent Canadians are buried there, including Toronto's first mayor, William Lyon Mackenzie, and *Globe and Mail* founder George Brown. It also contains a monument honouring Samuel Lount and Peter Matthews, who were hanged for their roles in the Upper Canada Rebellion of 1837.

During his time as a city councillor, Jack, dressed as William Lyon Mackenzie, had conducted tours of the historic cemetery. He was interested in these famous Canadians, but he also thought that the regular Torontonians buried there had stories worth sharing. He'd made the time to research some of these, and he shared them to the delight of tour participants. Listening to the service in the Necropolis on the first anniversary of Jack's death, I thought back to the days after his passing and realized the outpouring of emotion from regular Canadians had something to do with Jack's deeply held belief that everyone mattered.

That evening, just after midnight, I was back in Jack and Olivia's living room, listening to Ron Sexsmith give an impromptu acoustic concert from his perch on the couch.

"Anyone have any songs they'd like to hear?" Sexsmith asked the handful of Jack's former staffers, close friends and family. "They have to be Canadian," said Sexsmith, who went on to play some of his own music intermixed with songs by Leonard Cohen, Gordon Lightfoot, Neil Young and Joni Mitchell.

The group had gathered to mark the anniversary of Jack's death but also to celebrate his legacy. We were in the house where Jack, Olivia and an army of activists had developed strategies and launched campaigns for so many battles: AIDS funding and tenant rights, housing projects and campaigns against violence against women in the 1990s, and the NDP leadership win in 2003 that had morphed into a determined campaign to transform the party into a principled political machine vying for power.

In so many of the causes Jack championed, he was ahead of the curve. He had pressed for things that were right, such as marriage equality and an end to homelessness, before they were accepted by the mainstream. His deeply held convictions and lack of pretension were part of why Jack had an uncommon ability to connect with people. Guitar in hand and songbook at the ready, Jack would have been in his element that evening, singing along with Sexsmith.

WRITING THREE YEARS BEFORE THE NDP's breakthrough campaign in 2011, Paul Martin had dismissed Jack's vision in his book, *Hell or High Water*. "[Layton's] far-fetched plan was to have the NDP displace the Liberal Party as the natural alternative to the Conservatives," the former prime minister wrote.

Many inside the NDP had also seen the plan as far-fetched when Jack took the helm of the party. But Jack proved them wrong. In his years as NDP leader, he redefined the party, changing Canadian politics in the process. An important aspect of his enduring legacy was to instill in the party something that had been missing for more than a generation: a sense of confidence.

By the late 1980s, with conservative ideology driving privatization, reckless deregulation and job-killing trade deals, progressives had become trapped in an oppositional role, pushed far too often into merely defending the status quo. Social movements were active, but fewer and fewer progressives were devoting their time, talents and efforts to the NDP. "We no longer believed in ourselves... From day one, Jack didn't suffer from this lack of confidence. His leadership campaign *gave* us confidence," recalls David Mackenzie, a long-time supporter and friend.

That confidence ushered in an era of growth for the party and a sense that anything was possible, including governing the country. Jack handed down a party very different from the one he took over.

"Jack inherited a caucus that had become something other than a group who wanted to win power," recalls Ed Broadbent. "Social democrats should govern. He left the party with a sense that we could form a government. And that's a big achievement."

This confidence meant tackling the country's most pressing and difficult challenges with fearlessness. Jack systematically applied himself to each of the areas from which, for so long, the NDP had shied away. He believed our answers on crime, the economy and Canada's place on the world stage could capture the support of the electorate and make Canada better.

Jack's desire to govern gave the federal NDP an impressive track record. He accomplished more from his perch as leader of the fourth party than did other opposition leaders with more seats and resources. Whether it was negotiating an NDP budget deal in 2005, pushing for a government apology for past abuses at Canada's residential schools or securing a billion dollars for unemployed workers, Jack wrote the manual for how Parliament can and should work. His influence was captured on the cover of *Maclean's* magazine in December 2005. "Who Is This Man and Why Is He Running the Country?" asked the headline alongside a photo of Jack.

By the end of the 2011 campaign, this renewed belief in ourselves had moved beyond the borders of the party. Today, the idea of the NDP forming the government is no longer dismissed, nor is the idea that Tom

Mulcair could be elected the next prime minister of Canada. That level of confidence and credibility is also part of Jack's legacy.

JACK'S APPROACH TO POLITICS WAS motivational, and he helped define what leadership at the federal level can be. He worked to convince voters that Ottawa can be an agent for good in society and that Parliament can actually get things done to help people.

"Jack changed the way people think about politics and made it accessible for them. Jack brought a sincerity and realism to politics that turned people on to get involved. That might sound easy to do, but it isn't," says Libby Davies, deputy leader of the NDP and Jack's long-time friend and supporter.

Jack also inspired a generation of Quebecers who had grown up feeling rejected after the repatriation of the constitution in 1982 and the failures of the Meech Lake and Charlottetown Accords. They had witnessed the Liberal sponsorship scandal unfold and watched the Conservative enact policies that they didn't like. Jack showed them that there was an alternative to the old debates and that Canada was worth caring about.

"Jack worked hard. He stood on the shoulders of people like Ed Broadbent, who was always viewed very sympathetically in Quebec. There was always a reservoir of goodwill because of Robert Cliche and Tommy Douglas, David Lewis and Broadbent and so on, but someone had to translate all that good will into seats, and Jack had the skill, the vision, the moxy to do it, and he did," says Brian Mulroney.

After the 2011 election, Léger Marketing found that 45 per cent of Quebecers who had voted NDP agreed with the statement "I've had enough of the other parties and I wanted change." In the months following Jack's death, the party wanted to get a pulse of our new voters in Quebec. We conducted focus groups throughout the province to determine whether people were second-guessing their decision to vote for the NDP. The answer was no. Quebecers who had voted NDP did not regret their choice. They also said as long as the party's new leader articulated the same values as Jack, and respected Quebec as much as Jack had, they were willing to stick with the NDP in the future.

One comment in the focus groups in particular encapsulated this sentiment. "The grand bargain," a participant said, "was that we wanted rid of Harper. Voting NDP was the only way to do that. What happened in English Canada? We kept our end of the deal."

The rest of Canada *did* move towards the NDP, allowing us to catapult ahead of the Liberals in all regions of the country in the 2011 election. It wasn't enough then to allow us to pass the Conservatives. But we're getting pretty close. Despite some commentators suggesting the Conservatives have seen a big shift in support, it is the Orange Wave that has seen the greatest momentum over the last decade.

In the 2000 election, the last campaign before the Canadian Alliance and the Progressive Conservative Party merged, the two parties garnered a combined total of 37.6 per cent of the vote. In 2011, the Conservative Party received 39.6 per cent, an increase of two percentage points.

In the 2000 election, the Liberal Party garnered 41 per cent of the vote. In 2011, they received only 19 per cent. In Quebec, the Bloc's support dropped from 40 per cent of the popular vote in 2000 to 23 per cent in 2011.

Where did all of these votes go? In 2000, the NDP received 8.5 per cent of the national vote. In 2011, the party received 31 per cent, an increase of 22.5 points. The shift to the NDP has been at the expense of the Bloc and the Liberals. The Conservatives, meanwhile, have remained stagnant in their popular support. The Orange Wave, the astounding growth in support for the NDP, is the emerging consolidation of the progressive, non-Conservative vote. This is the goal for the next federal election in 2015 and beyond: to defeat the Conservatives and replace them with a truly progressive, New Democratic government.

So, how do we get there?

The first step will be to consolidate this new coalition of NDP voters across Canada: urban voters, youth, new Canadians, francophone Quebecers and aboriginal Canadians. Ipsos-Reid data show that on election day in 2011, 47 per cent of gays and lesbians, 43 per cent of aboriginals, 43 per cent of women voters under twenty-four years of age and 41 per cent of students voted NDP. The polling firm also showed that new Canadians who had been in Canada for fewer than ten years were more likely to vote NDP than any other party. This bodes well for us, since this group, along with young people and aboriginals, is among the fastest-growing segments of the Canadian population.

The next step is to build where the election will be fought and won: in the suburbs, with the support of young families, their aging parents and the ever-growing baby boomer vote. Ontario will have fifteen new seats in the next election, and B.C. and Alberta will receive six each. The West and Ontario's 905 region will play a huge role in deciding who forms the next government. Winning there will mean winning government. Jack Layton connected best with everyday Canadians when he spoke about issues that would help hard-working families make ends meet. With rising health care costs for seniors, record household debt, retirement insecurity and increasing suburban gridlock, it is among the audiences of this next tier that our message will resonate strongest.

Next, we must win as who we are: principled and pragmatic progressives. The NDP must not become what it has defeated. We have not come this far only to merge with the Liberal Party of Canada—a party that was the catalyst for our founding. The biggest threat to progressive gains is a political party that pretends to be progressive but really is not. Can a party that embraced the Reform Party's cuts in the 1990s be entrusted to bring about a progressive Canada? Can a party that hid behind the Supreme Court on marriage equality or has embraced social conservatives in their caucus be trusted to advance equality rights? Can a party that admitted to signing on to the Kyoto Protocol as a public relations move be the home for people who want action on climate change?

As Charles Taylor taught Jack, in an adversarial model like the Westminster parliamentary system, the best outcomes arise from a clash of competing values and ideas. The choice for the voter should be rooted in competing values that are real and significant. In Canada, those competing values are expressed by the NDP and the Conservatives.

The challenge for modern-day brokerage parties such as the old Progressive Conservatives and the Liberal Party of Canada is that they ultimately stand for nothing. They can be in favour of free trade one day and against it the next. Every core principle is on the table. What you stand for today is what your pollster told you yesterday. To have two parties, each with a distinct philosophical compass and belief structure, would serve the country better. In the last ten years, Canada has moved a little more in that direction. Offered the choice between the NDP vision and the Conservative vision, I have no doubt that Canadians will express their true progressive values.

IN POLITICS, MOVEMENT DOES NOT go in one direction. Unless the NDP entrenches our gains, we risk falling as quickly as we rose. Our May 2011 gains prove there is no permanent inheritance in federal politics anymore.

In 1987, according to a Gallup poll, the federal New Democrats were at 47 per cent in terms of popular support. We had lost more than half of that support by the 1988 campaign. Jack Layton's legacy is also learning that we have to work for every vote, take nothing for granted. The project that started around the kitchen table in Jack and Olivia's home back in 2002 made great strides in Canadian politics. But the Orange Wave is not just about what happened in the past. It is about the future. It is about achieving the power to create a more prosperous, generous society that ensures a better life for future generations.

Jack knew what we were up against. On June 6, 2009, the day his first grandchild, Beatrice, was expected to be born, he drafted a letter to her. It read in part:

> Thinking of you, about to arrive in our lives, makes me smile. I have a feeling you'll make me smile a million more times as the years go by. Olivia, your gramma, talks all the time about the many joys you'll bring.
>
> I do have a promise to make to you. I will do everything I can to make the world you'll live in a better place. I don't mind saying I'm worried about what's happening in the world right now... We're going to try harder to make the changes we need to make, but chances are that we'll be handing you some tough challenges ahead.

Jack was right. There are tough challenges facing Canada today, and indeed the world. But if there is one thing he taught us, it is to be optimistic about the trials ahead. Jack understood it would entail a lot of hard work to continue building the Orange Wave. We won't stop until the job is done.

ACKNOWLEDGEMENTS

It was late February 2012, just six months after Jack had died. My time on Parliament Hill was coming to an end after a decade-long run, and I was having a drink with an old friend.

"You need to write a book," Rick Smith declared.

"No way," I said. "You're crazy. I don't write books. I write speeches and memos."

Smith, himself a best-selling author and someone with whom I had fought a few political battles over the years, really put the screws to me. "Lookit, if you don't do it, nobody will. Your opponents will rewrite the history. Time is ticking. You gotta do it." Recognizing I wasn't getting out of there with a "no," I told Rick I'd think about it.

Rick ultimately got his way. At every step, I have been aided and abetted by a small army of friends, former colleagues and principal actors in Canadian politics for the past decade and beyond.

First, I would like to thank Olivia Chow for her unwavering and generous support in the telling of this story. She trusted me with Jack's personal emails, calendar and files, which give this book a unique and intimate perspective. I would also like to thank Jack's mother, Doris, his children, Mike and Sarah, as well as his sister, Nancy, for all of their help and support.

I would like to thank Tom Mulcair, the Leader of the Official Opposition, former NDP leaders Ed Broadbent and Alexa McDonough, former MP Bill Blaikie and MPs Libby Davies and Charlie Angus for their generous time. I would also like to thank the Right Honourable Brian Mulroney for sharing with me his conversations with Jack about the 2011 election, Quebec politics and caucus management.

Deciding which stories to include or exclude was the most challenging, and I am greatly indebted to many former colleagues and allies who reached back into their memories and sifted through their personal records to share their stories and perspectives. Thank you, Anne McGrath, Karl Bélanger, Drew Anderson, Brian Topp, Kathleen Monk, Bob Gallagher, Nathan Rotman, Ira Dubinsky, Raymond Guardia, George Nakitsas, Rebecca Blaikie, Nammi Poorooshasb, Elliott Anderson, Kevin Dorse, Jamey Heath, Ian Capstick, Éric Hébert-Daly, Heather Fraser, Dick Proctor, Chris Watson, Steve Moran, Pierre Ducasse, Gerry Scott, Franz Hartmann, Bruce Cox, Rick Smith, André Foucault, David Mackenzie, Peter Tabuns, Mel Watkins, Bob Penner and Stephen Lewis.

Olivia, Karl, Drew and Bob Gallagher also read parts of the manuscript, for which I am immensely grateful. Their comments made the book better, but any errors or omissions are mine. I am also indebted to Brian for writing a memoir about the 2008 coalition negotiations. *How We Almost Gave the Tories the Boot* was a vital source for me. A compilation of stories about Jack, titled *Hope, Love, Optimism*, was also helpful, so thank you to editors Jim Turk and Charis Wahl.

I would like to thank Erin Jacobson, George Jennings, Alice Funke and Rick Devereux for their kind help with photos, statistics and travel arrangements. They often dug up information on tight deadlines to accommodate many email requests that often included the sentiment "This should be the last thing" but usually turned out not to be.

I would also like to thank Laureen Harper and others for agreeing to have personal correspondence to Jack reproduced in the book, and Kory Teneycke and Tim Murphy for sharing their perspectives. L. Ian MacDonald's assistance was also vital, getting the ball rolling back in the spring of 2012 when he asked me to write a feature on the Orange Wave for *Policy Options* magazine. After the edits were done, Ian encouraged me to use the article as a blueprint for a book. Thank you for the encouragement.

None of this would have been possible without the fantastic team at Douglas & McIntyre keeping independent publishing in Canada alive and kicking, including managing editor Anna Comfort O'Keeffe, and publicist Corina Eberle. My editor, Barbara Pulling, was a joy to work with. Her patience and incisive contributions made the book so much better. I thank Trena White, who was an advocate from the beginning.

I would like to single out my agent, Rick Broadhead, who stickhandled me through the process from beginning to end.

I would also like to thank all of my colleagues at Hill & Knowlton Strategies in Ottawa for their generous support, notably Chief Executive Officer Mike Coates and President Goldy Hyder.

Finally, I owe my wife, Sarah Schmidt, immense gratitude for her incredible patience and determined assistance in getting this project across the finish line. This book would not have happened without her. To my kids, Addie and Harry, thank you for your understanding when I had to be away and miss so many dinners and tuck-ins while working with Jack and the team. And to my mom and dad, Joy and Lou, thank you for everything.

To those who practise the art of political campaigning in Canada, this book is written as a small contribution to the craft, with the belief it is best applied when done so vigorously, honestly and respectfully.

This book is dedicated to every Canadian who has been told by the powerful that change is not possible. It is. To everyone who believes that politics and government can be forces for good and that we don't have to accept the way things are, this book is also for you. This book is for the farmers on the Prairies in the 1930s who put their hard-earned nickels into the hat to build a party that spoke, fought and governed for them. This book is for the pioneers on whose giant shoulders the Orange Wave stands, and it's for those who will complete the project and build the Canada of our dreams. Don't let them tell you it can't be done.

Brad Lavigne
Ottawa, August, 2013

INDEX

Stewart, Jimmy, 50
Strategic Communications, 32, 51, 131
Strategic Counsel, 132
Stronach, Belinda, 90
Sun Media, 231, 233, 234
Sun News network, 234
Sun TV News, 230, 232
Supreme Court of Canada, 93, 122, 123, 267; Chaoulli decision, 93; Clarity Act, 123

Taber, Jane, 50, 68
Tabuns, Peter, 18, 133, 271
Taylor, Charles, 14, 116, 117, 121, 261
Teneycke, Kory, 156, 169, 171, 229, 230, 271
Thailand tsunami, 80
Thatcher, Ross, 113
Thériault, Jacques, 71
Think Twice Coalition, 111, 113, 153
Topp, Brian, 60, 61, 62, 66, 82, 88, 89, 90, 92, 100, 105, 108, 109, 112, 114, 123, 137, 145, 146, 148, 154, 156, 157, 159, 160, 164, 165, 166, 168, 169, 175, 212, 214, 216, 217, 231, 240, 241, 247, 248, 256, 260, 271
Toronto Board of Health, 17
Toronto Islands, 260
Toronto Star, 110, 237
Toronto Stock Exchange, 108
Toronto Sun, 229, 230, 235
Toronto Women's Hospital, 246
Toupin, Robert, 117
Tousaw, Kirk, 158
Tout le monde en parle (Radio-

Canada), 212
Trudeau, Pierre, 13, 14, 78, 79, 92, 117
Trudeaumania, 116
Trudel, Rémy, 118
Turk, Jim, 271
Turk-Browne, Jess, 229, 230, 231, 241
Turmel, Nycole, 121, 247, 249, 250, 253, 254
Turner, Garth, 130

U2, 54
Union Nationale, 12
United Church, 12, 46
United Food and Commercial Workers (UFCW), 58
United Nations, 48
United Steelworkers, 59, 261
Universal Child Care Benefit, 104
Université de Montréal, 135, 140
Upper Canada Rebellion, 262

Vachon, Paul "The Butcher," 118
Vaisakhi festival, 84, 85
Valeri, Tony, 82, 85, 86, 87
Vancouver Art Gallery, 260
Vastel, Michel, 43
Viewpoints Research, 190, 191
Vimy Ridge, 208
Vision Vancouver, 108

Waffle initiative, 1971, 22
Wahl, Charis, 271
War Measures Act, 14–15
Wasylycia-Leis, Judy, 106, 107, 108, 109, 183, 198
Watkins, Mel, 15, 17–18, 271

Watson, Chris, 56, 61, 271
Wells, Paul, 39
White, Randy, 73
White Ribbon, 18
Wikileaks, 49
Williams, Danny, 151
Wills & Co., 149
Woodsworth, J. S., 12, 167
World War I, 208
Wright, Nigel, 200, 201, 255

Wyman United Church, 260
York University, 16
Young Offenders Act, 159
Young, Dennis, 7
Young, Neil, 263

Zaccardelli, Giuliano, 107
Zarrug, Eiman, 200, 251
Zoom Media, 149